Nobody cared

Nobody Cared

*An Evil Predator, A Vulnerable Girl
Who Fought Back*

TERRIE O'BRIAN

PAN BOOKS

First published 2012 by Pan Books
an imprint of Pan Macmillan, a division of Macmillan Publishers Limited
Pan Macmillan, 20 New Wharf Road, London N1 9RR
Basingstoke and Oxford
Associated companies throughout the world
www.panmacmillan.com

ISBN 978-1-4472-0557-9

1 3 5 7 9 8 6 4 2

A CIP catalogue record for this book is available from
the British Library.

Printed and bound by CPI Group (UK) Ltd, Croydon, CR0 4YY

For my beautiful children,
who will always be loved in the way I never was

AUTHOR'S NOTE

This is my story, in my words, told in full for the very first time. Everything described in this book is true, although I have relied solely on my memory when retelling some events. For reasons of privacy and to protect the identities of those involved, most names in the book have been changed. Some people have been removed entirely, at their request.

CONTENTS

PROLOGUE

I sat outside the doors of the courtroom, trying desperately to take deep breaths but unable to get enough air inside my lungs. I stared at the clock as a million images ran through my mind, images of what he had done to me. I'd read through my statement the night before to refresh my mind. I didn't know what I was going to say, exactly, as I took the stand. But all I needed to do was tell the truth. That the man sitting opposite me had abused me again and again from the age of ten, how he had taken away my innocence, stolen my childhood.

It seemed as though the hands on the clock were barely moving, as though time itself was standing still. I glanced down at my smart outfit and smoothed my skirt, noticing then that my hands and legs were trembling.

Come on, Terrie. Pull yourself together. I knew this was the one and only chance I would get to tell the world what he had done to me and see him brought to justice. *He's not the one in control anymore; you are*. I had been a child when the sexual, and emotional, abuse had begun. But now I was older, and stronger, and the time had come for me to take a stand.

I pulled myself up straight, just as the polished wooden door swung open and an official-looking lady appeared, giving me a brief nod. I could hear people inside the courtroom, solicitors and court officials, speaking to one another in hushed voices.

'You can go in now, Terrie,' she said. 'Are you ready?'

I nodded. *This is it*, I thought. *This is what I've been waiting for all these years. A chance to put my sickening past behind me once and for all.* As I stepped through the doors and took a deep breath, I felt all eyes on me and became aware of the deafening silence. Then, from across the room, I saw him . . .

ONE

Cuddles From My Daddy

I spun around, turning my back to everyone and folding my arms across my four-year-old chest.

'No!' I cried. 'I don't want to get dressed here!'

Liz, my mum's friend who lived with us, laughed. 'Don't be silly, Terrie,' she replied. 'No one is watching you. Now, nightie off and clothes on!'

I looked at Liz and slipped the nightie over my head, shivering a little as I clasped my arms around my tiny naked body. Then I lifted one leg up to step into the underwear she was holding out.

'Good girl.' She smiled. 'See? No need to make a fuss.'

In our house, my clothes were kept upstairs in my bedroom, but for some reason my knickers were kept in a drawer downstairs in the living room. And part of my daily routine was to get dressed down there. The room was always full of adults, with my dad, one uncle and two great-uncles sitting around, and I always felt at least one pair of eyes on me, staring at my naked flesh. Even at that young age, it made me feel uncomfortable.

I quickly pulled my dress over my head. Now I could go and play with my My Little Ponies upstairs, one of the few second-hand toys I had. Over my shoulder, I could see my great-uncle

Pat leering at me. In his late sixties, he looked like a comic figure, always wearing jeans four sizes too big for his skinny frame, held up by braces. As usual, he had his Polaroid camera with him, ready and waiting to snatch a quick photo. Born with a cleft palate, Pat couldn't close his mouth properly and would drool when he smiled, covering the same blue jumper he always wore with patches of saliva. And whenever he took photos of me, he smiled.

'Stop it,' I said, trying to dodge him as he raised his camera in my direction again. I'd heard him snapping away when I took off my nightie but I hadn't said anything then – I knew it was best just to concentrate on getting dressed as quickly as possible. As usual, everyone else ignored his behaviour. My other great-uncle, Ron, carried on stirring his tea, Mum sat in her chair looking vacant, and Liz didn't seem to notice. Dad was in the bathroom.

I didn't know why Uncle Pat liked taking so many pictures, all instantly produced and then shoved into his pocket. Sometimes I poked my tongue out cheekily just before he clicked.

I lived with my mum, Carole, my dad, Reg, my two great-uncles, Ron and Pat, an uncle, Simon, my nan, Margaret, and Mum's friend, Liz – all in an ordinary four-bedroomed council house on an estate in Stevenage. From the outside we were one big, hectic family, with my father Reg at the hub. Stocky, with dark receding hair, Dad didn't have a single tooth in his head. 'I had some false teeth but a dog buried them in the garden,' he'd laugh. It didn't stop him from being able to eat, though; clamping down with his hard gums, he'd eat anything. He was a very popular man, and was always helping out friends and neighbours. He was seen as the local Mr Fixit, always doing DIY, always making time for people. Especially single women. If he heard that a woman was on her own, he'd knock on her door and offer to do any jobs. His drinking pals knew he had a vicious temper on him, but they loved him too. He would bowl down the road, a big smile on his face, waving to people as he went. But inside our four walls we saw a very different side to the man who all the neighbours thought was wonderful.

Even when I was very young, I knew that he had been convicted as a sex offender, and although I understood it was a bad thing, no one ever explained exactly what that meant. Abusive, both sexually and physically, my father used me as either his punch bag or sex toy, depending on what mood he was in.

It was obvious from the start that I stood little chance of a normal, loving upbringing. My mother was born on 9 December 1958, to my grandparents Margaret and Ted, and grew up in Hitchin, a few miles up the road from Stevenage. My nan was a lovely soft-spoken little lady, but she'd suffered from manic depression all her life. I only met Ted, my grandad, once, when he was being transferred from prison to a mental unit. I don't know what he was being treated for. Mum said he'd stopped talking, so he was sent to a secure mental hospital. I also don't know what he was in prison for on that occasion, but previously he'd served time for raping my mum. He carried out the attacks when she was between the ages of seventeen and nineteen, never having touched her before.

From as far back as I can remember, I knew of Mum's abuse by my grandad. Nothing like that was hidden in our family. Mum and the other adults openly talked about sex, and about Mum's background of abuse as though it was a normal aspect of everyday life. Mum had been terrified of my grandad, and was raped at night, when Nan was in another room, completely unaware of what was happening to her daughter. Perhaps my mother's own mental health problems were caused by the abuse she suffered, or perhaps it was hereditary. I will probably never know.

Mum eventually escaped my grandparents' house and met and married one of her first boyfriends, a man called Phil. He was her childhood sweetheart and looked the spitting image of Patrick Swayze, with the charm to match. But behind his Hollywood-esque smile, he was a man with a violent temper, who was always embroiled in fights and dodgy goings-on. Turning a blind eye, though, and happy to escape Grandad, Mum set up a new life. Feeling safe in her new home, one evening she plucked up the courage to confide in her new husband about the sexual abuse she'd suffered. 'He forced himself on me,' she said, tears streaming down her face.

She had hoped to unburden herself and finally to feel safe and protected by her new husband, but was shocked when his reaction was far from what she had expected. A rage descended over his face and he punched her hard repeatedly, crying, 'You dirty whore' over and over.

Mum fell to the ground, sobbing, but as broken as she was, somehow she found a determination to find justice. After Phil was finished, she stood up, and decided then and there to report her father to the police the very next day. I'm not sure what snapped inside of her. Perhaps this new violence was the final straw, or maybe she felt she had to prove to Phil that she hadn't deserved what her father had done. Whatever it was, this horrific beating made her want to tell the authorities.

Mum told me she pressed charges and, through her testimony, Grandad was sent to jail. My grandmother was horrified when she discovered what had been going on, and she had the first of many nervous breakdowns. Later it also emerged that Grandad's brother, Pat, who moved in with us, was a paedophile who liked taking indecent pictures of children. I've no idea what went wrong in that family to produce two perverts. Perhaps Grandad's father had abused them? Perhaps another family member? It's hard to know.

Born to a decent family in Vauxhall, both Nan's parents worked, her father as a metal sheet worker and her mother in a launderette. Although her brother Ron suffered from learning difficulties, her sister Vera did well for herself, working as a hairdresser. My mum's abuse at the hands of my grandad came as a big shock to Nan's side of the family. It was the sort of thing that had never happened in her family before. But, little did Nan realize then, it would trigger a cycle of abuse not to be broken for another generation. And one I'd suffer alone.

After Grandad's conviction, Mum spent a reasonably happy, although chaotic, few years married to Phil. She supported him through his ups and downs and the pair made a sociable, lively couple. Then one evening, Phil came home covered in blood.

'Take these to the launderette,' he growled at his young wife. Used to her husband getting into scrapes, Mum did what she was asked without a moment's hesitation. It was only when the police knocked on her door a day later that she began to worry that something really terrible had happened.

Phil was arrested and charged with murder. Mum was asked to testify in court and the story that emerged horrified her. Phil and a few accomplices had tried to mug an old lady, but through a haze of drink and violence it had turned very nasty. The woman was found almost split in two after she'd been sexually abused with a tree branch.

Totally devastated by what her husband had done, Mum didn't hesitate to stand up in court against him. She divorced him while he was serving his prison sentence. And while he was banged up inside for fifteen years without parole, it was then that Phil met my father, Reg.

Reg was also serving a sentence but for years after his release no one was sure what it was for. He had a daughter, Sarah, from a previous relationship, and he told people he was doing time for beating up Sarah's boyfriend for making her pregnant, but eventually it emerged that he'd been raping her himself and was in fact the father of her child.

Mum didn't know any of this when Reg knocked on her door shortly after he left prison.

Phil had asked Reg to 'look after' his now ex-wife, so, when he turned up, telling my vulnerable mum he was there to look after her, she believed him.

Lonely and rather naïve, my twenty-one-year-old mum, although wary at first, was quickly taken in by the dark-haired charmer, who always waltzed around with a trilby hat placed on his head at a jaunty angle. Despite an age gap of fourteen-odd years, the pair of them hit it off and were married a couple of years later in February 1981. Finally, Mum thought that she'd met a man who would look after her in the way a husband should. But he was known in the area as a sex offender. Did Mum know this when she married him and had a child with him? I can't answer. I would prefer to think that she didn't find out until it was too late.

I was born five years after they met, on 7 July 1984, when Mum was twenty-five and Dad was forty-nine. When I was two, we moved from our home in Essex to a four-bedroomed council house in Stevenage. This house would be the scene of a nightmare I would live through every day for the next eight years of my childhood.

My first memory is of falling out of a little buggy I was playing in over some brickwork dad had built in the back garden, bashing my head on the paving. Dad ran downstairs when he heard my screams. Sweeping me up in his arms, he took me into the bathroom, where he grabbed a yellow sponge and dabbed my head to mop up the crimson blood.

'You'll be okay,' he soothed.

I soon calmed down. 'Thank you, Daddy,' I said.

He gently tapped me under the chin with his index finger.

'I told you I'd make it better, eh?' he said. I smiled back at him and jumped down from where I was seated at the sink. As I left, he grabbed my arm. 'You're a terror, little Terrie, aren't you!'

That was his nickname for me. 'Terrie the Terror'. I didn't know what it meant then. Later on, I grew to realize that perhaps he saw in me the same spirit he'd managed to squash in Mum and everyone else in the family. A spirit I am very proud of today.

I ran outside again, to pick up my dolly to play. I loved pushing the baby doll around in the buggy, pretending to be a mummy. It was pure escapism, setting up tiny cups and saucers for tea and dressing her up. I spent hours chattering to myself, and my dolly, telling her how to behave. Maybe I liked playing mummy as I didn't see much of my own. She never seemed to be around when it came to caring for me and was probably upstairs in bed or sitting on her chair in the living room. After having me she became very depressed, just like her own mother, my nan, had done after the birth of my mum. Since the trial against her father, she'd suffered from depression, and having a baby appeared to tip her over the edge. She'd sit in silence for days without eating and only drinking when someone made her tea.

After singing to my dolly, I pretended to feed her some dinner. But I felt the plastic plate slip out of my hands as Dad looked in my direction.

'Making more mess, eh, Terrie?' he yelled. 'What have I told you about your toys?'

I held my breath, frozen with fear. Even then I knew Dad's moods could change like the wind. One minute he could be sweet as pie and the next he would give me a swipe with the back of his hand. I grew up anticipating his every move. I never knew what to expect.

'Sorry, Daddy,' I said, my eyes silently pleading for his mood to pass. Thankfully this time his face softened. I quickly picked up the plastic plate from the floor.

'Just keep your things in your bedroom,' he growled.

Soon after we moved into the house in Stevenage, our family unit began to grow. My nan was the first to come and live with us. She had been living in Essex but was finding it difficult coping without any family nearby, so Mum agreed to take her in. Then came my great-uncle Pat, my grandad's brother, and Ron, my nan's brother. Simon, Mum's brother, also came to live with us. Both Ron and Simon suffered from learning difficulties. I was told that Simon had grown up an intelligent child but that when he was eleven, his father threw him on to a bed during a row, and he hit his head on the iron bedstead. After weeks in hospital, he was released with a brain injury that he would never recover from.

Now in his late twenties, he was like a child in an overweight man's body. Unable to read or write, he never worked and sat all day fixing model aeroplanes in his bedroom. He had a playful streak and sometimes would flip over the dining-room chairs, and turn them into 'boats'. Very occasionally I'd play with him too, but most often he liked to play alone. Sometimes for fun he liked to burn pieces of paper in an ashtray in his bedroom. That always drove Dad mental, causing a terrible row. Every week when Simon collected his benefit money, he'd buy me a pack of Opal Fruits and a bag of cheese and onion Walkers crisps. It was the same every week and he never said anything when he gave them to me, but I always looked forward to them and would give him a big smile in return.

Ron was a big-built balding geezer in his late fifties, who hung around the house all day long as he had no friends at all. He'd spend most of his days peeling potatoes for Dad and helping him boil them. He was like a living shadow, always there but not taking part in any conversation unless it was to row with Dad, who hated him. On the whole, Ron and Simon kept themselves to themselves. It was Pat, who I called Pervy Pat, that I had to watch out for. But all the lodgers kept Dad in the money, so he let them stay. Ron and Simon paid £50 a week each just for their room, and Pat paid £90. Although he never worked, Dad was always rolling in money. Yet that didn't stop him from finding the cheapest (and most dangerous) way possible to heat our house. We had Calor Gas cylinders standing in the middle of every room with a naked flame on top to heat the area around them as that was cheaper than switching on the central heating.

'Go near fire, you get burned,' Dad would hiss at me. So I never did, although how there weren't any accidents, I'll never know. I only remember Liz burning her hand once.

Liz, my mum's friend, whom I called Auntie Liz, had just split up with a violent partner and needed a roof over her head, so she joined us too. A flighty, dark-haired lady, she was always trying to 'make' something of herself and signing up for college courses to try and get ahead. Compared to the other lodgers she got on the best with Dad. Sometimes I heard her laughing in his bedroom at night while Mum was downstairs sitting in her chair, and although Liz went out of her way to avoid Dad's temper like everyone else, she used to say that 'his heart was in the right place'. Liz was always in and out, busy doing something, but as far as the adults went in the house, she was the only one who appeared to pay me much attention. Well, positive attention.

With so many people living under one roof, it was a tight squeeze. Mum and Dad had the biggest bedroom, and Liz and I shared a room. She slept in a single bed, while I slept in a sleeping bag with a Coca-Cola logo, on a bare mattress with no pillow. Ron and Pat slept in bunk beds in another room and Simon was in the other, while my nan slept downstairs on the sofa. Eventually Pat moved into his own room when Nan got a new council flat and Simon moved in with her, as he and Ron argued like cat and dog.

The house was a reasonable size, but not only was it filled with people, it was also filled to the brim with junk of every description. Huge cheap chipboard dressers lined all the walls and behind their glass doors were masses of ornaments, clocks and brick-a-brac. The walls hadn't been decorated for as long as I could remember; the wallpaper was blue with pink flowers. The carpet was a dirty red colour, tatty and totally coated in our German Shepherd dog Kim's molted fur. Mum liked her trinkets and part of her illness meant that she'd grown addicted to buying things, shoving them away carelessly and never dusting anything. Dad meanwhile had an obsession with anything made from brass. He collected plates and figurines which he'd nail to the wall where they collected dirt and tarnished quickly. His pride and joy was a pair of swords hung above the living-room door.

Our cramped house and everyone in it was ruled with an iron rod by Dad. No one dared stand up to him as his patience was paper thin and his temper violent and unpredictable. From as far back as I could remember we were all scared of him. With just one look he could silence anyone, and he wasn't scared to use his fists either. It didn't take much to set him off: a burnt piece of toast, a cup of tea not made the way he liked it. Or even me just walking past him too quickly or too slowly. I was permanently walking on eggshells. His favourite way to slap was a hard back-hander aimed at the back of my head. Once, when I was about five, I accidentally got under his feet while he was in the kitchen. Bam! I felt the slam of his open palm cracking on the back of my head before he even said anything.

'Move!' he yelled, as I wailed, clutching my head. I hadn't meant to do anything to deserve a slap. But then I never did. Although his nickname for me was 'Terrie the Terror', the reality was that I was terrified of him. He used to always tell me I was 'trouble'. Sometimes he was joking, and sometimes he almost said it with a touch of pride. But most of the time there was nothing light-hearted about it.

'I will have to watch out for you,' he'd say. But I'd already learned that it was I who needed to watch out for him.

With Mum often asleep or in a trance due to her depression and the medication the doctor had given her, my nan occasionally looked after me but Liz was my main carer. I always felt as though she adored me in a way I wished Mum did, as she would get me up and dressed in the morning. She'd be the one to make me breakfast and help me in the bath at night, although when Dad did occasionally let us put the radiators on, Mum or Dad would hang my jammies on one to make them warm for me to jump into – one of the few times they showed genuine care for me. But Liz was rarely home all day as she tended to be at college and she was always talking about moving out and getting on with her life with whatever boyfriend she had at the time.

Living with Dad and his rules wasn't easy. He decided what happened, who slept where, what we had to eat. I never remember any meals apart from pork joints and boiled potatoes. With so many mouths to feed, Dad budgeted and cooked for everyone every night. He'd mash up the potatoes, boil the meat, and then dump it on the plates without any sauce or anything. No one complained. And my uncles, Nan and Mum couldn't afford to have anything else, so they ate what they were given. There was a small dining table extended out into a six-seater, but I wasn't allowed to sit at that. I had to go and sit on the floor in the room next door. I didn't mind, though. As long as I was left in peace to eat, and could maybe watch TV afterwards, avoiding Dad and Pat, then it was the best evening I could hope for. Often Dad put on a horror film for me before I went to bed. We had over five hundred videos, piled everywhere. From an early age I'd watch 18-rated films such as *Halloween* and *Nightmare on Elm Street*. I didn't find them scary, I found them funny, but compared to what I was living through it was little wonder.

I wasn't shown a huge amount of life outside our four walls. I was never taken anywhere except to nearby Hitchin town centre to go shopping or for summertime trips to the beach at Southend. Occasionally, Dad would take me to the Working Man's Club in The Oval, Stevenage, where I'd watch him get drunk with his friends. He'd sit me at a table, buy me a glass of squash, then say in a low, menacing voice, 'Sit there and DON'T MOVE'. And I didn't, all night.

I became good at people-watching, kicking my legs under the table, while I sucked on my orange cordial through a straw. Sometimes I also got a bag of cheese and onion crisps as a treat. The most important thing, though, was that I didn't move. If Dad told me to do something I carried it out to the letter. Maybe even then part of me wanted to please him. Just so that he'd be nice to me, which meant not hitting me.

Although Dad joined the other men who had labouring jobs during the week for a boozing session, he never worked himself. He had a forklift truck licence, so he must have worked before I was born, but I'd heard people talk about him 'being on the sick with a heart condition'.

For me, summer was the best time of year as once a week Dad took me to Southend-on-Sea for the day. It was here we'd meet up with my older half-sister Sarah. I don't remember much about the visits except that Sarah would ask him for £200 every time he came. There wasn't much love lost between them, although she always made a fuss of me and bought me ice cream. Standing by the van looking up at all the pictures of delicious-looking ice creams and lollies, I would choose the same thing every time: a 99 and, if I was extra lucky, I would get raspberry sauce on top.

'You remind me of me,' Sarah used to say, giving me a cuddle.

I loved my big sister; she was ten years older and seemed so grown up. Only later did I find out that she'd pressed charges against Dad when she was just thirteen for raping her and making her pregnant.

The only place we'd get food from was a cockle and whelk stand on the sea front, where Dad would treat us to a cone of seafood. I loved the smell of vinegar as we held the polystyrene cones in our hands. It was a treat I always looked forward to. I never asked to go on the fairground rides and only occasionally got to visit an arcade. I never ever dared to ask for anything extra, although just watching the colourful twinkling lights and listening to the screams of the kids having fun gave me pleasure as we walked past. It was an escape from Stevenage and our crowded house, even if I was just an outsider looking in at all the fun.

Dad didn't believe in buying me presents, but every week I got £5 pocket money, quite a lot of money for a six-year-old, but I was only ever allowed to spend it on sweets. I was never allowed anything extra, even though there was always spare cash around from all the rent the lodgers gave him. So once a week I'd go on my own to Woolworths and spend the lot on an enormous bag of pick'n'mix. The paper bag almost ripped under the weight of the sweets as I walked home with them, eating them quickly until I felt sick and my teeth were deliciously sticky with gooey sugar. Liquorice was always my favourite.

The first time I realized that Christmas was a time for celebration was when I started to watch Christmas films and visit friends' houses at Christmas time. I saw beautifully decorated trees in their living rooms with presents under them, a stark contrast to our bare living room, only ever decorated with Dad's brass tat and Mum's nick-nacks. Christmas simply didn't exist in our household. There were no decorations, no tree, no presents, no special dinner, and no family came to visit. The only recognition of Christmas Dad made was the £50 in cash which he handed to me on Christmas morning, and which I could spend a few days afterwards in the sales.

On Christmas Day we'd sit and watch the films in our house, listening to the neighbours' kids playing outside on their bikes, skateboards and new gear, laughing and joking. It was the only day of the year everyone on the estate seemed to be in a good mood. Everyone except us.

After Dad had given me the money, I sat in front of the blaring TV, just like all other days. Dad didn't believe in marking special occasions. 'Waste of time and money,' he said. It was the same at birthdays. I never got a single wrapped present to open as a child.

I remember one Christmas in particular, when I was five years old. I watched a film called *A Christmas Story*. It was a film about a very poor boy, Ralphie, whose family refused to buy him anything for Christmas; all he wanted was a ball-bearing gun. I loved it as it portrayed a family like our own: one with parents who didn't care and who didn't celebrate the day like other people. Very few films depicted such situations, unless they were Victorian tales like *A Christmas Carol*. It fascinated me and made me feel less alone, like there were other people out there who led lives like mine.

Dad didn't like Pat taking pictures of me and would scream at him if he caught him. But that was because Dad had his own 'uses' for me and didn't want anyone else doing the same. When I wasn't avoiding Pervy Pat I was being abused by my dad on a regular basis. Almost every morning, in his bed. It started as far back as I can remember. I can only imagine I'd been a toddler when it first happened.

While most children are woken by their parents telling them to get up and get dressed for school or to go downstairs to have their breakfast, I would wake to the sound of Dad calling me from his bedroom.

'Terrie!' My heart would start thudding like a drum. Mum never slept much at night; she seemed to sleep all day instead. So she'd be up by the time Dad called me. I was desperate to pull the covers over my head and ignore him, but I knew that he'd fly into an uncontrollable rage if I did, so I never dared. Instead, I leapt from my bed like a bolt of lightning and padded down the hallway to his bedroom. Then I'd have to push open his door, and step into the gloomy room, morning light streaming through the grimy curtains, which were always half falling down. The walls were covered in wallpaper tinged with yellow from nicotine; the carpet was deep red and the only items of furniture were a bed and a wardrobe. The bedding had mismatched chintzy patterns and it always smelt stuffy, sleep ridden, filled with a sweaty smell that made my stomach turn.

I'd have to slip under Dad's duvet as he grinned at me. After that brief glance, for the next ten or so minutes, he wouldn't look me in the face or eyes again.

He'd lay me flat on the bed, pull off my knickers and roll up my nightie to my waist in one swift movement. Then he'd position himself on top and I'd watch as he heaved himself on me, rubbing and groaning, working himself up more vigorously, his hard, hairy genitals rubbing against my own. I'd twist my head to the side, tears sliding relentlessly down my face on to the pillow. Sometimes I cried out loud, but usually I just sniffed in silence. Either way, Dad ignored me. Sometimes I opened one eye and saw the tattoos on his arm. He had the name 'Beatrice' on one side and a picture of a bird I didn't recognize drawn on the other. Mum said Beatrice was an ex of my dad's and it made her very cross.

I willed him to stop, but knew I'd have to be patient as he grimaced and puffed over me. I could smell his stale sweat mixed with the previous day's Brute aftershave. His breath was hot and meaty. I wanted to be sick but knew instinctively not to move a muscle until he'd finished. As he did every day, he grew more frenetic and then his face twisted as he sprayed my tummy with white goo.

Looking tired, he'd fall to the side. Then, pausing for a moment, he'd turn to me, as he always did. 'Go get yourself washed, Terrie,' he'd say, still not looking at me.

I'd slip out of the bed and run to the bathroom, where Dad, as part of his routine, stood over me as I turned on the taps quickly. I splashed water over my belly and the goo was always stuck on my fingers and under my nails as I rubbed my hands together under the scalding hot tap. I felt so dirty as I tried to get rid of it. That feeling never went away.

Briefly my eyes would flit to the mirror to see Dad staring hard at me. His face was tense, his fixated eyes sent an icy chill down my back as he watched me clean myself.

'Get it all off,' he'd order. 'Then skip off downstairs and get dressed.'

'Yes, Daddy,' came my reply. Dutifully, I'd turn off the tap, dry my hands and head off downstairs to start my day. And this is what happened almost every single morning of my childhood.

Dad would then lock the bathroom door behind me to get himself ready. Rarely showering, he just splashed on some more Brute to try to cover his stale smell, before appearing downstairs a short while later. Whatever he was doing, which usually wasn't very much, he looked smart and dressed to perfection every day. I'd never known him to have any kind of paid job, but he always looked the part in smart suit trousers and a shirt, as if he could step into a business situation at any moment. After running his hands through his hair he topped off his outfit with his favourite mustard-coloured trilby, set at its usual angle. This was the cheerful disguise he used for the outside world; so very different from the man I knew as 'Daddy'.

I didn't understand what it was my dad did to me during those morning 'cuddles'. All I knew was that it was wrong and I felt horrible and dirty afterwards. Most mornings I would carry on as normal, managing to block it from my mind. But some days it all felt too much to deal with so I would scramble back to my bedroom, tears sliding silently down my face, praying there was somewhere, anywhere, else I could be.

There was no point in crying loudly. No one would come anyway. So I would slip inside my sleeping bag, zipping it up as far as it could go. Then I would bury my head in the material and sob until my face was so wet that my cheeks would stick to the sleeping bag. I didn't know why Dad did what he did. I knew sex was something adults liked as people talked about it in front of me quite often. I'd seen some porn on the TV when I caught one of my uncles watching it. But I never saw any children involved. I hated looking at my Dad's thing and I hated the way he grunted as he moved backwards and forwards on top of me.

When the tears had run dry, I would lie inside the sleeping bag with my eyes squeezed shut, trying desperately to blank out what had just happened. Eventually, though, I knew I couldn't hide anymore and I'd have to get up.

My bedroom was pink with a huge mural of Snow White and the Seven Dwarves that Dad had got his friend to paint on the wall. I liked them at first; they were always smiling and cheerful, unlike most of the faces in my house. But sometimes it looked like they were just staring blankly at me and maybe laughing at me a little bit. My only toys were second-hand ones from car boot sales and I had a big Barbie house with lots of half-broken Barbies, which were my favourite toys. I'd play ordinary houses, with Barbie babysitting a little girl toy and talking to her friends over coffee. This is what I imagined life could be like. But sometimes, on my darker days, I would play 'Knock down Barbie'. I'd line them up on the roof, then say, 'Am I going to save you, Barbie? Nooooo!' as I pushed them over so that they fell to the floor with a clatter. Looking back, I realize this game was one way of releasing the anger that was building inside me. If I screamed out loud, I'd only get another beating from Dad. If

I cried or sobbed, no one was there to hug me. There was no one to complain to or talk to. So I began to find comfort in 'hurting' my second-hand Barbie dolls. If I hurt them, I reasoned, maybe I wouldn't feel quite so much pain.

TWO

Muddy Puddles

When I started school, at Wellfield Junior School, a whole new world opened up. Dad always took me each morning in his old red Cavalier, then he'd go to Woolworths in Hitchin for two crusty buttered rolls and a cup of coffee. It was part of his routine and nothing changed it. He'd stay there all day, chatting to his mates who popped in to see him.

It seemed as though my dad cared for my education, always making sure I got to school on time and sometimes helping me learn to read the 'Bangers and Mash' books I brought home from school. He'd sit me on his lap and we'd read the pages slowly together, me following his index finger on each sentence like a hawk. They were the only books in our house, as most of the adults couldn't read or write. We didn't even have newspapers; even the local one went straight into the bin. The only magazines were the porn mags in Pervy Pat's room and the ones Simon would sometimes leave lying around. So the only words I ever saw were in my school books.

'Good girl,' Dad said, if I got it right. I liked reading. It made me feel clever. Reading words meant you could lose yourself in another world. You could pretend you were someone else.

But the reality, I think, was that Dad wanted me out from under his feet and school was a convenient place for me to be babysat for free. I'd soon grow to realize that when it wasn't so 'convenient' for him he'd be quick to stop me going to whatever school I was attending.

School wasn't any more fun than being at home. Although it was lovely to get out of the house for six hours a day, the school was run down and full of kids who liked to tease me. They told me I looked like a scruff and that I was stupid. Some of the other kids were from very poor families on the estate and didn't have good parents either, and most of them were bullied too. After just a few months of being at school I'd grown to dislike the teachers and being told what to do because I had enough rules to follow at home. But my instinct was to be a good girl, try my best in lessons and keep myself out of trouble where I could.

During my early school days I became best friends with a girl called Laura who lived across the road from us. Sometimes I was allowed over to her house for dinner and stepping across the threshold into her neat and tidy ordinary house was always a revelation. Her mum and stepdad went to work every day, and Laura was served a different dinner every evening by her mum and had to sit at the table while she ate it. They even had a vacuum cleaner, something I'd never seen before. Our house was always dirty and the carpets were only ever swept with a hard brush. Laura was allowed out to play after her dinner 'went down' and she had to be home by a certain time, unlike me. Dad never minded what time I got in or went to bed. The only time he'd stop me from going out to the little park near our house was when it was raining, but it was more about having to wash my clothes again than caring that I might get wet.

One Sunday afternoon he'd said I couldn't go out, but I was itching to. I saw Laura across the road, splashing about in puddles with wellies and a rain mac on, and I wanted to join her. But, of course, I didn't have any waterproofs or boots.

'You're not going,' said Dad, turning back to the TV.

'Please, Dad,' I whined. 'Let me!'

I didn't usually ever ask twice. I knew I was risking a slap, but the idea of staying stuck in until bed time was unbearable that afternoon.

'Please, Daddy,' I said, hoping it was in a sweet enough voice not to make him angry.

'Go on, then, you little terror,' he snapped. 'See if I care if you get soaked in the rain!'

Feeling giddy with excitement I grabbed my little coat off the peg and ran outside. It was too small for me, as were most of my clothes. Dad said I wasn't to get anything new 'until it fell apart'.

Laura and I had a lovely time for a couple of hours, playing on the wet swings and chasing each other.

Then I spotted an enormous puddle by the side of the park. 'Let's go for it!' I yelled.

We ran across and Laura jumped in with two legs, her feet safely dry with her plastic boots on. I only had my trainers on, but with Dad's words echoing in my head about how he didn't care how wet I got, I threw myself in, screaming with laughter. We kicked our legs up high, watching in delight as the water splattered on our coats, faces and hair. After a few minutes we were both soaked, our cheeks flushed with laughter.

'You're dripping!' Laura laughed. The rain had long stopped, but with the fun in the puddle, I was soaked.

'Yeah.' I grinned. 'I'll go home and get changed.'

Laura walked with me. She never said anything about Dad or my family, although secretly I thought that, deep down, she must feel sorry for me, as her parents were so lovely.

I pushed open the front door, which led almost straight into our living room. Dad looked up and before I'd even stepped into the house properly he leaped up, grabbing me by the hair.

'You little bitch,' he screamed in my face. 'Look at the state of you! Soaked through!'

Raising his hand, with his palm open flat, a smack landed on the side of my head, sending me reeling across the room. I had no time to cover my head; the blows came so fast, my ears were ringing.

From the corner of my eye, I could see Laura standing there, open mouthed, watching. Through the pain, a new feeling emerged: humiliation. Sobbing, I tried to cover my face as I saw Laura silently turn and leave. After slapping me at least ten times, Dad breathed in deeply.

'Dad!' I sobbed. 'But you said you didn't care if I got wet!'

'I meant if the rain got you wet,' he screamed. 'I didn't mean that you could go and jump into every puddle you saw! You've got such an evil streak, Terrie. You manipulative little cow.'

Howling now with pain and embarrassment as Laura had seen what my dad was really like, I ran upstairs as he landed one last blow on my bottom. Lying on my bed, I tried to rub the red hand marks left from each smack. I felt the hatred flood through me. Why couldn't I have been born into a family like Laura's?

Laura never mentioned Dad's beating. The next time I saw her she just looked at me sadly. 'I wish I could give you my rain-coat,' she said.

*

When I was about five, Dad bought an enormous rigid plastic paddling pool and built the rest of our garden around it. Filling it with water, it attracted all the neighbours' kids who loved splashing around in it, playing boats or just dipping their toes in whenever the sun came out. These are some of the nicest memories I have from my childhood. For once I had something in our house to be proud of and kids on the estate 'knocked' for me instead.

Just like me, all the kids avoided the lodgers when they came over. Simon and Ron mainly kept out of our way but Pat would lurk around, giggling to himself as he watched us. But I didn't mind as for once Dad seemed to leave me alone when the pool was full and he was much scarier than Pervy Pat.

As I grew up, I became increasingly aware that I lived a 'different life' from other children. One day after school, I went to Laura's and we had a Chinese takeaway. It was chicken chow mein and it was absolutely delicious. I never knew food could taste that good. Laura also had new toys, and a walk-in wardrobe, where all her clothes were piled up neatly, unlike my heap of second-hand clothes all squashed in a chest of drawers. I never told Laura much about our house. And she didn't ask, not after she'd seen my beating. I never invited her back, unless it was to play in the pool; I always went to hers or we played outside instead. In all likelihood Laura's parents were scared of my dad, who could show his charm but also had a reputation for being free with his fists, so although I often visited Laura's house, I was never allowed to stay too long or sleep over. I always had to make my way back home with a heavy heart and just look in on Laura's world with wide eyes and silent jealousy.

*

By the time I was six years old, clothes had become an embarrassment for me. I always had the cheapest trainers, which quickly grew holes in the soles, and I'd gaze enviously at my classmates' shiny white branded versions. When I got home one day I started to complain to Mum and anyone who would listen.

'I want proper Fila trainers,' I snapped. 'It's not fair!' The second the words had left my mouth, I wanted to bite them back in case Dad went mental. But at the same time I felt that I couldn't keep my anger inside; I could feel it boiling over. It was so unfair and kids had started to poke fun at me. Dad tried to calm me down, and then he disappeared for half an hour, returning with a brand new pair of Fila trainers. Flinging the box at me, he looked at me with his hard stare.

'Now will you keep quiet?' he snarled.

Looking back now I'm sure he didn't buy them from the kindness of his heart. He was buying my silence. As I was older and mixing with other kids and teachers at school, Dad was probably scared that one day I'd tell someone what my home life was really like. Or about his morning 'cuddles'.

The following day Liz was downstairs in the kitchen, flicking on the kettle, sorting out her college books. As usual, the TV was blaring, Mum and Ron were sitting on the sofa, while Pat was drinking tea, drooling it down the side of his mouth.

'Morning, sweetie,' she said.

I looked at her and smiled. I loved Liz and the way she gave me a quiet wink. It felt sometimes like she was the only one who noticed me in a nice way.

'Would you like some toast?' she asked.

'Yes please,' I replied.

It never occurred to me to tell her what Dad was doing. I just knew that it would make him more cross than ever. Now he'd started to let me walk the five-minute journey to school by myself, so, after my toast, I said goodbye to Mum. She looked at me with her blank gaze. Then she went upstairs to do the washing as I left for school. She was always doing the washing; it was the only form of housework she did do. The machine downstairs was constantly humming. But she used the bath to wash sheets and towels. In the previous few months, Dad started to pay for gas to heat the radiators. And now every radiator in the entire house was always boiling, and draped with clothes of every description. But even the smell of clean laundry couldn't disguise the smell of cooking, dirt, sweat and the general sticky, musty air that pervaded every nook and cranny of our house.

Occasionally on the way to school, I found myself wondering if Mum knew about Dad's 'cuddles'. There had only been one time that she was still in the bedroom when I arrived. She was just getting up, groggy eyed as usual, as I approached Dad's figure lying under his filthy duvet. I was already trembling at the thought of what would happen next, but was flooded with relief when I saw that Mum was still there.

'Hello, Mummy,' I said.

'Morning,' she yawned.

Dad was staring at me with his hard look already, a smirk forming on his lips. 'Come on you,' he said, patting his side of the bed. 'Get in for your cuddle.'

I looked at Mum, my eyes pleading. 'Mummy?' I asked, my heart starting to thud again. 'I don't have to, do I?'

For a split second, I waited as my mum, the woman who was

supposed to care for me, looked straight through me as if I was made from glass. Her mouth twisted.

'Just get into bed and give your dad a cuddle!' she snapped. Abruptly she stood up and stalked out of the room, her nightie flapping around her knees.

And, as if my heart was made from glass, I felt it shatter. For a moment I struggled to hold down a sob in my chest, as my face grew hot with a growing, terrible realization. Mum didn't care. My own mum, the one person who was supposed to love me more than anyone, wasn't going to save me. Did she know what Dad was about to do? Or did she think it really was just a cuddle? I'd no time to think, as Dad's hand was now slapping the mattress impatiently.

'Get. In,' he commanded.

I climbed up, my limbs feeling like lead. I felt so worthless. I didn't even try and stop the tears as they dripped off my chin, making my sleep-fuzzy hair wet. Pulling off my knickers, Dad was just staring at my pale little body. In the usual routine he rolled up my nightie and licked his lips as he started rubbing and rocking himself, gently moaning. All while I listened to my mum's bare feet creeping downstairs to the kitchen for breakfast. Leaving me behind. My stomach felt sick with the betrayal, even if, back then, I didn't know the meaning of the word.

Arriving in the playground each morning, I saw other mums kissing their daughters 'cheerio' on their cheeks, handing them lovingly packed lunches and waving them off. I had free school meals and knew I'd walk myself home to find Mum weeping on the sofa. She'd been doing a lot of that lately.

Although Mum wasn't a big presence in my life, one particular afternoon she suddenly disappeared. I'd sensed something was wrong as she'd grown even quieter recently and the crying fits had lasted longer. Now her chair was empty.

'Where's Mum?' I asked Liz.

'Oh sweetheart, she's gone to hospital,' she said.

'What for?' I asked.

'She's just tired,' Liz said, by way of explanation.

I didn't understand. I was often tired. I always went to bed late, after watching a horror film Dad put on. But even after staying up really late and feeling completely shattered, I didn't need to go to hospital like Mum. Maybe she just needed more sleep?

A few days later, Dad took me to see Mum. She was wearing a hospital gown and looked pale, her face a complete blank. Mum was rocking in silence as we sat opposite her across a plastic table, our chairs nailed to the floor. She smelt like chemicals.

Dad just kept saying, 'She's not well.'

Mum only spoke and looked at Dad, not me. She told him they were giving her something called 'electric shock treatment' and it made Mum cry when she described it. 'They hold me down,' she said, pointing to a passing doctor. The fear I saw in her eyes made me shiver. I just sat and kicked my feet under the chair, wondering when we could go home. I decided then and there that I didn't like hospitals.

For the next year or so, Mum stayed away as she'd suffered a severe nervous breakdown, although this was never properly explained to me at the time. Dad insisted I went regularly to visit her, even if sometimes she could barely recognize me. I didn't miss Mum particularly, as Liz was the one who, in effect, looked after me, especially since the council had found my nan another house and she wasn't living with us any more. The hospital was a cold, horrible-smelling place and all the people looked ill, shuffling around in their pyjamas, shaking, muttering or rocking themselves. Mum rarely spoke and just looked vacant – until Dad kissed her goodbye, when she'd manage a smile or try to cling on to him.

On one visit, I walked into the meeting room and said 'Hello, Mum', but as she looked in my direction she just started screaming.

'Get her out!' she shrieked, pointing at me. 'Who is this child? She's not mine! She doesn't belong to me!'

She became so upset that nurses ran towards her to pin her arms down and drag her away. All the while she turned her head to try and look me in the eye. 'You don't belong to me!' she screeched. While her words rang in my ears, Dad dragged me back down the hospital corridor to the car park.

'Terrie the Terror, why did you go upsetting your mum like that?' Dad snapped. He glared at me as though it was my fault. Then he bundled me back in the car and we drove home in silence.

'We're still going to see her next week when she's better, Terrie,' he said. I didn't want to go, but I knew I couldn't say so.

But the following week something else happened that stopped any planned visits to see Mum. I was sitting watching *Thundercats* on TV while Dad was pottering in the kitchen, rolling one of his Golden Virginia cigarettes, when he suddenly stiffened. As if in slow motion, he grabbed his heart, the veins on his neck protruding as he fell forwards like a felled tree. He bashed his head on the kitchen surface as he collapsed on to the floor.

I watched him twist with pain, shocked at what I was seeing. My scary dad, a great brute of a man, was in agony on the floor – I'd never seen him look so vulnerable. Unusually, everyone happened to be out of the house. I had no idea what was happening to Dad, but knew it must be serious: he'd gone a funny colour and was gasping for air. I flew out of the front door and ran to our neighbours, Tracey and Keith, and began screaming through the letter box.

'My dad is on the floor dying!' I cried.

Tracey followed me and ran inside, as Keith called an ambulance. Within minutes, I was standing in the kitchen watching as paramedics knelt by my father, trying to resuscitate him. Strangely I felt quite detached, like an audience member viewing a play I wasn't enjoying. At the age of six, I was old enough to realize that my dad might be dying or badly hurt, but I didn't care about that. I wasn't afraid to lose him.

After he was carted off on a stretcher, Tracey gave me a quick hug. 'Hopefully he'll be okay,' she said.

She looked genuinely upset. She liked my Dad. 'He's the salt of the earth,' she kept saying, as though she meant it. I'd forgotten how people viewed Dad outside the house. Reg was seen as one of life's good guys.

'If you need anything, just ask,' said Tracey as she left, assuming that the lodgers would take over looking after me.

That evening, when my uncles returned home, the atmosphere in the house changed. No one knew what to do. Ron, Simon and Pervy Pat argued over who was cooking. Liz was crying.

'He's got to get better,' she sobbed. 'He's got to!'

With no beatings and no 'cuddles' to endure, I felt relieved – relaxed, even. I got myself some bread and butter for dinner that night and went to bed. For the first time in a long time, I closed my eyes without dreading the following morning.

THREE

A Silent Evil

The next afternoon Tracey walked me to nearby Lister Hospital to see Dad. None of the lodgers wanted to see him. Liz was going to visit after college, and Mum was in hospital herself still, so I was the only visitor. He was lying with tubes poking out of his face and hands. He looked thinner, his receding hair suddenly making his face look like a skull, ageing him beyond his fifty-five years.

Tracey asked the nurse about his stroke and she explained that he'd been left unable to speak. The stroke had led to a huge heart attack. But he knew who we all were. The look in his eye hardened when I walked into the room.

'Hello, Reg,' said Tracey softly, as if talking to a child. 'I've brought Terrie in to see you.' She placed a bottle of lemonade on the shelf next to his bed. He liked lemonade, but he couldn't drink it as he was being fed with a tube.

'You just need to rest up now,' she said, as he stared at her.

She popped out of the room to the toilet, and I was left alone with Dad. My new silent, ill dad, who couldn't speak but still made me feel uncomfortable just being in his presence. Pointing to something on the small chest of drawers next to him, Dad indicated with his eyes and eyebrows that he wanted me to pick it up.

I walked over and saw a small, long pot. Unsure what it was, I picked it up, then passed it to him. He managed to raise a hand and take it from me. Then he held it over his groin area. Staring at me hard in the face, he smirked as much as his stiff face would allow. And I realized that it was a patient's bottle for weeing in. I shivered as he stared at me. He didn't actually use it; he didn't need to. But he was trying to show me that without needing to utter a single word, he still had the ability to make me feel dirty. And I was left in no doubt as to who was in control.

Life at home was incredibly hectic during the week Dad was in hospital. With the adults rowing over who needed to cook what, we sometimes ended up eating round at Tracey's house. As much as I hated being around my dad, he provided a framework and routine for our house and when he wasn't there it quickly descended into chaos.

Uncle Pat loved Dad being away as he was free to take more pictures of me than ever with no one there to stop him. One morning he filled up the paddling pool outside in the garden. Pulling on my swimming costume, I was excited to have a go. But as I started splashing around, Pat jumped out of the back door, a manic grin on his face.

'Come and give me a smile, my lovely,' he said, raising his camera. Instinctively, I wrapped my arms around my body, a familiar uncomfortable feeling rising in my chest.

'No!' I snapped. 'I don't want to, Pat!'

He glared at me. 'What? Why not? Come on! What's wrong with you, eh?'

Liz had recently moved out to live with her latest boyfriend, and on this particular day she had popped back to pick up some clothes she'd left behind. She poked her head round the door when she overheard Pat's raised voice. 'Aw c'mon, Terrie,' she chided. 'He's only after an effing picture!'

I stood with my arms folded and poked out my tongue at Pat's camera, as I watched dribble starting to ooze from his lower lip. But despite the battles with Pat, I felt freer and happier than I could remember.

Then, after only a few days, we ran out of food. Ron and Simon were incapable of doing any shopping, and although Liz popped back occasionally, she was busier than ever in her life, always moving from one college course to another. I was now seven, and I think there was a presumption on her part that I was able to look after myself. So I just took myself off to school as it was only five minutes away. And when I was hungry I made myself a bowl of cereal as that was one thing we always had in the cupboards – whatever brand was on offer in the shops at the time. But after a few days of eating it for breakfast, lunch and dinner, I found that even that was running low.

One evening, I was so hungry, I decided to go shopping myself.

'Can I, Ron?' I asked. He looked at me blankly and fished out £20. He was on benefits and never seemed short of money.

'Only get frozen stuff,' he said, by way of direction.

I walked into town, a mile or so away, and pushed a trolley around Iceland. Dumping in as many pizzas, sausages and loaves of bread as I could gather, I popped in a few other bits like sweets and chocolate, then paid at the till.

'Is your mum with you?' asked the cashier, peering at me.

'Yes, she's waiting outside,' I lied. At just over three feet tall and weighing only a few stone, I looked much younger than my seven years. I was so hungry, I crossed my fingers, hoping there wouldn't be any trouble so that I could get home as soon as possible and eat some of the food I was buying.

'Okay, pet,' she said. She scanned the food, her eyes flitting back to me with concern. She looked like a warm, loving lady. I found my mind wandering for a few moments, wondering what it would be like to have her as a mummy. After scanning the items, I bagged them up and heaved them into the trolley. It weighed a ton.

'How you getting it home, pet?' the lady asked.

'Just pushing it to the car park,' I said, cheerfully. 'My mummy's waiting.'

Confidently I pushed the trolley out of the door, but not to any waiting vehicle. When no one was looking I carried on pushing the trolley past the car park, into the street, down the road, and all the way home. Navigating kerbs and pavements with a trolley was a nightmare, and I struggled to push it up and down but I couldn't stop smiling. All I could think of was having a full stomach that night. Back home, I put the oven on full blast and filled up our blackened dirty baking trays with pizza. They emerged burned at the edges and soggy in the middle, but I couldn't care less. I polished mine off in minutes.

A week later, Dad was discharged from hospital and our mini holiday from Reg's regime was over. He shuffled in with a walking stick, helped by Keith.

'If there is anything at all we can do . . . ' Keith said.

Dad winked at him, looking every inch the grateful, charming neighbour. He even managed to smile, although he was still struggling to move his face properly. The smile remained until the door clicked shut and then his eyes scanned the room. Still unable to speak, he moved slowly, one foot dragging behind him. Picking up a mug on the sideboard, the nearest thing to him, he held it up high as he flung it with full force across the room above the heads of Ron and Simon who were watching TV. The shattering porcelain forced everyone to fall into an uneasy silence. Dad still couldn't speak but it was his way of telling us he was home. Shortly afterwards he banned me and all the local kids from using the giant paddling pool. He asked one of the lodgers to buy a load of fish and put them in instead. Using his hands and miming, he managed to get all his instructions across. Everyone was desperate to understand what Dad wanted as fast as possible. His patience was at an all-time low.

For the next three weeks, Dad was still in recovery and would disappear every few days to hospital for treatment and therapy. He was gradually growing stronger, though, and, as his strength grew, so did the force of his temper. His frustration at not being able to shout at or hit anyone meant most of the crockery was smashed on walls or on the floor, then swept into the bin. I could just look on helpless. I couldn't deny that I was enjoying the relief of him having a disability, of him not being able to slap or 'cuddle' me any more. It might sound horrible, but for me Dad's heart attack was one of the best things to have happened for ages.

Slowly, however, I could see Dad's ability to move improving every day and my relief began to be replaced by fear.

I tried to avoid Dad whenever I could, especially by staying in my bedroom. Then, one afternoon, I was playing with my Barbies in my bedroom when Pervy Pat started banging on our ceiling with a broom handle. That was his way of telling me to pipe down. If I made any noise at all he hated it – even if I so much as laughed, which I didn't often do. This time, I was chucking my Barbies on the floor, and it was disturbing him.

'Shut up!' he yelled.

Then I heard some tramping of feet. It sounded like Dad with his stick knocking on the stairs. Then the door slammed open, causing my dressing gown hanging on it to fall on the floor. Standing at his full height, Dad started slapping me as hard as possible over my head and face. I cowered, dropping to the floor, as I screamed and cried. I used my arms as shields, but he just pulled them apart and then slapped even harder, catching my ears and pulling my hair. I curled into a ball, as his fists landed on my sides and legs. After a few minutes spent slapping me, he left the room panting and flushed with the exertion. As he left I thought once again how much I hated him. I pulled myself on to my mattress and lay there sobbing, knowing I had no one to comfort me. I knew it was Dad's way of telling me he was fit again and able to hurt me as much as ever.

The next morning I woke up to hear a familiar voice calling down the hallway. 'Terrie,' croaked Dad. I almost sat bolt upright as Dad's voice penetrated my sleep. He was quieter than usual, a little bit slurred. But it was unmistakably him.

'Time . . . for . . . your cud-dle,' he stuttered, the first proper sentence he'd said since his heart attack.

And so it began again. My holiday from Dad's abuse was over. He'd recovered sufficiently enough from his heart attack and stroke to get aroused again. And when I pushed open the bedroom door that morning he couldn't have looked happier.

While Dad was recovering, it was Mum's turn to come out of hospital. Ordinarily, a child would be thrilled that their mother was coming home after such a long absence, but I wasn't looking forward to it. In truth, by now, my own mother disgusted me. She looked terrible, with her straggly hair and wild, staring bug eyes, due to all the medication and electric shock treatment. Before she'd gone in she was depressed and tired. Now her behaviour was even worse as she'd lost all sense of co-ordination and would sway and fall over all the time. Her memory had been affected and her moods seemed more unstable than ever. Before she'd gone into hospital she'd grown addicted to dyeing her hair and the local chemist now refused to serve her as it had started to fall out. Her hair was wild, a riot of shades of orange with patches of baldness from the electric shocks. She reminded me of 'Fraggle' from Fraggle Rock, so that's what I started to call her when Dad wasn't around. I didn't like calling her 'Mum' anyway, especially now that her appearance and behaviour had started to frighten me. I didn't know what a real mum was supposed to be like, but she definitely didn't match up to the image I had in my mind.

Dad drove her home and she shuffled into the living room like a shadow, looking around blankly. She sat in the corner like a statue, staring at the TV.

'Now Mum's back,' Dad said, 'it's up to you to look after her. She'll need washing and feeding. If you don't do it, you'll know about it.'

That evening, after our meat dinner, Dad slammed a pot of yoghurt down in front of me.

'Feed your mum,' he snapped, before turning to the TV.

Mum looked at me, her eyes half lolling around her head. She smelt terribly of urine and body odour. I pulled the lid off the yoghurt and stuck the spoon in. As I tried to put it in her mouth she poked her tongue out, smearing the white stuff over her lips. Within a few seconds she looked like a middle-aged toddler. I felt my stomach turn as I tried to get the yoghurt down her. The whole of her face was coated and she leered at me, half smirking, as if she found the fact that I was struggling funny. Even then I knew something was very wrong. To me, a small child feeding an adult felt like the world had gone mad. I knew I shouldn't be feeding my own mum, even if she wasn't much of a mother to me.

'Come on, Fraggle,' I said. 'Eat it!'

Afterwards, Dad told me to bathe Mum. I led her upstairs by the hand like a child, and then took off her clothes. She was so thin you could see every single rib and her collarbone stuck out like a carcass. Her skin was papery like an old woman's and she smelt dreadful. Somehow I understood it was degrading and embarrassing for us both. I pointed to the bath and she leaned on my narrow shoulders to step in. Then she sat there looking at me like a baby, waiting to be washed. I squeezed out a warm flannel and rubbed her body with it. I closed my eyes, barely wanting to look.

I went to bed that night and stared at the ceiling for ages. *I hate living here*, I thought to myself. I was just a little girl but I hated my life. I hated the people who lived in my house and I even hated my own parents. I closed my eyes and thought of Laura, who lived with her family only a few metres away, but they might as well have been on a different planet. Their house always smelt lovely, was always as warm as toast, and her mum couldn't do enough for her. Laura could laugh, sing, play, and just breathe normally from the moment she woke up to when she went to bed.

Now on top of having Dad back, and avoiding Pat, I had to look after a mum who acted like a kid younger than myself. Just the thought of having to live like this made me want to scream. But there was no escape. I pulled my sleeping bag tight to my chest, imagining that it was someone giving me a warm hug, telling me everything was going to be OK. I wiped away my tears; as usual, there wasn't any point in crying. No one was really going to hug me.

Dad was in and out of hospital constantly over the next two years and by and large I fended for myself for food. Pervy Pat often cooked for Ron and Simon. They made proper meals and ate them at the table together. They never offered me any, or noticed me looking at them while they ate. I never dared to ask them for any of it either. They saw themselves as paying lodgers who had nothing to do with this annoying kid. Mum didn't make food for anyone, even herself. She lived on tea and biscuits. So I carried on doing the shopping every week, unless Dad was at home and able to do the occasional run.

I only ate pizzas or sausage sandwiches for dinner. Not knowing how to cook them properly meant that often I just grilled the sausages on one side and ended up eating them half-raw. A couple of times I woke up with terrible stomach pains, throwing up at the side of my bed. As I screamed in pain, enough to wake the neighbours, Mum managed to find it in herself to ring for an ambulance to take me to casualty a few times with food poisoning. I was never told how to cook them properly, though. As long as they sizzled in the frying pan and smelt and tasted good, I ate them up.

One day, when I was still six, Dad took me out of my first school suddenly and sent me to Giles Primary School, a short walk away from the house.

'You won't be going back to that school next week, Terrie,' he said. 'You're going to a new one. I'll walk you there until you know the way.' And that was the only explanation I was given.

Looking back, I realize that he probably didn't like the fact that I was making friends at school, and he didn't want me getting close to any of the teachers. I think he reasoned that if he moved me on before I felt comfortable enough to confide in anyone, he would be able to carry on getting his 'cuddles'. Also, I'd started to get involved in a few fights in the playground and teachers had begun to complain about me. It was nothing serious, just small, petty rows over silly things. But my behaviour had been pointed out to Dad during one of his drop-offs and he didn't want me drawing attention to myself. I wasn't sad to leave my old school behind, as it wasn't especially nice, and I definitely didn't miss the playground taunts. And I suppose it made things easier for Dad as he didn't have to drive me anymore.

The Sunday evening before I was due to start at the new school, Dad came into the living room and threw me a pair of jogging bottoms and a white T-shirt.

'There's your uniform,' he said.

I looked down at the clothes on my lap and my heart sank. Yet again I would be known as the 'poor' kid, the one who couldn't afford a proper uniform like the rest of the children.

'Well, what do you say, you ungrateful little cow?' Dad's angry shout snapped me out of my thoughts.

'Sorry, Dad. Thanks.' I gave him as much of a smile as I could muster.

'That's more like it,' he replied, as he headed into the kitchen to make a cup of tea. I remember feeling angry as I knew that Dad could have quite easily found the money for my uniform if he had wanted to.

I was never happy at Giles Primary; I always looked scruffy and all the kids singled me out as different from them, so I never felt like I fitted in. Then, a few months after I started there we had a rounders lesson taken by a teacher called Mr Rustkin. I was standing by the side as I saw him watching a girl who was messing around, doing a handstand as she waited in the queue for the bat. I felt my palms break into a sweat as I spotted the all-too-familiar gleam in his eyes as his gaze roved over her knickers when she kicked her legs into the air. Well, that's how it appeared to me at the time. I couldn't believe this was happening in school; it was so wrong. I was filled with a fury I couldn't control, and I wasn't going to let this teacher get away with it.

'You pervert!' I screamed in the middle of the lesson. 'What do you think you're doing?'

Mr Rustkin spun around, his mouth open with shock. He narrowed his eyes as he spotted the culprit – me.

'Terrie O'Brian,' he yelled. 'How dare you speak to me like that!'

Grabbing my arm, he started dragging me to the Head Teacher's office. 'You need a proper speaking to,' he said. 'Rude little girl.'

I found my feet dragging on the shiny corridor floor as he

pulled me up the stairs to see the Head. I could feel the anger building inside me, my sense of outrage even stronger now that he was manhandling me like a sack of potatoes.

'You're nothing but a disgusting perv,' I shrieked, as we arrived at the top of the staircase.

Trying to grab me again, he lost his grip, and without thinking I turned round and pushed him with all my might. I watched in slow motion as he swayed a little and then began to topple, step by step, bashing his back and shoulders again and again before landing in a crumpled heap at the bottom.

I gasped out loud and my heart felt as though it had stopped for a few seconds. I couldn't register what was happening. What had I done? I'd never been this naughty at school before. But then I'd never spotted a teacher being a perv, either. The Head flung his door open to see what the commotion was about. When he saw Mr Rustkin picking himself up, he grabbed me by the shoulders and stood me in front of his desk, while Mr Rustkin got his breath back, brushed himself down and recounted the story.

'I was just taking a lesson as normal when Terrie began shouting obscenities at me in front of the other kids,' he said.

Naturally, he denied that he was a pervert and, naturally, the Head Teacher believed him.

'You, young lady,' said the Head, 'are now in deep trouble.'

I glared at him and at that moment stopped caring. I knew he'd never believe me. No adult ever listened to me, no one cared. I just stared out of the window as he told me he'd ring my parents and tell them.

As if they're going to do anything, I thought to myself.

The next day, Dad, fuming, brought me in to school. I'd told him the Head wanted to see him, but hadn't explained exactly why. Standing in front of the Head as he recounted the previous day's events, Dad started shouting, spittle flying out of his mouth as he spat his words.

'If my daughter says that a man's a pervert, then he's a pervert!' he raged.

Even the Head looked a bit scared after a few minutes. He could barely get a word in edgeways as the full force of my father's anger raged.

'Right, well, Mr O'Brian. Let's end this conversation now, as Terrie is obviously beyond help. I was going to expel her anyway. So from this moment she is expelled . . . '

He stood up and indicated for us to leave.

'You're all dirty bastards,' snarled Dad, as he led me away by the hand. On the way home he never said a word about it. Part of me saw, even then, how Dad was being a hypocrite. He was as pervy as Mr Rustkin, probably much worse, but he didn't seem to see it.

Looking back, I don't know whether Mr Rustkin had been eyeing up the girl, or whether I'd simply grown paranoid about this sort of behaviour and had imagined the whole thing. I suppose I'll never know for sure. The only thing I do know for certain is that I wasn't yet seven years old and already my trust in all men had disappeared.

FOUR

He Can't Hurt Me Anymore

The next school I was sent to was Moss Bury Primary. Dad told me that I could never bring any kids from my class home for tea. 'You have your old friends on the estate,' he said. I think this was because they already 'knew' our family, and many of them, I suspect now, had family problems of their own, so they didn't concern themselves with our business. Dad didn't want any more outsiders in. The nearby neighbours were used to hearing the rows and the chaos in our house, but he didn't want other parents questioning it. So once again I found myself in a school where I knew no one and I didn't have the proper uniform. I'd long grown out of the Fila trainers and they'd been replaced by a pair of cheap trainers that I had to wear all day as well as for PE. Right from the start most of the kids gave me a wide berth. I was used to it by now, and it didn't matter anyway as, after only a few months there, Dad suddenly told me one morning that I was to join yet another school.

The next day I was sent to a school called Bandley Hill, miles away on the other side of Stevenage. It meant that Dad had to drive me to and from school every morning. But even that inconvenience didn't stop him. He seemed determined that my school would be the one furthest from our house. If Dad couldn't drive because he was too ill, he'd pay for a cab for me.

To my own surprise, I actually really enjoyed going to Bandley Hill. Because I was so far away, no one knew me or had heard of me and my family. I felt I could start afresh. I quickly found a group of pleasant enough friends, and never breathed a word to anyone about my dad or my strange family set-up. I just pretended all was well with the world. I was a real tomboy and found that I loved playing football with the boys at break or climbing trees. In some ways I felt I could be myself for once. I had recently become a bit of a troublemaker, but at Bandley Hill I tried to be good and behave. Because the kids were from nicer families they were kinder to me and didn't tease me about looking scruffy all the time; they saw beyond that. I began to look forward to each new day and would sit tapping my foot on the floor of the car as Dad drove me to school in the morning, desperate for us to arrive at the gates.

For the first time I started to get along with a teacher. The Head, Mr Harris, insisted on having private meetings with me every week to see how I was getting on. He had a gentle, kind manner, and although I never fully trusted him, as I never did any man, I felt drawn towards him as he took a genuine interest in me. He seemed to actually care. Most likely he guessed, just by the look of my 'uniform', that things weren't right at home and that I wasn't from a 'nice' family like the other kids.

I never told him about Dad, but I did once tell him something wasn't right in my house. I explained about cooking sausages every night for dinner and watching horror films. I told him how many adults lived there.

'No one really talks to me much, though,' I said, shrugging.

He'd listen with genuine concern in his eyes. 'Is that why you act up in class sometimes?' he asked.

I shrugged again. Sometimes I still got sent out of the room or kept in at playtime for some row or other, even though I loved my new friends. But I really didn't know why I did it.

Mr Harris would listen with interest, but didn't ask a lot of questions. He didn't ask if I was ever hit or whether I was being abused. But he started ringing the house every day to have a 'chat' with Mum or Dad, depending on who picked up the phone. Mum would happily talk to him when she could. Doctors were constantly trying new pills on her and sometimes she had moments of being quite lucid and was able to chat on the phone. 'What a lovely man,' she'd say, putting the phone down. Dad on the other hand, would be a bit short with him, while still trying to show his charming side as much as possible to avoid any suspicion.

Afterwards he was never happy. 'Why does this Mr Harris keep ringing?' he raged. 'None of your teachers has ever rung up before.' I didn't know either really. Although I was the dirty kid with the wrong uniform, I never had any bruises on show. Nobody knew about anything that went on at home or that Dad hit me. I think Dad was careful never to leave any marks. He would often turn to me with an angry, suspicious look on his face and ask, 'Have you been saying something, eh? Terrie the Terror, eh?'

'No!' I would cry, running upstairs, bracing myself for a quick kick on the behind. 'I'd never say a word.'

During all the time Dad was in and out of hospital, it didn't stop him from abusing me. Only the first big heart attack made him stop for a few weeks. Not once did he have to threaten me not to tell anyone. He ruled the whole house with such terror, I'd never dare breathe a word to a friend or teacher, or anyone, about the 'cuddles'. Instinctively, I knew it would lead to the beating of my life and no good would come of it. He never threatened me directly, but he never needed to. There was a constant atmosphere of threat hanging in the stale air.

Just once did he say, 'If you tell your mum what's happening, she'll get ill again and have to go back to hospital. She'll end up a vegetable and it will be your fault.'

And so the 'cuddles' carried on, most mornings, around 7 a.m. The routine never varied through all the years. He ignored my tears, never looked at me, and always rubbed himself on top of me. But as much as I hated him, I also knew he loved me in his own messed-up way. Once I was shouted at by a friend's mother across the estate for being rude. When Dad found out, he raced out of the house like a madman. He came back, sweating, telling us how he'd punched the dad and no one was ever to speak to me like that again. 'No one can criticize you, Terrie,' he said. 'No one.'

He might regularly have been abusing me, but somehow he didn't want anyone else to do it.

Gradually Mum grew a little better and we were able to hold conversations with her. 'How was school, Terrie?' she asked one afternoon. Mum was taking an interest in me – I was almost too shocked to answer. I managed to say something about liking my English lessons and the book I was reading. Mum soon became vacant again, but at least she'd attempted to have a normal conversation. It was more than I usually got. I never knew if it was the medication stopping her or the fact she didn't care. Maybe it was a mix of the two.

Dad's rule over the house was absolute again. He'd never particularly liked Pervy Pat but relations between him and all the lodgers were especially strained. One evening I was watching TV downstairs when we heard an incredible racket – a door banged and there was screaming coming from the bathroom upstairs.

'You dirty bastard!' Dad was screaming.

The sound of Pat's lisping voice crying in pain was heard in between cracking sounds of knuckles on bone. My nan, who was staying at the house again for a while, was shrieking like a banshee. She came running out of the bathroom clutching a towel to her wrinkly, naked body.

Pat suddenly emerged, flying backwards out of the bathroom door, rolling down the stairs, knocking into the bannisters and the wall as he came. In an absolute fury Dad charged down after him.

'You piece of filth!' Dad screamed, standing over him. 'You disgust me!'

'What's going on?' asked Ron. 'What's the commotion?'

'He's been taking photos of Margaret in the bathroom,' cried Dad. 'And I'm teaching him a lesson.' I watched as Pervy Pat curled into a ball, dribble mixed with blood pouring down his jumper, while Dad continued kicking him. My instinct was to run out of the house, perhaps to the park, but I didn't want to draw attention to myself, so I turned up the TV to drown out the sound, feeling sick to my stomach.

Later on we discovered that Pat would pay Liz and Nan £50 for taking pictures of them naked. Nan had actually agreed to do it for some extra money, but this time Dad had caught him. And, naturally, as the man of the house, he didn't approve. Nan's mental state had never been good. She was easily led and Pat probably bullied her into it.

During the incident, Dad broke the lock on the bathroom door and never got it replaced. This made the lack of privacy even worse. By the age of nine I had started puberty and was more mindful than ever of Pervy Pat's roving eyes.

Where the lock used to be there was a hole that I would stuff with toilet tissue before I jumped in the bath. I could never fully relax and always had a quick wash in case Pat was lurking around. One day, though, after securely covering the hole, I allowed myself to lie back in the bubbles when I heard a scraping sound. The tip of a ballpoint pen was being shoved through. Bits of tissue fell to the floor and I could hear Pat's heavy breathing on the other side of the door before his leering eyeball emerged into view.

'Stop it!' I screamed, grabbing a towel and stepping out of the bath.

I could hear him laughing behind the door, a horrible, low cackle. 'Only a game, Terrie,' he whispered.

Without hesitation I poked my index finger through the hole, jabbing him straight in the eye.

'Leave me alone!' I shrieked.

'Owwww!' he yelled, clutching his eye. 'You little cow!'

He never did leave me alone, though. Every time Dad was asleep or out, and I was using the loo or having a bath, he'd creep upstairs and cheekily push the tissue out of the hole. I couldn't relax behind that door for a single second. There was nowhere to hide.

There was also little to do in the house now that Dad had put fish in the paddling pool. Sometimes I'd peer at them, watching them peacefully swimming around. Sometimes I'd put my hand in and watch them gently nibble. How I missed playing in the pool with my friends!

One hot afternoon Dad caught me dipping my toes in. 'Get out of it!' he yelled. 'That pool is only for fish now.'

I leapt up, shaking my feet dry. It was so unfair. I wanted my pool back, the one good thing about our house. I ran upstairs to the bedroom, grateful he'd not slapped me this time. The following day, Dad filled it with tiny little piranha fish he'd got one of the lodgers to buy from a dodgy pet shop in Stevenage.

'You'll get nipped!' he laughed, the next time I went near it. 'Go on, try it! Go on!'

I didn't know that Dad had put the piranha in there but I knew something wasn't quite right by the look on his face. Gingerly, I dipped a toe in the water, watching Dad's face crack up with laughter as the fish went into a frenzy. I gasped in horror, as a terrible pain tore through my big toe.

'Argh!' I squealed, nearly falling backwards on to the concrete.

As blood dripped down my foot, Dad was roaring: 'Ha! ha!' I told you, you little terror.'

I limped off, sobbing. I knew Dad could be cruel but this was so deliberate I felt even more crushed than usual.

A few days later Dad was showing off to Ron how dangerous the fish were. 'They are vicious little bastards,' he boasted, poking his finger in. He didn't remove it quite fast enough, and instantly a fish bit his finger, causing him to yelp in pain. Red blood dripped into the pool as he turned and waved his injured finger. 'They'll keep all little hands and feet out of that pool,' he said proudly as he shot a look in my direction.

*

A few months after I started at Bandley Hill, I came home from school to find Mum in tears yet again on the sofa. This time, though, she was sobbing loudly and looked even more distraught than usual.

'Dad's in hospital,' she cried. 'He collapsed again.'

Not understanding what had happened, she had called a doctor to ask him to bring a wheelchair, but he'd advised her to send for an ambulance. Dad was now in intensive care and they didn't know if he'd survive.

'Will he get better?' I asked. I didn't feel much. No panic or big upset. Seeing Mum in tears was such a normal sight, anyway. I was used to it.

'Liz is moving back in to take care of you,' she said, not answering my question.

I sat on the floor staring into space as Ron and Simon sat on the sofa behind me watching TV. No one uttered a word. I felt nothing. No upset, no concern, no relief, just nothing. My Dad could be dying, and I didn't care.

Mum was taken by Tracey and Keith to visit Dad and Pat was in his room, so I sat downstairs watching another horror video before bedtime. I slept soundly that night, knowing that in the morning there would be no call for a 'cuddle'. At 4 a.m., I was woken by the telephone and then the sound of Liz sobbing uncontrollably. I went downstairs to find her shaking with tears on the sofa.

'It's Reg,' she said, looking up as I came in. 'The hospital says he is deteriorating.'

She called a cab and jumped in to go and visit him too. I went back to bed, wondering what would happen next. The following morning, there was still no news, so I flicked on the TV and tried to enjoy the peace. Eventually Pat came downstairs and spotted me sitting there, waiting. 'What you waiting for? A bus?' he said.

'It's Dad,' I said. 'He's "deteriorating". What does that mean, Pat?'

Pat's face lit up as if he'd won the lottery. 'It means your father is going to die!' he cried with a cruel laugh. Then he started doing a little jig on the carpet. 'Reg will be dead!' he sang, with an evil grin. Even though I had mixed feelings towards Dad and his illness, watching Pervy Pat dance like a devil knowing my dad was dying made my stomach twist into a knot.

A few hours later Mum came home with Liz. Both were sobbing and holding each other.

'He was so special,' Liz cried, as Mum blew her nose.

'I don't know what I'll do without him,' Mum replied, her voice sounding like a little child's.

Seeing me on the sofa, Mum's face hardened a little, before becoming an emotionless blank again. 'Your dad's dead,' she said very simply. Then without so much as looking for my reaction, she went upstairs to bed. It was Liz who fell to her knees, covering me with kisses and hugs.

'Your dad was a good man, a good 'un!' she kept repeating.

Her tears surprised me. She was utterly devastated, crying as if it was her own husband who had died. I suspect now that she was having 'cuddle time' of her own with my dad. I would hear her laughter coming from Dad's room at night, and remember the way she looked at him sometimes. It didn't mean much then, but now I think that she was in love with him.

I didn't cry. I felt shocked, but not a single tear for my father escaped my eyes. I wasn't sure what it meant, but knowing the abuse was going to stop made me want to weep with relief. Yes, my own dad had died but my days of living with a knot in my tummy and constantly flinching from anticipated slaps were over. And that could only be a good thing.

Although Mum didn't seem to care one way or another whether I was upset or not, she insisted I was taken on a trip to the mortuary to see Dad's body.

'You need to say goodbye,' she said.

I didn't want to go and felt my heart beat in panic during the bus ride to the funeral parlour. I didn't want to see a dead body. Especially Dad's. When we arrived, we stepped inside a room filled with white flowers and pictures of different kinds of coffins for relatives to choose from. The whole place gave me the creeps, but nothing prepared me for seeing Dad in the side room.

He was laid out in a coffin already but as I walked closer, I hesitated, resisting the urge to run away. Rigor mortis had already set in and he was as stiff as a board, but his arm was pointing slightly upwards with his index finger pointing out. And his waxy finger was pointing precisely in my direction. I gasped and squeezed my eyes shut, but it was no good. When I dared to open them again, Dad was still there, his skin the colour of ash and his finger pointing sinisterly at me.

I moved to the side, as far away from him as I could get. Mum was sniffing into her tissue, drying her eyes repeatedly as tears still came. 'Reg,' she whispered tenderly. She reached out and prodded Dad's body in the side. Prod, prod. I watched as my mother poked his corpse. Over and over, as if she couldn't quite believe he was dead. I stepped closer and, copying Mum, I reached out a finger and gave Dad a good prod as well. He felt hard and like plastic, as though he were a mannequin in a shop. I felt nothing as I poked his side, his stomach, his shoulder. He didn't move. It felt almost good. The big beast of a man who'd hurt me so many times was now totally helpless. Mum watched as I stood poking my father like a piece of meat, neither of us muttering a word. Then abruptly she told me to say goodbye. It was time to go.

Mum insisted that only close family should be at the funeral. She dressed us both in new black outfits that Liz had bought us and, together with everyone else, we filed into the church. We must have looked so ordinary. A nice well-turned-out grieving daughter and widow about to say goodbye to a loving father and husband. There were flowers everywhere. Mum and Liz had organized masses of bouquets and wreaths.

Some were simple white, round wreaths; another one spelt out 'DAD'; some were from our neighbours, people who believed that Reg was a decent human being.

I stared at those letters: D-A-D. Thinking of what they meant. I knew other dads didn't do what he did to me. My friends at school never spoke of 'cuddles' and I knew they didn't get hit like I had. But now it was over and I could be grateful for that, if nothing else.

Mum was putting on a good show for the funeral. She'd gathered strength from somewhere over the past few days, deciding on flowers and food. She was able to speak to the few guests who came, too. 'Thank you,' she kept sniffing. 'Thank you for coming.' But I didn't know how long her recovery would last. I didn't trust it to be for long.

As the music began and we all turned to see the pall bearers carrying in Dad's wooden coffin, I was caught off guard by a sudden overwhelming sense of sadness. Dad really was dead. He was gone. It seemed so final. He might have been a pervert, but my dad was still my dad. He had never let anyone else lay a finger on me, and even though he was the person who had hurt me most, without him I felt more vulnerable than ever. He'd taught me to read. He had cooked my meat and potato meals, however horrible they were. He had put my pyjamas on the radiator so that they were warm when I put them on. I started weeping, covering my face and not wanting anyone to look. Dad was dead. He was dead! Sniffing, I gradually regained some composure and began trying to make sense of my feelings. How could I feel so sad and yet so relieved at the same time?

The vicar in the church gave a reading, talked about God and 'dust to dust'. He made no direct comment about Dad or his life or what sort of man he was. It was very simple and direct. Then we walked out of the chapel, to follow the coffin for the burial. That's when Mum's new face of strength broke. 'Reg!' she screamed, as the wooden box was lowered into the cold, hard ground. 'Don't leave me!' Then, to our horror, she started edging towards the muddy hole, putting one foot into it, almost losing her balance. My uncle, Mum's brother, stepped forward to stop her. 'What the hell are you doing, Carole?' he cried. He grabbed her elbow and pulled her back sharply, until both of them almost pitched backwards. 'Get a grip on yourself,' he cried. Mum's face dissolved into yet more tears as she was led away. I followed her, feeling strange, almost like I wasn't really there.

I rarely saw this uncle and he left shortly afterwards. He absolutely hated my dad and I think he only turned up to check that he really was dead.

Dad was buried under a simple cross with his name, date of birth and date of death. I never visited his grave again. As I left, I wiped away the tears from my cheeks. I didn't know whether to be angry at myself for crying, sad that he was gone, or just relieved. My emotions were such a whirl, clouding my mind, making me feel sick, that I felt numb by the time we got a taxi home.

Back at the house, Mum cleared out all of Dad's things into bin bags, only keeping his driving glasses and the mustard-coloured trilby hat he always wore.

'There you go,' she said, passing the hat to me. 'Keep it in your bedroom. A memento.'

I took it from her. Dad's familiar smell of Brute still clung to it. Then I put it on my chest of drawers. I thought about throwing it away but, actually, I didn't want to. You'd think it would fill me with fear but seeing his precious items made me certain of my true feelings. The sense of peace in the house already told me that it was over and I could feel that there wasn't an ounce of sadness left in me. Only relief. For, all the while his trilby was sitting on my chest of drawers, it wasn't on Dad's head. And that meant that he could no longer hurt me.

After Dad's funeral, Mum's new-found spirit quickly shrivelled like a popped balloon and she took herself off to bed, staying there for six weeks. She refused to eat or wash. Ron and Pervy Pat tried a couple of times to tempt her out of her bedroom but soon gave up. Liz was around sometimes, but she was so caught up in her new life that she didn't have much time to deal with Mum. She simply told me to keep giving her tea to drink 'to keep her going'.

So I did as Liz suggested and brought up tea on a tray for her, with bits of toast which she nibbled at, but other than that I tended to avoid her as much as I could. I hated going into her smelly, sweaty bedroom, the very place Dad had abused me in. When I saw her bizarre orangey hair sticking up in tufts over the duvet cover, I began to feel an urge to ruffle it and tease her. Her helplessness just made me angry now. I needed a mum now that Dad was gone, not this useless childlike woman. She looked so pathetic lying there, crying or just sleeping. Now even the washing wasn't being done. Dirty clothes were piling up and I was expected to wash my own. I had to cook, clean and wash clothes while she just hid under her duvet. I couldn't avoid life, so why should she?

'There you go, Fraggle,' I said, handing her her tea one morning. 'Drink that.' And then I shut the door on her for the rest of the day. Although it seems cruel to taunt someone as ill as she was, I was just a little girl who'd had enough. I wanted her to look after me for a change.

Just having been in that bedroom made me want to go and wash. Though washing was something else I couldn't do with ease. Not only because of Pervy Pat trying to cop a view through the keyhole, but also because of my dad. He might be dead, but every single time I leaned over the bathroom sink to brush my teeth or wash my hands, I'd look up into the mirror and nearly jump out of my skin. I'd 'see' him still standing behind me, glowering at me, as he used to do after our 'cuddles' and I'd feel the shivers running down my spine.

In certain ways, though, the first few weeks of my life after Dad's death felt amazing. It took a while for it to sink in, but my day-to-day existence had changed for good: no more shouting, no more beatings and no more being made to feel dirty and disgusting.

Finally, I could relax more in my own house and I planned to make the most of it. I was nine years old and could make every decision from the moment I woke up to when I went to bed. I got six weeks off school for the bereavement but I didn't bother going back after that. Although I missed my friends, I'd started to get told off regularly by teachers for talking and now I didn't have Dad to drive me there and back and no one offered to pay for a cab. Besides, no one cared whether I went or not, so why should I bother? I was still thrilled to be soaking up the more relaxed atmosphere at home. If one of the lodgers tried to call me back indoors when it grew dark I'd laugh in their face. Mum, especially, was powerless to stop me from doing anything I wanted. The sheer feeling of liberation was overwhelming and the last thing I wanted to do was to go to school and be told to behave by boring teachers. I was free!

Of course, I still had Pervy Pat to deal with, but I started to find the strength to stand up to him and to tell him to get lost. After all, who could stop me? One day, not long after Dad had died, I spotted Pat angling his Polaroid camera at me while I sat outside in the garden. 'Oi,' I said. 'Just because Dad's not here any more . . .'

He started laughing, raising the camera to his eye. This time, something snapped inside me and a flash of anger shot through me. I didn't need to bury my emotions any more. I was angry and for once I was going to show it.

I breathed deeply, my chest expanding with air as I lunged for his camera. Lobbing it as hard as I could across the garden, I watched him pathetically scrabble on the grass, trying to put it back together, and I couldn't stifle the bitter laugh that rose up inside me.

'You're a pervert!' I shouted. 'Pervy Pat!'

'Stop it,' he cried.

'You're a dribbler,' I taunted. 'That'll be your new name now, Dribbler!'

'I can't help having a cleft palate,' he insisted, trying to lick his lips.

'Ha! Ha!' I laughed. 'You're just a pervy, disgusting dribbler! And you make me sick!'

I laughed in his face and ran back inside. I couldn't believe it. I was no longer Terrie the Terror, bullied by Dad, and chased by old Pervy Pat. This was a new Terrie, who could stand up for herself. I could watch what I wanted on TV, eat what I wanted, play when I wanted. But, most of all, I could get my own back however I liked.

This new-found sense of freedom, combined with years of suppressing fear and anger, soon created a bit of a malicious streak in me as I began to go out of my way to taunt Pat. I even started to turn my attention towards Ron.

One afternoon, I grabbed a tin of polish and ran upstairs to his room. He was lying, snoring, on the bed, even though it was only 4.30 p.m. Looking at his bald, shiny head, I decided it would be funny to 'polish' it. Scooping out some polish with a cloth, I started rubbing round and round, chuckling and giggling to myself. I did it gently at first, so as not to wake him, and then rapidly rubbed harder as I started laughing out loud. He woke up, and batted me away.

'Oi! What do you think you're doing!' he cried.

I flung the polish at him and ran off. He ran after me down the stairs, but before he could reach me, I grabbed some of the rotting potatoes Dad had bought in his last shop, which were still under the sink, and started pelting him with them.

Giggling, I laughed harder as he ducked and dived to avoid the rock-like spuds.

'Ow, ow!' he cried.

'Ha ha! You're a total div,' I giggled.

Later on, I filled up a water pistol and sprayed Pat's trousers. 'Hey, Dribbler!' I laughed. 'You've wet yourself now, ain't you!'

I also liked to taunt him about his age. He was pushing seventy now, and I kept thinking how great it would be if he hurried up and died too. So, some mornings, I burst into his bedroom. 'Aren't you dead yet, Grave Dodger?' I would yell, pulling back his filthy curtains. I feel ashamed now, but at the time it felt wonderful to be getting my own back finally, after all the years of him taunting me with his camera. At last I had a voice and I could shout as loud as I liked. All my life I'd had to sneak around, being controlled by Dad and his moods, putting up with Pat. Now, even if I was being cruel to Pat, it was nothing compared to what I'd been through. I didn't want to be the one crying into my sleeping bag upstairs; for once I wanted to be the one in control.

After Dad died, I took on the responsibility of looking after Kim, our dog. No one else liked walking him, so when he whined at the door, I'd grab the lead and march him around the park a few times. He was a vicious thing and sometimes, when Dad was alive, he would give me a nip. But, as if he knew that I was the only one who cared now, he had stopped doing it.

One day shortly after Dad's funeral when I was taking Kim for a walk, I felt a strange wetness in my knickers. When I got back, I went straight to the bathroom and found blood everywhere. I was shocked, and I had no idea what it was. I spent the rest of the day pulling my hair out with worry, thinking I was dying, imagining the worst. So when Liz popped round later that day, I told her what had happened.

'Periods,' she said, briefly. 'Every woman has one every month. You've started yours early – most girls start them when they're a couple of years older – but it's all normal. Don't stress. They only stop when you're up the duff.' And she went out and got me some sanitary towels. I'd no idea what she meant about it being 'normal'. I'd never had any sex education apart from what I was hearing and seeing at home.

It was six weeks after the funeral when Mum finally got up. She sat down in a chair, put her head in her hands, and said simply, 'I want to die!'

I looked at her. I wanted to feel sad but I couldn't. I just stared at her, wondering what she was going to do. Dad was dead; was it Mum's turn next? Even though Mum wasn't much of a mum, the thought frightened me. I'd be left truly alone then. So I found the number for her mental health worker and gave them a ring, which is what Liz told me to do if Mum ever 'went funny'. I called and explained so that someone could come over the next day and 'review her medication'.

After that she started shuffling downstairs more often and eating a little more. We still didn't talk much, she didn't take much notice of me, but in some small way it was nice to have her back in the land of the living. Late one night, Pat started to get his camera out again after I had put my nightie on and was sitting next to Mum, watching TV. I pulled it over my knees down to my ankles and told him to get lost. But he didn't stop, he just smirked and knelt down, holding up his camera to get a better angle.

'Smile!' he said.

'Mum!' I cried. 'Tell Pat to stop trying to take pictures!'

Mum's eyes didn't move from *Coronation Street*. 'I'm not kicking him out,' she said, simply. 'I need his rent money.'

Pat winked at me, smiling in his drooling way, and left the room. There was still a war between us. He'd taunt me with his camera and I called him Dribbler and any other insult I could think of. He had begun to enjoy our running battles.

But now I was able to give as good as I got, and so I jumped off the sofa and ran upstairs. Pat was just coming out of the bathroom, still with the camera around his neck. I ripped it off him and ran back downstairs, with him chasing me.

'Dribbler!' I screamed, flinging the camera back outside again. My only regret was not flinging it hard enough so that it broke for good. Later he tried to sit down and watch *Emmerdale Farm*, his favourite TV programme, but I stood in front of the TV so that he couldn't see it. As much as it was his challenge to take horrible pictures of me, it became an equal challenge for me to wind him up to the point of madness. He'd hop from foot to foot, looking like a mad elf, shouting at me, the dark patch of dribble on his jumper spreading as he did so.

'You little cow!' he would yell, shaking his fists. Not once did he try and hit me, though. In any case, I was too fast for him.

No one could catch me now and it was wonderful.

FIVE

Rebel

Despite having to dodge Pervy Pat's camera, I was still determined to enjoy every minute of freedom without Dad there. Every morning I'd get up and have an enormous bowl of cereal to try and fill me up. Then it was pizzas or sausage sandwiches for dinner. In between, I did whatever I liked. I started to roam the estate during the day, meeting up with teenagers who were hanging about.

I soon got to know a crowd of them: a bunch of delinquents, drugs users and criminals. To them I was nothing but a little nine-year-old kid who could be helpful to them in their 'activities'. Soon I was recruited to do some of their dirty work, such as breaking into garages or spray-painting cars. Once I spray-canned the word 'Cunt' on some poor bloke's Nissan in a revenge attack I didn't understand at all. But I loved the way they'd smile and joke with me. They were always pleased to see me and it felt good, even if I felt a little uneasy or scared by some of the things they asked me to do. I liked the feeling of being popular for once.

I still saw my old school friends on the estate. However, when they were called in by their parents, I'd stay out. Sometimes Mum would try and call me in, but I'd ignore her or run off and deliberately stay out for ages. So, after a while, she gave up. Occasionally, our neighbour Tracey tried to call me in too, but she soon grew tired of it. I was rapidly getting the reputation of being a real handful.

Once, Dad's friend Ben came over to try and help Mum. 'I will talk to Terrie,' he said. 'She's a lovely girl really.'

I listened to him politely about how important school was and how I needed to get home at a certain time after playing outside. 'You should try and be good for your mum,' he said. 'See that you get yourself back to school. That's settled. I only want to help you.'

But I didn't believe a word about him wanting to help. I didn't believe he cared. Not really. When he said he was doing it 'for your dad', I really switched off. Any friend of Dad's was no friend of mine. So I just nodded in the right places until he seemed satisfied I was listening and went home. Then I went back to doing whatever I liked.

Around this time, I started to develop a fascination with the local pet shop and begged Mum for a rabbit. She went out and bought me one to keep me quiet. I was thrilled. I loved picking it up and stroking it. Dad would never in a million years have let me have my own pet. Now I could ask Mum for anything and it was brilliant. Next day I went back to the shop and asked the man behind the counter to order me a guinea pig. Then I went home and told Mum that she had to pay up or else. Unable to argue or control me, she went trotting down to the pet shop and dutifully did as she was told. Realizing that I was on to a good thing, I waited until I saw signs announcing the arrival of a new animal in the window and then I'd order it, forcing Mum to fork out.

Within a few months our house was crammed with cages and

pets of every variety. Eventually, we had a chipmunk and a budgie in the living room; hamsters in a tank upstairs; chinchillas in the shed; love birds on the landing; gerbils in Mum's bedroom; and rabbits and guinea pigs in the garden. Mum spent a small fortune feeding them all but never cleaned them out, and I didn't either. Our whole house was soon teeming with flies, so she bought loads of sticky fly tapes and hung them everywhere. The entire house absolutely stank of fetid animal droppings, but Ron and Pat just ignored it.

For so long I'd rarely been bought anything at all, not even at Christmas or for my birthday. But now, without Dad around, I could tell Mum to buy me whatever I liked, including, for the first time in my life, fashionable clothes. I took her to the market and told her to replace all the rubbish cheap things I'd had to wear until they fell apart. I got Naf Naf jeans and a Spliffy jacket the first time. I was thrilled. Mum never argued. She was always too tired or doped up on whatever medication she was on. She always had plenty of money, too. Dad had left her some and now she was on maximum benefits for a mentally ill person. On top of the lodgers' rent money, she was never short.

Another time, I booked a perm in a local hairdresser's, which cost £40. She forked out for everything without complaint; she obviously didn't feel she could stand up to me.

All the while she was spending money on me, I carried on taunting her. 'Call yourself a mother!' I'd cry as I cooked my own sausages. 'You're having a laugh. You can't even look after yourself, Fraggle!'

Today, I feel ashamed at my behaviour, because I know that she was ill. But at the time, I didn't understand mental illness and it was my childish way of releasing the pure, unadulterated anger I was feeling. For so many years I'd been hurt, physically and mentally, by my dad, and not once had Mum stepped in to stop it. I'd been bullied and tortured by him, waking each morning with a sense of dread at the prospect of having to give him a 'cuddle', never being able to relax in my own home, with a mother who did nothing to comfort me. The sickening betrayal and the knowledge that the one person who should have helped me never did, was a pain that wouldn't go. Now, for once, I had control and could hurt other people. I never hurt anyone physically, but just taking the mick out of the lodgers and my ill mum was enough for now. At the time, it was the only way I knew to deal with all the emotions running through me, and however wrong it was, it helped to dull some of the pain I was feeling.

Mum had some friends, a couple called Derek and Sheila. Sheila had severe learning difficulties herself, but was actually a very good and loving woman. She started to drop in occasionally, knowing Mum was having trouble too.

'You need to go to school, Terrie,' she said softly. Again I'd listen politely but I would ignore her advice. I didn't know how to get to school on my own anyway; it was too far to walk.

Christmas that year was a little different as Sheila noticed that we didn't have a tree.

'It's not fair on Terrie,' I overheard her telling Mum. 'Now Reg is gone, you should get her one.'

Obviously not trusting Mum to buy a tree, she dropped one off a few days later with some cheap decorations. That evening I sat, my face aglow in the fairy lights, thinking how life was changing and how much happier I felt. It almost didn't matter if I still didn't have any presents to put under the tree. It was a big deal just to have a tree. Perhaps, piece by piece, things would fall into place and, one Christmas in a few years' time, I'd get 'all the trimmings' like they talked about in the festive Disney films. I spun a decoration round and round until it fell off, and stared at the angel sitting delicately on top of the tree as I felt a huge, beaming smile spread across my face.

My hopes for a change that year were soon dashed, though. Mum didn't cook any dinner on Christmas Day; I grilled a few sausages and had them with some ketchup. There were no presents, just £20 instead of Dad's customary £50 and, as usual, I sat in front of the TV, dreaming of the Christmases other children were having.

That new year, Mum was still having occasional therapy and was asked to keep a diary and write down her feelings as part of her way of dealing with bipolar, one of the many conditions she'd been diagnosed with (although I didn't understand fully what it was at the time). Once, while rummaging through her room, I came across her scrawled notes. In the diary she'd written how much she loved Pete, our window cleaner. Bizarrely, despite how dirty our house had grown, Pete, who was an old mate of Dad's, still came to clean our windows once a week. He was a cheerful soul, a dark-haired, good-looking guy with a wife and couple of kids. In her diary, Mum wrote about how in love they were, how they were in a relationship and how happy she was. It was one big fantasy. Once I pulled back her duvet to find she'd written, 'I love Pete' in lipstick on the mattress. She was probably caught up in an imaginary world to distract her from her real life. I knew that Pete wasn't seeing my mum; he was a happily married man, who was trying to be kind. I'd never seen him show her any special attention, not for a moment. And not for one minute did I think he'd be attracted to someone like my mum.

I felt sorry for Mum. She was totally deluded. She had no chance of happiness with a normal marriage and a normal life. She could barely function, let alone find a nice, normal man like Pete to love her. For the first time, I felt proper pity, as her diary revealed a side of her that longed for a romance that even my child's mind knew she'd never have. Other times I read the diary and she admitted that she wanted to kill herself. However, I didn't take her notes that seriously.

But one day she came downstairs and started opening all her pill pots one by one. After emptying them on to the kitchen table, she stared at them. I knew what she was doing and guessed what she'd do next, but I felt paralyzed to stop it.

'Mum?' I said, as she ignored me completely, reaching for the first pill. Like a greedy child with sweets, one by one she popped them into her mouth, her eyes closed, rocking herself like a mad-woman. I watched as she choked and gagged, downing a glass of water with them. I don't know why I didn't stop her, but she didn't seem to notice that I was there. I suppose I was in shock. I closed my eyes and when I opened them all the pills were gone. Then I got up and calmly dialled 999 as she grew groggy.

'Please come and help my mum,' I asked, tears springing into my eyes.

Mum had started to drop off on the sofa when the ambulance men arrived. 'Don't worry,' I said to her. 'They will look after you now.'

'Have you got anyone to take care of you?' one of the para-medics asked.

'Yes,' I lied. I'd no intention of going with Mum. Not back to a hospital. Not after what I'd seen in the mental places where she had been held in the past. 'One of the lodgers will be back soon.'

The ambulance drivers told me she was in safe hands and I turned back to the kitchen and started frying myself some sausages. Humming to myself, I was a bit worried about Mum deep down. I didn't want her to die – who would I live with then? But the other part of me just felt numb. Just like after Dad died. I suppose, because by then I had been through so much, I had started to switch off a bit to protect myself. I didn't want to be hurt any more.

Mum was only kept in overnight. She came home the next day looking tired but a bit less pale. She sat down in her favourite chair and started channel hopping again, without saying a word to me. I watched her, thinking how calm she looked. They had washed her hair in the hospital and for once she actually had colour in her cheeks. I wondered what it would be like to go to hospital. To have all that fuss and attention from the ambulance men. To be taken away on a stretcher and have someone look after me . . .

My mind started racing. I began imagining what it would be like if I decided to act like Mum and take an overdose. I quite liked the idea of people being worried about me, the drama, nurses fussing over me. Maybe then Mum would start to love me more? Maybe she would start to look after me properly, cook for me, give me a hug. Maybe even start noticing me and caring, like a normal parent, like Laura's mum. The idea grew in my mind and, without thinking, I grabbed a bottle of paracetamol. As I poured the pills on to the table, Mum glanced up. In between her blank phases she could be completely lucid.

'Don't do it, Terrie,' she said suddenly, as if she'd read my thoughts.

I grinned. Her words were like a red rag to a bull. One by one, I started to neck the pills, looking Mum in the eye while I did it. Incredibly she didn't stop me. She just stared as I washed them down. Then, just like I'd done, she dialled 999.

My tummy started to hurt and I began to feel really sleepy. I don't know how much time had passed but eventually I could see the blur of the blue flashing lights through the living-room window and I began to feel quite scared. What had I done? Was I going to die? In a way I hoped not, just in case I ended up seeing Dad again. But then again, I also didn't really care. Mum sat in the ambulance with me, as the sirens wailed above us. She was staring at the ambulance equipment, fascinated by the buttons and the wires, not looking at me or saying a word. I wanted her to hold my hand or something, but then thought the better of it. She was lost in her own world.

When we arrived, Mum explained to the doctors what I'd done and I was made to drink some chalky black liquid. It was disgusting and I threw up most of the contents of my stomach quickly. Physically, I felt dreadful but I appreciated having nice clean, smooth bed sheets to sleep in, and nurses to hold my hand and call me things like 'sweetheart' and 'love'. It felt good just to have people looking at me, asking me questions. But all too soon I was well again and discharged with Mum. Doctors wrote off my behaviour as that of a silly child. 'We don't want to see you back here,' one of them said, ruffling my hair.

But this was the start of a new idea for me. I took two more overdoses of paracetamol shortly afterwards. Each time the same thing happened and I was discharged the next day. Both times doctors again put it down to 'attention seeking'.

Mum was growing angry with me. 'Why are you doing this?' she asked.

'Because I want to,' I snapped back. I didn't like being sick but I liked the drama I'd created; it felt good. For once, it was all about me, even if only for the day. But nothing changed at home, Mum didn't do all the caring things I'd wanted, she simply grew more angry, which, in turn, seemed to make her even more exhausted and even less of a mum.

A few months later, I managed to get hold of Mum's medication for her psychological conditions. I plucked them out of her bag after she'd been to the chemist's and she caught me nipping out of the door with them. 'Terrie! Terrie! Don't you dare take those!' she screamed. 'Come back!'

This time I could hear the desperation in her voice that told me that taking these could be dangerous. Maybe this time I could stay in hospital for even longer? Or maybe I didn't want to be anywhere at all. I ran as fast as I could, down the road, off the estate and on to the grey pavements of Stevenage, glancing over my shoulder only twice, to make sure no one was following me. I knew that Mum would never be able to keep up anyway. She was too weak and breathless at the best of times. Running a bit further, I decided to head for the fields near a big park. I wanted space and peace, away from anyone who would try and stop me. I stopped at a newsagent's to buy a bottle of Coke, gasping for air as I handed over my money. I felt giddy with excitement. I was really going to hurt myself this time and no one could stop me!

I carried on until I found a quiet spot by a tree in some long grass. Sitting down, I poured the pills into my hand. They were large capsules, lurid pink and yellow. They looked more dangerous, and more exciting, than plain white paracetamol. Pop, pop, pop into my mouth they went, tasting bitter and spiky in my throat. But I kept going until I felt myself shiver, my eyes roll, and then, like a pair of curtains closing down my brain, darkness descended.

I woke up three days later. Liz was standing over my bed, sobbing. 'What did you do that for?' she cried, hugging me closely. 'You silly girl. We nearly lost you, Terrie!'

I felt sick. A tube was running into my hand for a drip. A nurse was looking at me, saying that the doctor was coming. I half closed my eyes. I was still alive. I wasn't sure if I wanted to die or not but I knew I didn't want to go back home. Later, I was told that someone had found me unconscious in the playing field.

'You could've died,' said Mum when she arrived. But I ignored her. She still didn't look very upset to me. I had to stay in hospital for a few days and, this time, doctors finally alerted social services. After I was sent home, a social worker came round to see me and Mum.

'I can't cope,' Mum mumbled, in tears.

The social worker started making notes. 'I understand that Terrie hasn't been in school for almost . . . ' she paused as she looked at a sheet of paper – 'a year.' I wondered why she was talking about school when I thought she was here about the pills I'd taken.

I watched this softly spoken woman look first at Mum and then at me, her big eyes reflecting concern, and I quite liked her. She was a woman whose job it was to help kids. Maybe she could actually help me? Suddenly I felt a desperate urge to jump up and grab her coat collar, to make her listen.

'Can you tell Pervy Pat to stop taking pictures of me?' I blurted out instead.

The woman turned to look at me. Then at Mum. 'What?' she said.

'Yeah, Pervy Pat always has his Polaroid camera and likes to take pictures of me getting dressed . . . ' I went on.

'Is this true?' the social worker asked.

Mum sighed. 'Yes,' she said.

'Well, tell him to stop,' said the lady, turning back to her notes. Mum said nothing. 'Now about Terrie's schooling . . . ' the social worker continued.

A wave of terrible disappointment and betrayal washed through me. I just couldn't believe she'd dismissed what I'd said as if it was nothing. Part of me wondered if she'd understood what I'd meant. But how else could I have described it? I'd called him Pervy Pat, I'd told her he took pictures. But the reality was, she didn't seem to care. Mum wasn't going to stop him. I already knew that too.

She went on and on about my starting back at school so I agreed to everything and was offered a key worker, someone to help 'ease me in'. But as soon as she left, clicking the door shut behind her, I turned to Mum and said simply, 'I'm never going back to school and you can't make me.'

Finally, our neighbours Tracey and Keith stepped in. They told Mum they'd like to offer me somewhere to live as they could see she was struggling. I'd never seen Mum's face light up so fast.

'If you're sure,' she said, not waiting for a reply. And so I went up to my room, packed a few clothes and my Barbies, took a last look at the Snow White mural, and left. I wasn't sorry to go. I was fed up with Mum and still hated having to avoid Pervy Pat like the plague. It was a relief to be rid of them – for a while, at least. That evening, Tracey made a lovely home-cooked pizza and told me how pleased she was that I was staying there.

'We've known for a while that things might not be quite right for you at home, Terrie,' she said kindly. 'So we're happy to give you a roof and a warm bed and something nice to eat every day. How does that sound?'

I smiled and acted grateful, but it was outside my experience, this kind of life, and I couldn't imagine it. She told me what time I needed to be home every day for lunch and dinner at weekends, and how she hoped that I'd be back at school the following week. I didn't know how to feel, so I felt nothing. She made it all sound so lovely, but I wasn't sure how I'd manage after missing so much school. I'd fallen so far behind that I knew I'd never be able to catch up now.

The next day was Saturday and I went for a wander down to the pet shop to see what they had in. I missed the lunch deadline and Tracey wasn't pleased. 'Don't be ungrateful for what we're giving you,' she snapped. For a moment I was speechless. I'd never heard Tracey speak to me like that before; she'd always been nice. Now she was glaring at me, frowning, and her voice was cold. I would have brushed it aside from a member of my family, but because this was Tracey, for a moment I felt hurt.

That afternoon I went out to hang around on the swings, missing the dinner deadline too. I didn't have a watch anyway, so how was I supposed to know the time?

As she opened the front door, Tracey was obviously annoyed. 'Listen, Terrie,' she said sternly. 'This cannot carry on. If you won't listen to me and let me look after you properly, I can't see how you can stay here.'

I shrugged and went to my room. I didn't know what to say. Within a few days Tracey was already at the end of her tether, and I was resenting her for trying to control me and take away my new-found freedom. Although normality was something I'd craved throughout my childhood, I just couldn't leap from a completely chaotic life to a more normal one overnight. Part of me liked Tracey and Keith, and wanted to fit in and be a good girl. But I didn't know how to. There were so many rules and it was all so different; having to do this and that and be places at certain times . . . it all seemed so strict. So, by the end of the first week, I decided to leave.

I went home briefly, but by now Mum was almost on the verge of another breakdown, so when Liz dropped in for a visit, she told Mum she'd take me back to hers instead.

'I will try for full custody,' she said to Mum. I didn't know what she meant, exactly, but it sounded better than living at home with all the flies and Pervy Pat, so I just agreed. This time, I had my bag packed and ready hours before Liz picked me up. I felt comfortable with Liz, even if I'd not seen her much over the past few months. She'd been busy as usual with a new boyfriend and yet another college course. She smiled at me as I held her hand when we walked off. 'You'll have a great time at mine, lovely,' she said, squeezing my hand.

Her home, a few miles away from Mum's in Stevenage, was a tiny one-bedroomed flat that she rented, and I had to sleep on the pull-up bed in her bedroom. She was on the list for a council flat, and I overheard her telling friends she hoped that 'taking Terrie in would speed this up'.

She told me that social workers would come and assess it soon to make sure it was all above board. Meanwhile, she was being paid £600 a month to foster me officially. It sounded like a huge amount of money and she seemed very pleased about that. 'It certainly helps pay the bills,' she giggled.

After I'd put away a few of my clothes and had got used to where everything was, she popped out to buy some fish and chips and then told me she was heading out for the evening.

'Oh,' I said, through a mouthful of food. I'd sort of imagined we'd spend the first night watching a film or chatting. 'Where are you going?'

'Only to the pub,' she laughed. 'You'll be okay on your own for a couple of hours.' Liz was always laughing. She never made much of herself, but looked good for her age, with her dark hair and skinny figure. I knew men liked her. I wanted to make a fuss, and to beg her to stay in with me. Just for the first night. But as she pulled on her jacket, I realized that it had all been prearranged and she was going out anyway.

'Okay,' I said, turning back to the TV.

So I spent that first evening in Liz's flat alone. Eventually I fell asleep in front of a late-night film and after she arrived home, Liz led me, half groggy with sleep, to my pull-up bed.

For my tenth birthday Liz didn't make a fuss or buy me a present. However, her boyfriend bought me a birthday card. It had a black-and-white picture of women laughing on the front and it read, 'Good girls go to Heaven and bad girls go everywhere.'

Liz laughed at my confused face when she read it.

'Don't worry, Terrie,' she giggled. 'You'll understand when you get older.'

*

I was excited to be ten. I liked the idea of growing up, being double figures. It felt like a new start again. Dad was dead, and I barely saw Mum any more, so her and her madness no longer troubled me. I'd also made some new friends – Tasha and Lucy. They lived in the area and we hung around sometimes when they got back from school. Tasha was fourteen, but she seemed even older. She knew loads of adults and was always hanging around the town, drinking or shoplifting. She was cool, though, and seemed to take me under her wing a bit. I looked up to her. Lucy was my age. With her long red hair and cheeky grin, she looked every inch the innocent school girl, although nothing was further from the truth. She was out of control, always bunking off school, and she already had a taste for boozing. Looking back, I couldn't have chosen worse people to make friends with, but at the time their friendship was exactly what I needed. For the first time in my life I'd begun to feel like I really fitted in.

SIX

Over and Over

Liz encouraged me to go back to school at Bandley Hill. 'You have to get back into the routine,' she said. 'Have a normal life. That's what you want, isn't it, Terrie? A normal life?'

I agreed. I wanted it more than anything. Now, thanks to Liz, perhaps this was finally possible. A few weeks after I'd moved in with her, I was beginning to feel quite happy and settled. I found myself listening to Liz and doing as I was told. We often had a natter while she made me toast for breakfast. 'What are you up to today, Terrie?' she'd ask, always listening to what I had to say. After school, she'd quiz me about my friends, my teachers, my day. I liked her easy-going style and even though she seemed to be forever popping out to the pub, leaving me for her friends, I grew not to mind it. I started to see it as the best of both worlds – I was able to keep the sense of freedom I'd grown used to but I had someone to look after me and to turn to if I needed them.

Liz always had lots of people around her and they seemed nice enough. She was a good talker and liked nothing better than sitting down for a chat over a cup of tea. One evening her friend Jim came over. He was a tall, gangly fellow, a builder on a local site, and he had got chatting to Liz in the street a few months previously. Being such a sociable person, Liz was soon inviting him over for chats when she wasn't busy with college work.

I was watching TV and Liz was cooking tea when Jim came into the living room and sat down next to me.

'You must be Terrie,' he said. 'Liz has told me a lot about you.'

'Oh, right,' I said, not really knowing what to say.

I still didn't like being alone with men. In fact, I didn't like men full stop, if the truth be told.

I carried on watching TV, while Jim chit-chatted away about his job. I could tell he was trying to get me to talk, but I couldn't be bothered. Then he got up and walked into the hallway.

'Pssst, Terrie,' he said, calling me. He was out of sight.

'What?' I said, slightly grumpily. I couldn't be bothered with any games.

'Come and see what I've got, Terrie,' he said, sniggering.

I sighed and reluctantly got up, my eyes still glued to the soap opera I was watching.

Slowly I walked out of the room and turned the corner into the corridor. As I did so, Jim grabbed my wrists. Then, holding them together in a vice-like grip with one hand, he plunged his other one into my underwear. I opened my mouth to scream but no sound came out. My heart was banging so hard I thought I'd be sick then and there on the hallway carpet. Jim's eyes were bulging as he looked at me.

'Feels nice, doesn't it?' he leered.

Swallowing hard, I could still hear Liz banging around in the kitchen.

'Liz,' I managed to croak. 'Liz!'

Jim grabbed my face, squeezing my cheeks together. 'Shhhhhh,' he spat.

He carried on for a few more minutes as I held my eyes shut, then he pushed me away, glaring at me in a way that sent a chill down my back. I heard Liz switch the TV channel next door and the music for *Coronation Street* began. The kitchen and living room were open plan, so she liked to keep an eye on the TV as she cooked.

'Liz! I cried. 'Come here a minute!'

There was a pause. 'What's up?' she said. '*Corrie*'s just started.'

Jim pointed to the living-room door to indicate that I was free to go. Brushing away my tears, I walked into the living room. As I saw Liz sitting on the sofa, glued to the telly, a terrible feeling of disappointment swelled in the pit of my tummy. Liz barely batted an eyelid as I sat down. And then a hideous thought struck me – did she know what Jim had been up to? And did she actually care? She looked as if she hadn't a clue, or was she just good at pretending? The ground shifted beneath me, my feeling of safety draining away. I hugged a cushion, my cheeks flushed. Liz turned to me and smiled.

'Tea's ready,' she said in a sing-song voice. 'Egg and chips tonight.'

Jim called out, 'Cheerio' and Liz shouted 'See you later!' She told me to get on with dinner and to be a good girl. I picked up my knife and fork but even the tiniest mouthful was hard to swallow.

That night I barely slept a wink. I tossed and turned with anxiety, feeling every spring and lump in the mattress, my mind whirling as I wondered whether Liz knew what Jim was really like. I couldn't believe she'd allow something like that to happen. Would she? But then I couldn't prove anything either. The same betrayal I'd felt when Mum had told me to cuddle Dad returned to haunt me.

From then on, every few weeks Jim would 'drop in' for a cuppa and as soon as Liz's back was turned he'd shove a hand inside my knickers. I hated it and him. But he was very clever, always catching me on my own, even when I tried to avoid him. And, of course, Liz always seemed to make herself busy. I never cried out, never told anyone. I felt resigned to the fact that it was going to happen. Why did men seem to want to do this kind of thing to me all the time? I didn't know. Maybe I'd been born dirty.

It took social services six months to carry out a risk assessment at Liz's house. Even though I was sleeping on a pull-up bed next to Liz, a thirty-something single woman, they didn't think it was a strange set of circumstances. I was being well-behaved, I hadn't taken any more overdoses, and I looked well fed and clothed. To the social worker, it meant that there had been progress.

'All looks fine to me,' the social worker said, beaming, just before she left. She seemed very pleased with Liz as she snapped her file shut.

'We'll pop in every few months,' she said. She never asked about school. Or how Liz was caring for me. She was easily charmed by Liz's happy-go-lucky manner.

Liz always had money on her now, thanks to the foster money and, although by this point I had begun to suspect that she'd only taken me on to get the cash, she did buy me any new things I needed for school. She bought me a brand new school uniform, a proper PE kit, and extras like a tennis racket – things I'd never dreamed of having before. But despite getting all the new stuff, I was still struggling to go to school every day. I'd missed a lot of classes already, had fallen behind, and I missed the freedom

I'd enjoyed after Dad died. At every opportunity I bunked off. I'd say goodbye to Liz in the morning, pretend that I was going in, and then hang around with Tasha. The school took months to notice and complain, and when they eventually did, Liz wasn't bothered.

'If you don't want to go, don't go then,' she sighed. 'I can't force you.'

I think making the journey every day was quite inconvenient for her as she had to pick me up and drop me off, and in between her college work and her hangovers from the pub, it felt like too much hassle. We both preferred it this way.

As suddenly as Jim had appeared on Liz's doorstep, his visits stopped. Liz found a new boyfriend and he didn't like her spending time with other men, so her friendship with Jim ended, along with my ordeal. All I could do was sigh inwardly with relief again and bury the memories as fast as possible.

I started spending more and more time hanging around with Tasha, who didn't go to school either. She lived with her mum, who was never there and always had a different boyfriend on the go. I admired the freedom Tasha had and what she did with it. She seemed to get on well with Liz, too. I wasn't sure why, but Liz always had time for Tasha.

With Tasha as a friend, Dad, Pervy Pat and Jim all out of my life, and the freedom to do what I wanted, I felt as though a new chapter in my life was about to begin . . .

I was right, and this chapter was going to be worse than anything I could have imagined. I was about to meet the man who would almost destroy me. A man called Adam.

SEVEN

The Nightmare Begins

After finally being allocated a new council flat, Liz was terribly excited and couldn't wait to start decorating it. Tasha recommended a local odd-job man, Adam, to help.

The first time I met him was when Liz and I had popped over to the flat to check it out before moving in and he was laughing out loud in the kitchen. He was about five feet nine inches tall, had gingery hair, piercing blue eyes, and a wide, generous mouth. He seemed like the life and soul of the room when I walked in and saw him for the first time; he was chatting away to Liz in depth about the decorating.

'I want magnolia,' she said. 'But is that a bit boring?'

'No!' he laughed. 'All the best people have magnolia, including my good self.'

He kept touching Liz's arm as they chatted. At thirty-three, he was around the same age as she was, and I wondered whether he fancied her. When I came into the room, he gave me a big, charming smile.

'Hello, Terrie,' he said, shaking my hand as if I were a grown-up. 'Lovely to meet you, girl.'

I smiled shyly. I was still very wary of all men. But he did seem genuinely warm and friendly, so I smiled back. Then I went to go and look around the new flat.

It only had one bedroom, but it was much nicer than the rented place. I was still going to be sleeping on the pull-up, but I was excited anyway. Liz bought a big new TV and unit, a second-hand blue carpet and some green chairs to try and spruce the place up a bit. And with all the decorating going on, I thought it would be lovely.

'We'll be even happier when Adam has decorated it to perfection,' she giggled after he had left. 'I've chosen pink and blue for the hallway.' I found myself becoming as excited as Liz was. A proper fresh start in a freshly painted house. What more could I ask for?

On the day Liz got the keys to her new flat, Adam turned up on a pushbike, wobbling with all his paint pots and brushes. He reminded me a bit of a clown and I couldn't help but laugh. He threw me a huge grin and waved when he saw me at the window. I opened the door.

'It's Terrie!' he cried, as if genuinely pleased to see me. 'Hello, babe.'

I said hello and let him in. He went to find Liz to work out where he needed to start. It was the weekend and, a bit later, I heard a knock on the door and some familiar laughing. It was Tasha and Lucy. I'd told them I was moving and they'd popped over to see if I was there.

By that point Adam and Liz were sitting in the living room with a cup of tea, and Adam stopped chatting and looked up as soon as Tasha and Lucy walked in. He said hi to them both and started a general conversation about school and the local parks. He soon had them laughing, too.

He's a right joker, I thought. He seemed cool, though, always seeing the sunny side.

After half an hour or so, Adam suddenly looked like he'd had a brainwave. 'Hey! I know!' he said excitedly to us girls. 'Why don't you take the keys to my flat and go and listen to some music or something while us boring adults talk paint?'

Tasha and Lucy looked at each other as if he'd offered them a free holiday.

'Brill!' cried Lucy.

'If you don't mind!' Tasha said.

'What do you think, Terrie?' asked Adam, turning to me.

'Great,' I said. I liked the way he'd asked me, as though he cared what I thought.

Looking as pleased as we were, Adam handed over the keys and we ran to the address he'd given us.

His flat was privately owned and up a flight of stairs in quite a posh modern block nearby. We ran up the steps giggling, unable to believe an adult would allow us complete freedom in their own place.

'What a nice guy he is!' giggled Tasha, as we fiddled with the lock.

'Or what a stupid one,' Lucy said, grinning.

We burst inside. The first thing that struck me was how immaculate the whole place was. It was well decorated, and everything in it was new and matched perfectly. Straightaway we ran from room to room to have a nose around. He had a big expensive TV, a lovely coffee table, and a huge DVD and CD collection neatly stacked away behind a glass cabinet.

Tasha went over and opened it.

'Fancy putting some tunes on?' she said.

Lucy and I nodded. As she picked the album, I peered into his bedroom. It was immaculate, and it looked like no one had ever slept in the bed. I jumped as the quiet flat began booming with loud music. I went into the living room to find Tasha and Lucy dancing to 'Hey Macerena' as Tasha rummaged in the drinks cabinet.

'Look what I found!' she said, holding up a bottle of Mad Dog. Tasha and Lucy started taking gulps as I danced along to the song. They offered me the bottle but I shook my head. I'd never tried any booze and didn't like the idea, and the way they winced and squeezed their eyes tightly shut as they drank it proved to me that it couldn't be very nice. As we danced about like mad things, I looked around the room, thinking it was so clean and lovely that it didn't look like a man's flat at all. I wondered if a woman lived there too. After two hours of dancing and giggling, ignoring bangs on the wall from complaining neighbours, we all collapsed. Tasha and Lucy were pretty drunk now, and slurring.

'Nothing like a few too many,' hiccupped Tasha. We chatted about Adam and how nice he seemed. Then, as we'd left the front door open, he sauntered in.

'Aye, aye,' he said, in his good-humoured way. 'What've you naughty girls been up to, then?'

We all laughed again, thanked him for the keys and said goodbye.

'I'll see you soon,' he said to me as we left. The way he looked me directly in the eye, as though he could see into me, made me shiver a bit. *Why was he looking at me like that? I must have imagined it*, I thought, as I walked down the stairs and made my way back to Liz's.

The next day he was back again with his pots and brushes. He seemed like a hard worker, paying attention to detail with his handiwork and clearing up afterwards. He didn't cut any corners.

After another full day of work, he had a quick chat with Liz. 'If you ever need a babysitter for Terrie, let me know,' he said. 'I'm always around in the evenings to help out.'

Liz's eyes widened. 'Really, Adam?' she said. 'Gosh, that would be so handy. It's hard trying to manage sometimes, I admit. I've had to leave her on her own a bit lately, but I'd feel much happier knowing someone's looking after her.'

'Well, that's sorted, then.' Adam beamed. 'How about tomorrow night?'

Wasting no time in taking up his offer, Liz arranged to go out and Adam suggested that I bring a friend over to his flat too, so I rang Lucy and invited her. Lucy was the same age as me and she was a bit of a tearaway, so her parents struggled to cope with her and often let her do exactly what she wanted. She didn't hesitate to say yes. She thought Adam was the bee's knees.

That evening, we turned up at Adam's at around 7 p.m. He was all freshly showered and clean after another day's painting when he answered the door with wet hair.

'Hello, Treacle,' he said, grinning at me.

A large bottle of vodka and a bottle of Coke sat on the kitchen worktop.

'Would you like a little one?' he asked.

I shook my head, but Lucy jumped at the chance. 'Yes, please!' she said. He poured her a weak one, and then automatically poured me one too, so, wanting to join in, I took it. It didn't taste too bad, as it was so weak. It just made the Coke taste funny. I took little sips and smiled after every mouthful. Wanting to keep us entertained, Adam put on the computer and soon we were transfixed by a racing game. It was so much fun. Adam didn't mind messing around and being childish. I'd never had a computer of my own before, I'd only ever played computer games at Laura's house. To have one to ourselves all night was such a treat.

'Go, Terrie! Go!' he yelled at the screen when I was winning. Punching the air if I won, he'd do a high five with me and then ask for his turn. He was so friendly, and chatted away. He asked me all kinds of questions about school, and seemed properly interested. Although he was an adult, he was cool and acted like one of us. While we had our eyes glued to the screen, he had been regularly topping up Lucy's drink until, soon, she was hammered. I didn't notice at first. We were all laughing one minute, the vodka making me giggle as much as her. Then, slowly, she started slurring, swaying to the music of the computer game and turning down her go. 'I can't see the screen properly,' she said. Then her eyes half closed and she could barely stand. 'I'm so tired,' she slurred. So Adam scooped her up and laid her on his bed.

'She needs to sleep it off,' he chuckled.

I carried on playing the game for a bit, and then felt tired myself, so Adam said I could lie down on the sofa. I'd started to sway myself. I'd not drunk as much as Luey had, but objects in the room were swimming in front of my eyes. My head hurt.

'I like looking after you, Terrie,' he said, sitting on the floor by my feet. 'I really do. I want to take care of you. You're such a lovely girl. Really special. I'd do anything for you, you know.'

I looked at him. I tried to say something but no words came out. I just felt so warm and woozy, but also happy. It felt wonderful to hear such kind, caring words. He looked me in the eye and seemed to really mean it. I smiled. It was a lovely feeling, and suddenly I thought how I wished my dad had been a man like Adam. Kind and caring. Someone who noticed me and took the time to talk to me properly. My head was pounding a bit now, but at the same time, I couldn't help but grin to myself. Adam was lovely and I was so very lucky to have a new friend like him.

As if he read my mind, he carried on. 'I know things haven't been easy for you,' he said, gently. 'What with your dad dying and your mum being ill. But I am here now. I only live around the corner. So if you need anything, anything at all, you come to me.'

'Thank you,' I managed to say. I relaxed now, put my legs up on the soft sofa and closed my eyes. My body just sank into the cushions. It felt wonderful to be in such a nice flat, all warm, cared for, safe.

I felt myself beginning to drop off. Just as I was drifting, I felt a pair of hands hold my face on either side. I looked up and Adam's face was very close to mine. I could feel his hot breath on my lips and nose. I almost leaped out of my skin but, in total shock, remained as still as a stone. My heart pounded all of a sudden like my head. What on earth was he doing?

'Terrie,' he mumbled. Then he planted a kiss on my lips, pushing his tongue into my mouth, all wet and slippery. His spit tasted like a mix of alcohol and toothpaste, turning my stomach. I was shocked, but was unable to move or say anything. What was going on? What was he trying to do? He was holding my head very firmly now, pinning me down. From somewhere I found some strength in my arms and I put my palms on his chest to try and push him off. But he didn't move an inch. His strength was overwhelming, his muscles taut and hard like rock. I was absolutely no match for him at all. After a couple of minutes of his tongue whirling around mine like a slimy snake, his saliva filling my mouth, he suddenly let go. Then he went and poured another drink. I quickly sat up, wiping my mouth with the back of my hand. I wanted to say 'urgh' out loud and spit into my hand, but somehow I felt too scared to. The woozy feeling vanished in an instant, as the shock had woken me completely. I couldn't believe what he'd done. I simply couldn't. I hadn't seen it coming at all. I felt sick again. The familiar sick feeling after my dad had 'cuddled' me and each time I'd met that Jim character. Now Adam too? Was this what all men I ever met would do to me? Perhaps it was. After all, Lucy was sleeping soundly next door, without a care in the world. Why had he picked me? Why did men keep thinking it was okay to do this to me? Adam reappeared with another drink. He sat down and put on the TV like nothing had happened. Then he turned to me. 'I'm sorry,' he said. 'I had to do that as I'm in love with you.' He looked at me with real affection in his blue eyes, as though he meant every single word.

I was completely gobsmacked. He was a man and I was a child and that was enough to tell me that this whole situation was very, very wrong. But then he was also being so nice to me. The confusion was all consuming.

'Okay.' I shrugged.

After a bit, he handed me his mobile and asked me to ring Lucy's dad to come and pick her up. We waited in silence for him to arrive. When Lucy's dad turned up, he seemed to be a bit drunk himself and struggled to get her in the car. He eventually managed, calling her a 'right one' and chuckling as he drove off.

Adam drove me back to Liz's, chatting again like nothing had happened. 'See you soon,' he said, pecking me on the cheek as I got out of the car. I turned my face, feeling the rough bristle of his cheek on mine.

'Thanks for looking after Terrie,' Liz said, grinning.

'No problem,' he replied. 'Any time. We've been playing computer games!'

Liz ruffled my hair. 'Fun, was it, Terrie?' she asked, without waiting to hear my reply.

I mumbled 'bye' to Adam and went straight to my pull-up bed, clutching my blanket tightly around me as Liz carried on chatting with Adam. I pulled the blanket right over my face as silent, hot tears sprang to my eyes and ran down my cheeks. It didn't occur to me to tell Liz. I didn't think she'd do anything about it even if I did.

EIGHT

Innocence Lost

The following evening, Liz told me that Adam was babysitting me again.

'You don't mind, do you, Terrie?' she asked, not waiting to hear my reply. She was straightening her hair in the mirror. It looked glossy and shiny.

'Do I have to?' I asked. I felt a bit sick and panicky. 'Are you going out again?'

Liz grinned at me in the mirror, tossing her hair to one side. 'I've got a date tonight,' she squealed. 'And you don't want to be sitting around here on your own, do you? How boring would that be?'

She turned to face me. 'And Adam is such a sweet guy. You'll have a fun evening with him.'

I bit my lip and swallowed hard. Part of me wanted to scream and tell her what he'd done. But then, would she believe me? And would I get Adam into trouble? Maybe he was just trying to be nice. He did seem to properly care about me, after all . . .

'Okay,' I said instead. I was used to not having any choices any more. I could only hope that he wouldn't try to kiss me again. Arriving at his flat my nerves soon vanished, as Adam acted as though nothing had happened and just talked to me as a friend. He let me play the racing game again and then asked me all about school. I'd recently started going again as I was still seeing a key worker and she had told me that I had to try to fit in. I hated going back, though, as my class teacher insisted I wasn't ready to join the class again after so many months off school. So I'd been segregated and made to sit outside the Head Teacher's office on my own to do my work. I felt bad and guilty for just being there.

'Aw, that isn't fair, is it?' Adam said. 'Poor you, Terrie. Those teachers sound like a bunch of prats.'

'I know,' I replied, grateful for someone who understood. 'They are.'

He seemed so caring. In all honesty I was having a great time with him and when he didn't attempt to touch me all night, I was so relieved and thought to myself that he'd obviously realized he'd made a mistake the previous evening. Then, as he dropped me home later, he turned to me: 'If there is anything, anything you want at all, Terrie, just come to me and I'll sort it.'

'Thanks, Adam,' I said. I grinned, thinking how sweet it was of him to say that. He made me feel so lovely inside. He held my hand gently as we waited for Liz to answer the door, just like I imagined a normal dad would do. I said goodbye as they chatted on the doorstep.

After he left, Liz turned to me, smiling. 'Isn't he so lovely?' she said.

For the next three visits to Adam he didn't touch me. I'd started to think I'd imagined what had happened that first night. He just let me play the racing game on the computer or watch motorbike racing, which I loved, on the Sports Channel, all the while laughing and joking with me. He couldn't do enough for me – he was always making me beans on toast or leaping up to get me a drink or some sweets, as if he really wanted to look after me. I felt so grateful. I didn't know why he was taking such care of me, but it felt so good that I didn't question it. He was lovely and I felt special.

Although I hadn't completely forgotten what Adam had done the first time he had babysat me, I put it to the back of my mind. It was obviously just a one-off, a silly mistake, and I'd been wrong to judge him so harshly.

His next-door neighbour Sally often popped in to say hello and she seemed just as friendly as Adam. She was a young teenage mum with her head screwed on, and she liked to sit down and chat to me, taking a real interest in how I was getting on. One evening she popped over to have a cup of tea with Adam as I was finishing off a game. 'You're turning her into a champion driver, Adam!' she laughed.

'She's a good kid.' Adam winked. 'Just had a hard start in life but that's all changed now. Now she's got me to care for her and help her, eh, Terrie?'

'Poor you, Terrie,' Sally chipped in, as if she'd already heard my story. 'No mum and dad must be hard. Well, luckily you've got nice guys like Adam to look out for you now. And I'm always around if you need to bend my ear too.'

I smiled at her as Adam patted my leg. For once, I felt welcome and part of things. Once again I thought Adam couldn't be a bad guy if lovely people like Sally liked him. For the first time in years I truly felt that perhaps things had turned a corner.

Lots of nice people were coming into my life now. Things were changing.

Later that evening after the racing had finished and Sally had left, Adam made me a plate of beans on toast.

'You're a very pretty girl, you know,' he said, as he handed me the steaming plate. I felt myself flush. Nobody had ever said that before.

'Thanks,' I said shyly.

'Beautiful big brown eyes,' he said, looking at me intently. 'Gosh.' He looked away, as if he was overwhelmed, a strange smile curling his lips.

I felt a bit funny inside. Flattered but uncomfortable. Why was he staring at me like that? I took a knife and fork and started eating as Adam changed the subject and began chatting about skiing. My key worker had taken me on trips to the nearby dry ski slope. The idea was that I'd be taken out every week by someone who would treat me to whatever I wanted to do – they obviously hoped that I would start to trust them and open up about my life. I'd chosen to go indoor skiing as I'd always wanted to try it out. I'd heard a few kids at school talking about skiing and it sounded so cool. They'd come back with brown faces and white circles around their eyes where their ski goggles had been and had told the class all about it. Being a tomboy, I was desperate to have a go.

My key worker was all right, a quiet young woman, always asking me personal questions. But I didn't trust her or feel comfortable with the set-up. After all, I knew that she was only doing it as a job and was getting paid. I doubted she really cared about me or my life.

'I want to go to Switzerland one day,' I told Adam. 'Go on a proper ski trip.'

'Oh yeah?' he said excitedly. 'Wow, you've got plans, then. Well, why not? How about I take you on holiday myself?'

I stopped mid chew and stared at him. 'That would be amazing!' I cried.

He hugged me. 'Yep, I think a girl like you deserves a big treat like that. After all you've been through you deserve the world.'

I found myself smiling from ear to ear. I couldn't believe someone was going to take me to Switzerland. I wasn't even sure where it was, but I'd seen beautiful pictures of pure snow and people whizzing down the slopes in adverts in travel agents and on TV. It looked like a piece of heaven to me. And now I could be part of it. That evening, as every evening, I fell asleep on the sofa while Adam dropped off in the chair next to me. He never went to his own bed. This time I was dreaming of whizzing down powdery white slopes. I couldn't wait.

But on my next visit, everything changed. Adam opened the door wearing only his boxer shorts as he let me in.

'Ooops, sorry,' he said. 'You caught me just out of the shower.'

'See you soon,' said Liz, kissing me on the cheek. She didn't seem to notice that Adam didn't have many clothes on.

'Bye,' I said.

I stepped inside. Adam smelt of shower gel and shampoo.

'You okay, Terrie?' he asked, not waiting for the reply. 'Look what I've got for you!'

He picked up a bottle of Mad Dog 20/20. It was Kiwi flavoured. On the last visit he'd got me chatting about what drinks I liked, and it was the only one I remember Lucy talking about. I wanted to appear cool and 'in the know'. I liked the idea of impressing Adam. I wanted him to think I could keep up with adults – after all, he treated me as if I were one.

'Oh, thanks,' I said, wondering if he expected me to drink it.

I didn't have to wait long. Adam was reaching for a glass and filling it to the brim.

'There you go, girl,' he said. 'Get that down you. It's the in thing to drink at the moment, you know.'

I nodded. It smelt very strong, overpowering, like something to clean paint brushes with. But Adam was staring at me, and I so badly didn't want to let him down now. I took a sip and it burned my tongue and lips. It felt warm as it slipped down my throat. I felt a bit sick, but fought back the feeling as I took another slug.

'That's it! You can do it,' said Adam, encouragingly. 'Not too bad at all, eh?'

I shook my head. 'No,' I said, my eyes and throat stinging more and more.

Over the next hour, I kept taking glugs. I was determined to finish the glass, just so that I could prove myself. And the more I drank the easier it got.

Adam put some music on and soon Boyzone was blaring from his hi-fi system. I started swaying, taking more sips, feeling quite giggly now. The room was spinning a little but this was fun. More fun than I had imagined. Adam was laughing in front of me, dancing in a silly way, making me laugh out loud.

'Ha! ha!' I cried. 'You can't dance at all.'

'Ha, ha,' laughed Adam. 'I can't keep up with you, Terrie, can I?'

I started swaying to the music, feeling on top of the world. I loved this song. I loved this living room. This was a real laugh. I jiggled and danced, until my glass was empty. Within moments of putting it down, Adam picked it up and topped it up again.

'We don't want an empty glass for our guest now, do we?' he laughed.

My heart sank a little. I had to drink even more now but, like before, the more I drank the easier it got, until I barely noticed the burning sensation. Then, as quickly as the tipsy feeling had started, a heavy, sick, spinning feeling set in. Overcome, I stumbled to the sofa where Adam helped to lie me down.

'I feel sick!' I cried.

'Okay, okay,' he said, his tone changing slightly. Was he annoyed with me now? I didn't want him to be. Suddenly I felt so bad. I wanted to cry.

I looked up and the glass cabinet was flickering up and down. The coffee table at my feet was spinning as if I were on a fairground ride. I closed my eyes, but the sick, dizzy feeling grew even worse.

'Urrrrgh,' I said, trying to sit up.

'No, no,' said Adam, laying me down again. 'Best thing for you is to lie down and relax.'

I put my head on a cushion, feeling anything but relaxed now. The music hurt my head and I wanted it to be switched off. In fact, I wanted to switch everything off. I felt a horrible mix of being out of control and exhaustion and it made me anxious. But I did as I was told and laid my head back, closing my eyes and willing the feeling to pass.

After a while, I don't know how long, I opened my eyes to find Adam looking at me, and I didn't like the look in his eye. A horrible sharp prickle of discomfort shot down my spine, making my tummy turn over. Something about this reminded me of Dad. So I shielded my face with the crook of my arm. If only I could go to sleep and wake up feeling all right again. A few moments later I opened my eyes again as I realized I felt very sick and needed the bathroom. But Adam was still staring at me, and now he was pulling down his stripy boxer shorts. He then sat down completely naked on the sofa next to me. Before I knew it he started unbuttoning my trousers, all the while staring me straight in the eye.

I lay there and watched as he struggled to undo them and pull them down my thighs. I was literally rigid with icy fear, hardly daring to breath. I knew now that in a few moments he was going to do something horrible to me. Just like my dad, just like Jim. Except that I didn't know what. I was petrified. I completely froze and my body felt like lead. I wanted to get up and scream, run away as fast as possible. But I was glued to the sofa, my head feeling woozy, my limbs wobbling like jelly. The drink had taken full effect and I seemed to have no control over my body.

He quickly pulled down my knickers, then swiftly heaved himself on top, pushing, pushing so hard. I was so small his big man's chest was squashed on my face, even though he was still trying to look me in the eye. Then I felt a horrible, searing pain, a pain so terrible that I thought he'd split me in two. I opened my mouth to scream and, unlike the times with my dad or with Jim, this time a loud, high-pitched shriek emerged.

'Urrrrrrghhhhhharrrghhhhhh!' I screamed, tears flowing down my cheeks. The pain was unreal. It was horrible. But he didn't stop, whatever he was doing, he kept going, grunting and panting like a dog, the orange hairs on his sweaty chest grating against my face. After what felt like hours, he finally made a loud grunt and then stopped, pulling himself out of me. For a second I lay in shock, then I curled into a ball. Still looking at me, he pulled on his shorts.

'Go and have a shower,' he said, sweetly. 'I love you, Terrie.'

Scrambling to my feet I ran into the bathroom. My head was spinning, I could barely see straight through the tears and my drunken haze, but somehow adrenaline and fear gave me the strength to move. I felt so disgusting. I didn't know what full penetrative sex was so I had no idea what he'd just done. This was something new and even worse than anything I'd ever experienced or could imagine. Standing under the hot shower, I didn't want to use the same gel he did, as it smelt of him, but desperate to wash him off I did anyway.

Afterwards, I picked up a fresh towel and wrapped it close to me. I stared in the mirror. I didn't see a little girl looking back. I felt so detached that it was like I was a ghost now. For a split second I 'saw' Dad standing behind me.

'Wash yourself, Terrie,' he growled. I snapped my eyes shut again, trying to extinguish his image.

'He's dead,' I told myself. But now Dad had gone a new man in the shape of Adam had arrived. And little did I know then, he'd be even harder to escape.

I didn't want to go back into the living room, in case he did it again. But at the same time, I knew I had absolutely nowhere else to go. I had no one to call. I had no phone. I could have run out into the street, but I had no money and no one to visit. Liz had said she would be out all night. I had no idea where and had no key to her flat anyway. So I took a deep breath and went back into the living room.

'Hey, Terrie,' Adam said, breezily. 'That all better now?'

'Yes,' I said quietly.

'Good,' he replied.

I took another deep breath. I still felt sick, but not as drunk. I felt so tired but I didn't want to sleep anywhere near this man.

'Please may I sleep in your bed?' I asked. Adam never slept in his bed. He always, for some unknown reason, kipped on a chair in the living room. It was hopefully a safe bet that I'd be left alone there tonight.

'Sure!' he said, brightly. 'Let me put the night light on.'

I slipped under the sheets. Even though I felt so dirty, the smooth, fresh, clean sheets made me feel a bit nicer. Then I curled back up into a ball and tried to drift off, although my mind was spinning with images of Adam on top of me. After a few minutes, I heard the floorboards creak. Adam was in the room. Slowly, the duvet crackled as he lifted it and slid in next to me. Then he turned his body and pressed himself next to me, sliding his arms around me and holding me very tight. To begin with I was tense. But he didn't try and touch me, he didn't kiss me. He just held me, very close, very tightly.

'I love you, Terrie,' he whispered, just as any boyfriend would to a girlfriend. A mix of emotions was rising up and then disappearing. I was angry, hurt, but then the warmth of him enveloping me actually felt very nice. Warm and secure. I didn't know why I felt this way but I did. In all my life no one had ever held me like this, so close.

'You'll always be safe with me,' he murmured. 'You're so beautiful.'

He pushed a strand of hair away from my ear gently. 'You belong to me.'

Never had my mum and dad told me that they loved me.

Slowly, I started to drift off. Feeling sore down below, but some-how also bizarrely comforted in the arms of my abuser.

I woke up and was alone. I'd bled through the night and tried to clear up the mess. I got up, making sure that I was covered up. The night's events slid through my mind like a film reel, but I closed my eyes, trying to blank them out.

Adam was in the kitchen, cheerfully whistling. The smell of toast filled the air.

'Morning!' he said. He was busy buttering toast.

'There you go,' he said, handing me a plate. 'Sleep well?'

'Yes, thank you,' I found myself saying. He looked like nothing had happened, like nothing was wrong. Maybe it wasn't, then. Maybe this *was* normal? After all, my life had been anything but normal so far.

'What you up to today, then, Terrie?' he asked brightly.

'Probably just playing SimCity,' I said, saying the first thing that popped into my head. It was my favourite game at Liz's.

'Oh, I love that,' he said.

And so we talked about the world I'd created and the char-acters. I loved the imaginary computer game. I especially loved building worlds and then creating disasters, like earthquakes and fires to destroy them all. I liked the feeling of watching buildings coming crashing down. After our chat, Liz came over to take me home.

'Had a good night?' she asked, but I couldn't bring myself to utter a word.

The next night I was back at Adam's again. It had started to become part of the routine. Liz would come home from college, sometimes make me some tea, and then drop me off at Adam's.

She was out every night now in the pub, drinking, dating, catching up with her many friends.

'I'm too young to be sitting at home,' she laughed. 'And if Adam is offering, it seems silly to turn him down.'

It would have been natural for me to feel frightened or upset, but some defence mechanism had kicked in and somehow I just felt detached. I didn't want him to do what he had done again, but at the same time I knew I had little choice. Also, in my confused mind, I liked the way he made me feel sometimes. *Wanted.*

This time he handed me a glass of ouzo. It was an incredibly strong drink and I could smell it as he poured it. 'This one will put hairs on your chest,' he laughed.

I pulled a face. I didn't want hairs on my chest, I was a girl.

'Oh, not literally,' he said. 'It's just a funny saying.'

I took a sip. The liquid burned my lips again and tasted revolting, but Adam's expectant, encouraging face made me start to sip more. I'd started to not want to let him down. I liked to please Adam. If he was pleased, I felt good inside.

'Good girl,' he said, whenever I took a bigger swig.

We watched some TV, and then he turned to me. Grabbing my face gently but firmly he twisted my head slightly and kissed me. This felt worse. I absolutely hated the feeling of him holding my head. It felt more intimate and even worse than him having sex with me. I badly wanted to be sick. Or to scream. I felt like I was going to burst holding it in.

He pulled back after a few minutes.

'Mmmmm,' he said. 'I do love you, Terrie.'

I said nothing. I turned back to watch TV, drinking a bit more to wash the taste of his spit away.

As time went by I tried to find any excuse I could not to kiss him. Sometimes, when he'd ask, 'Can I kiss you?' I'd say, 'No, I don't feel well' or 'No, I haven't brushed my teeth.' Sometimes he listened to my excuses, sometimes he didn't.

The kisses always progressed to him forcing me to have sex on the sofa. He never had to hold me down, apart from my head. When he held both sides of my forehead in a vice-like grip, I couldn't move it an inch. He used just enough pressure not to bruise me, but enough for me to understand his silent message – any thoughts of escape were impossible. He never threatened or hit me, but by holding my head in such a manner he didn't need to. I became robotic, detached. I let my body go floppy and tried desperately to avoid his gaze as he always tried to stare me in the eye while he was doing it. I viewed his actions as something men did to me. Except that when he wasn't doing it, this horrible thing, he was being tremendously kind to me. Making me feel like I'd never felt before.

At first he didn't use any protection and then, after a few times, he pulled a strange plastic circle out of a box. Slowly he unpeeled it on to himself.

He caught me looking at it. I didn't ever like looking at his bits but I couldn't understand what he was doing.

'It's a condom, Terrie.' He smiled. 'Just to be safe.'

I had no idea what he meant. I didn't feel safe. Not while he was doing this to me, so how would this little circle thing help? Sometimes afterwards, when he held me, and the relief that it was over flooded through me and I knew that I could have something to eat, it made me feel better.

'You okay, babe?' he always asked when he'd finished. 'Tell me if anything is wrong.'

Aside from the sex nothing was. I had everything I needed, games, food, and something I'd never ever had – love. In every other way Adam was loving and kind towards me. He was always making sure that I was okay, always hugging me, always asking me if I needed anything. That's what was so confusing.

Just a few weeks after I had met Adam, I turned eleven. I went to Tasha's house and Adam was there. He knew Tasha's mum and had done some decorating for them in the past. I didn't know this until he appeared that day. And Tasha thought Adam was lovely; she was always laughing in his company. Part of me wanted to scream at her, tell her what he'd been doing to me, but somehow I knew I couldn't. Adam had been told by Liz that it was my birthday and he was holding out a box. I couldn't believe my eyes when I saw it.

'Is it for me?' I said.

No one had ever given me a present in a box before. A proper posh, soft, furry-feeling box, like it was something special. For someone special.

'Open it,' he said, grinning.

Inside was a gold chain with the initials 'TB' hanging off the pendant part. I held it up to the sunlight, watching it glint, feeling on top of the world.

'Thank you! Thank you!' I cried. I felt so made up. If I didn't know before, surely this was proof that he cared. I didn't mind when he tried to kiss me on the lips this time – well, not so much. Tasha didn't bat an eyelid. I think she assumed that he was messing around.

I hugged him and he whispered in my ear. 'Nothing is too much for you, babe.'

Adam had to leave for another decorating job so Tasha and I hung around for a bit longer.

'Do you like Adam?' she asked.

'Yeah, he's nice.' I grinned.

'Be careful, Terrie,' she said. 'He is a nice guy, but he's not one to be messed with. I mean, I heard a few weeks ago that he beat up a bloke for something or other. I think he's lovely myself but, you know, best to keep on his right side.'

I swallowed hard, thinking of how he held my head in between his two palms like a nutcracker. 'Yeah, he's just a good mate,' I said, shrugging.

A couple of months later it was my first day of senior school at Barnwell School. I turned up at a new school with all the proper gear for the first time in my life. For once, from the very beginning, I wasn't the scruffy kid. From the very first day I was just like everyone else, except when people asked me where I lived and who I lived with. I wanted to lie and pretend that I had a mum and a dad and a normal life, but most of the time I just dodged their questions. People didn't need to know everything about me. But my honeymoon period at school didn't last long. After missing so much of primary school I lagged behind everyone else. And in subjects I didn't understand much of I played up. I chatted with my friends, or threw paper around, driving the teachers crackers. Within weeks I was missing lessons and then whole days . . .

NINE

Unloved

One afternoon I was in the town centre hanging about with Lucy and a few older teenagers who she knew from the estate where she lived, when Adam turned up. We were drinking a bottle of Mad Dog, bought from the off-licence. I'd started to get a taste for alcohol and had begun to drink more regularly now – I liked the happy, free feeling it gave me, the way it made me feel as though I didn't have a care in the world. I'd just been to get my nose pierced in the Stevenage indoor market. The man in the tattoo parlour where I'd had it done hadn't questioned me or my age, even though I still looked younger than my years. I was so thin – even though I now had meals cooked for me, I only ever ate erratically – that my seven- to eight-year-old's clothes hung off me. Lucy and I thought we were having a good time, and were a bit tipsy, jumping in the fountain, messing around. And I felt even more grown-up with my new nose stud to show off.

'It makes you look like a teenager,' Lucy laughed.

Adam looked pleased to see us as he ambled up. He sat down on the edge of the fountain, as we giggled. Then he took my hand firmly as I tottered past him and sat me down on his lap.

'Do you know how much I love you?' he said, wrapping

his arms around me. 'When you're older we'll get married one day . . . '

Lucy laughed. She thought Adam was hilarious and was just playing around as usual. He was a touchy-feely guy anyway.

I giggled too. I didn't know what he was talking about. Married? I'd just turned eleven! But I nodded and went along with it.

'Yeah, maybe,' I said, giving Lucy a funny look. I liked being drunk, I felt happier. The bit before everything started spinning was nice. Nothing seemed to matter so much. It made me forget about having a bad day at school, or Mum not really caring or Liz going out all the time. Adam lifted me up on to the edge of the fountain. Standing on it, I was the same height as he was.

'Come with me,' he said, pinching my cheek.

Soon we were walking towards a jeweller's. I'd never been in one before, but Adam held the door open as if I was a princess. We walked inside and started looking at the dazzling display of diamonds and silver. I couldn't believe how they sparkled under the lights. They were beautiful.

'Which one do you want?' he asked.

I gasped. I felt like my breath had been taken away.

'What?!' I replied.

'You can have any one you want,' he said. Then, in a lower voice, so that the shop assistant couldn't hear, he added, 'For an engagement ring.'

I couldn't believe what I was hearing again. No one had ever bought me anything so expensive. They all cost around £400, an absolute fortune.

Almost blindly I pointed to a twinkling diamond cluster ring. Adam nodded approvingly and the shop assistant picked it out for us. It was reduced from £400 to £209. Still a small bomb, though. Adam waited until we'd got outside, then he opened the box and put it on my finger. My tiny finger was far too small, so he took it to another place to reduce the size. Afterwards, he wouldn't let me wear it on my engagement finger, so I wore it on my middle one.

Even that was a bit loose, but the sparkly bits kept catching my eye and I couldn't help but hold it up and admire it, squinting through one eye as I buzzed with happiness. Wearing such an expensive thing made me feel so special. It was for me. Me! Maybe it was a bit weird for a grown man to buy a young girl a ring, but I wasn't going to say anything out loud. Why spoil the moment? I was just a bit drunk, and happy for the attention. Even though I knew we were never going to get married, and I knew I didn't want to marry him, it was exciting. Yes, Adam was a grown-up, but he made me feel like one too. He took me seriously; he thought I was worth it; he saw something inside of me that deserved to be made to feel special. And how amazing was that? I pushed all the horrible sex to the back of my mind.

Spending so much time with Lucy that day had been fun, and I fancied more of the same, so I went to Tasha's that evening. Tasha was always up for a laugh – although she'd started taking some weird powder in her kitchen sometimes and that made her even more giggly.

'Ah, this stuff is sooo much better than booze,' she laughed, as she started dancing around. Sometimes I'd watch her pour it in a drink or rub it on her gums, but I never asked to try it. I preferred to stick to my drink. She told me that it was drugs. The only thing I knew about drugs was the needles I'd seen lying near our local park and it made me shudder.

But that evening she asked if I wanted a go. 'I know you're only young,' she said with a grin. 'But you're never too young to start, eh?'

Casually, she poured some powder into a glass of water before handing it to me.

'Drink it!' she said. 'It's brill.'

'I dunno,' I said. I didn't like the idea of drugs, or any medicines. My last overdose had put me right off.

'Go on!' She grinned, spinning on one foot. 'Look at me! Do I look like it's a bad thing to do?'

Her cheeks were flushed and her eyes were like deep black pools. She looked so carefree, happy. I took a swig as she watched my face. Within minutes the room was spinning more furiously than ever and I could feel my heart beating so strongly that it was like a drum and bass song in my head. I started to sweat and felt completely out of control with my emotions; tears began spilling on to my cheeks.

'Help me,' I gasped to Tasha. 'Make it stop. I think I'm dying!'

An overwhelming feeling of panic gripped me as I laid my forehead on the cold work surface.

'I feel so ill,' I moaned, hugging myself with my arms.

Tasha started laughing. 'Aw, Terrie, it's only a bit of base, come on, you'll be okay. First time is always a bad one.'

I tried to take deep breaths as she suggested. Feeling a little better, I sat on her sofa as she cranked the music up. The top of my head started to fizz and as I jiggled to the music I started to feel a little better. Maybe she was right, this wasn't so bad after all . . .

*

Within weeks I was taking base, a type of speed, almost every day. Tasha always bought it from someone she knew, she'd said, with money she took from her mum, and we'd dance or just sit around and giggle. To me, it made me feel light and breezy inside. A pleasant feeling, and a welcome escape from my life.

For the next eight months, Adam babysat me virtually every night. The only time he told Liz he couldn't was when he knew I was having my period. Liz told me that he couldn't help out as he was 'busy working'. During the day I would either hang out with Tasha, Lucy or the bad crowd of hangers-on we had, out-of-work older teens, who had nothing better to do but to shoplift and get drunk. Very occasionally I went home, but Mum was usually in bed or sitting looking blankly at the TV. The lodgers always ignored me or told me to get out of their way. It wasn't a fun place to be and because I was far from welcome, my visits grew even rarer.

I still saw a key worker from social services about once a week to go skiing or ice skating. She always tried to chat to me about what I was doing, but I would never reply or I would lie and pretend that everything was fine. Instinctively, I knew that if I mentioned what Adam was up to I'd be in a lot of trouble. Just like I would have been with Dad. Either I'd get the blame or he'd hurt me in some way. Tasha had already warned me about Adam, and through the gang we'd been hanging about with I had heard more and more stories of how he wasn't a man to be messed with. I also overheard Liz one day on the phone telling a friend how Adam had been questioned by the police after another fight.

'He's a bad boy,' Liz had giggled. 'Best to keep him as a friend, you know that!' The key worker also encouraged me to go to school again, repeatedly saying, 'You've just started secondary school. It'll be a fresh start for you, won't it?' So I just kept nodding in agreement. I almost felt sorry for her. I knew there was nothing she could do to change my life for the better.

Every Saturday and Sunday, I went to visit my nan to help her with her cleaning. She was now suffering from arthritis and couldn't manage cleaning her flat at all. I didn't mind helping out; I loved my nan. I'd rarely got to visit her when Dad was alive, but she'd always been pleased to see me and was very sweet. I didn't ever dare tell her what was happening in my life, though. I saw how very vulnerable she was. She wouldn't have been able to handle the thought of anyone hurting me in that way. She probably wouldn't have understood anyway. She was too old, too ill and I didn't really see her as an adult who would know how to help me. By now my uncle Simon had moved in with her. They were always rowing about his porn magazine collection. Right in front of me too.

'Simon, I've found more filth,' Nan would cry, as she struggled to get up from her chair. 'I was tidying around and found it!'

'You were having a nosy!' Simon yelled back.

I didn't understand the concept of porn. All those naked pictures of adults that made parts of their body look weird. Why anyone would want to look at something like that I'd never know. As upset as Nan was, though, Simon still went out and bought them with his dole money. He didn't care.

Very occasionally Mum would also turn up at these weekends. We didn't really talk much. She asked about how I was getting on at Liz's sometimes and what I was up to.

'That's nice,' she always answered. She still looked half asleep, vacant, as if she wasn't sure where she was. She was even thinner now too. Without anyone to take care of her, her health was suffering. No one in my family really knew how to help her, and she didn't eat or sleep properly and just lived in a bubble, getting by with a bit of help from Pat, Ron and Liz here and there.

I'd been living at Liz's for a while when two social workers turned up at the door out of the blue, carrying a thick file on me. They said they weren't happy with my progress and as I wasn't going to school they wanted to put me into care. After they'd gone Liz sighed out loud.

'See, if you went to school, Terrie, all this bother could be avoided,' she said, sounding annoyed. I'd been given a few weeks to 'turn things around', the social worker said, or they'd get a care order for me to go into a home or be fostered elsewhere.

Later on I was dropped around at Adam's and I told him what the social workers had said.

I was terrified of going into care. A few of Tasha's friends had ended up in care and she'd told me that you never got to leave the building and lived a very restricted life, as if you were in prison. I was used to so much freedom, I simply couldn't face it. He looked thoughtful for a moment.

'Hey, I know,' he said. 'Why don't I decorate your bedroom at home, make it look all nice, and then social services might let you go back and stay at your mum's house?' This was one option. If I managed to make living back at Mum's work, I knew social services were less likely to get a court order.

I nodded enthusiastically. I wasn't sure about going back to Mum's, but no one had bothered with my bedroom since I was tiny. I liked the fact that Adam cared enough about it to try and help. We went and chose the colours together.

'I'll paint you a beautiful moon and some stars too, Terrie,' he said.

I beamed. He could be so kind.

By now I had started to try and attend Barnwell School more regularly. When I did go, I found myself enjoying the social side a bit more. There was a real mix of pupils. Because of this they were less judgemental and I quickly made new friends, even with a few boys who were my age. One was called Lee. He was lovely. He was taller than me and had dark hair and big eyes. He loved skate boarding, and we'd chat during break times. He was from a nice family, who lived in a big detached house down one of the posh roads. He was popular, too, and I felt chuffed to bits that he seemed to want to talk to someone like me. He didn't see Terrie the 'foster girl'. He liked me for who I was, a funny, friendly girl who liked a laugh. But getting up for school was growing harder, as I was still hanging around with Tasha and Lucy and then, of course, at Adam's in the evenings. I was getting drunk and high more and more often, and was regularly waking up with a hangover. I enjoyed feeling like a normal girl when I was at school and I revelled in the routine, but it was such a contrast to life after school when the only routine I had involved drinking and being forced to have sex.

One afternoon after school I popped in to see Mum. In spite of existing in her fog of mental illness, she had started noticing the amount of time I was hanging out with Adam.

She was sitting having a cup of tea at the kitchen table. She'd just taken her tablets and seemed unusually calm. I was flicking through the *TV Times*, wondering what was on the box and whether I should stay in and watch telly or go and meet Tasha or Lucy for a drink.

'You off out tonight?' Mum asked.

'Yeah, maybe,' I said. 'Might go to Tasha's.'

'Or Adam's?' Mum asked.

I stopped reading and looked up. 'Yeah, maybe.' I shrugged. I hadn't planned to, but he'd started to pop into Tasha's on the way home if he was working. I suspected I would run in to him if I was there. I was surprised that Mum had mentioned his name.

'It's not normal for a man of his age to be around you so much,' she said. This was the only time she acknowledged the strangeness of the situation, during a rare moment of lucidity.

I didn't say anything. She was shaking her head. 'I might call social services myself,' she said.

'Whatever, Mum,' I said, shrugging. Deep down I was touched that she cared. I didn't know what she was meaning to do, though. How could social services do anything? At the end of the day Adam seemed to care about me a whole lot more than she did. As soon as Liz got her council flat she stopped really taking an interest in me, so it was Adam who was giving me money for lunches at school and feeding me of an evening. He'd also just splashed out on a pair of new trainers, after Mum had said that she couldn't afford them this time round. He was so much nicer to me than any member of my family. Adam was just so generous in comparison. Sometimes I even imagined he was my family.

The next day Mum rang social services, but, as always, they were more concerned with my poor school attendance. And I decided not to listen to anything Mum had to say. In my eyes she had no authority over me whatsoever.

But eventually another social services meeting was arranged. Although I was still living at Liz's, by now Adam had redecorated my bedroom at Mum's, painting over the Snow White mural and changing it to baby-blue walls, with a dark blue ceiling covered with stars and a moon in yellow. It looked great and I couldn't thank him enough. When he'd finished, he curled his arm around me and we gazed at the ceiling, admiring his handiwork.

'Anything for you, Terrie,' he said, kissing my cheek. 'You know that, babe.'

Mum's concern for me was short lived, however. She seemed reluctant for me to move back in permanently.

'I can't cope,' was all she kept saying. The social workers said they thought it was in everyone's best interests if I went into care.

'No,' I said, firmly. 'I want to come back and live with my mum.'

I stared at her while I said it. She looked blank as usual. I wanted her to say she wanted me. I wanted her to hug me and act like a normal mother. But, of course, she didn't.

'Do you want Terrie, your daughter, to come and live with you?' one asked. The social workers looked at Mum and waited for her to respond.

'I CAN come home, can't I, Mum?' I urged.

She paused for what felt like ages and then she looked at me, almost fearfully.

'You don't have a full care order for me, do you?' I frowned at the social worker. 'Only an interim one?'

The social worker looked a little taken aback. I was eleven years old and savvy enough to know these things by now. I knew that without a full care order they'd have to let me stay at Mum's if that's what Mum and I both wanted. I carried on staring first at Mum and then at the social worker for answers.

'Well, yes,' said the social worker hesitantly. 'You're actually right, Terrie.'

'Mum?' I snapped again.

Then Mum nodded. 'Okay.' She shrugged. 'Stay here, then.' But her face dropped as she said it.

The social worker's face brightened as she scribbled something down. 'Okay,' she said quickly. 'I'm sure this is a step in the right direction and the best thing for you, at least until we get a full order in.'

Even though I'd won for now, I felt a burning sensation in my tummy rising to form a lump in my throat. I couldn't believe that my own mother could sit there and not even disguise the fact that she didn't want me. Bold as brass. It was only because I knew the system that I could stay. It was only because I spoke up and insisted. I wanted to cry, but what was the point? Even if Mum felt bad, she'd let me down again, just like she had a million times before. I wanted to scream and get out of there, maybe meet Tasha and have a drink, just so that I could forget about it all.

It turned out that moving back was far from the best thing I could have done. As soon as my bag was unpacked I felt miserable being in that house again. Pervy Pat was up to his old tricks and within a day of my being back he burst into the bathroom as I tried to shower.

'Get lost!' I screamed, throwing my soap at him.

I quickly realized how little I'd missed being chased around by him, and all the flies and smells from the pets I'd made Mum buy. Not to mention the worry of whether there would be food in the cupboards. Mum's attitude towards me made me feel horrible too. She barely noticed that I was there. She never asked anything about me. I sensed I was unwanted just by walking into the room. I didn't miss Liz, though. I'd grown fed up of always being left on my own or sent off to be babysat. Deep down I'd realized long ago that she had only been keen to foster me for the money she got.

As for Adam, he'd started ringing the house all the time, to 'see what I was up to'. Mum glared at me sometimes when I took the call, but it wasn't like she wanted me around anyway. Her moods were up and down like a roller coaster. I couldn't keep up with her and she couldn't keep up with me. We were like two strangers, existing side by side and just snapping at each other now and then.

Within two weeks, I had started to stay out all night, mainly round at Tasha's. Then Adam started turning up. At first he met me at Tasha's too. We would have a few drinks and a laugh. Then Tasha's mum came home and wanted us all out, so one night I had two choices: to go home or to go back to Adam's.

'Why don't you just come with me, babe?' he said, taking my hand. 'I'll cook us some dinner.'

I hesitated. I didn't really want to go. I didn't want to do what I knew he'd make me do. I froze, quickly thinking of my options. But Mum had no food in, as usual, and I didn't fancy another row. I looked at Adam's smiling face as he stroked my hand. Despite everything I felt myself melting a bit.

'I love having you around, Terrie,' he said softly. 'Come on. You don't want me to be sitting indoors all lonely, do you?'

I felt a stab of guilt. I didn't know why he liked me so much, but he did. And despite the horrible sex bit, I didn't want him to stop liking me, not completely. Who would care about me then?

Tasha wanted me to go as well. She was desperate to move out of her mum's home, as they kept rowing, and thought that I was really lucky to have another option.

'Go on, Terrie,' she sighed dismissively. 'Just go with him.'

'Okay,' I spluttered. 'Let's go.'

Knowing I liked Chinese food, Adam started making me his own version as a treat. Out of cans he heated up noodles and water chestnuts and bean sprouts. Sitting in his nice clean flat, I felt really grateful. 'Thank you,' I said, eating hungrily.

'No worries, babe,' he said, staring at me intently. I relished every mouthful of the food, but felt my heart deaden as I thought about what would happen after I'd eaten. He poured me a drink and asked for a kiss. I still tried to come up with excuses, but more often than not saw it as something to get out of the way. The sex part was still awful, but I knew the routine by now. My clothes came off and he climbed on top. I'd close my eyes, try and detach as much as possible, and wait until he'd finished. It never lasted long, a few minutes or even seconds. I told myself it would be over soon, sometimes even hugging myself while he did it. Then, it was finished. The worst part of it physically was the way he held my head. One hand, either side, and I couldn't move.

A few weeks later, after which time I'd practically moved in with Adam, Mum called me at his flat.

'The police are looking for you,' she said. 'They've got an order to put you into care now.' She didn't say it as a threat, just as a matter of fact. As usual, her voice sounded tired and resigned.

'Whatever.' I shrugged. But my insides were churning. A care order! This was just what I'd been dreading. I tried to tell myself that there was nothing I could do. I'd just have to wait.

But suddenly events seemed to be racing ahead beyond my control.

They'd initially had an interim order, but then got a full court order when they realized that I still wasn't going to school from Mum's house. Over the past couple of weeks I'd been bunking school again. Adam never encouraged me to go and I'd had some raging hangovers after nights of drinking. My form teacher had noticed that I'd not been turning up and had notified social services.

I'd just finished dinner at Adam's when the doorbell rang. Six police officers and a policewoman were standing there. Adam smiled widely and let them in. I could tell he was a bit nervous though.

'We have an order to take Terrie to any accommodation social services sees fit,' said the WPC to Adam.

He welcomed them in. 'Yes, yes,' he said. 'That could well be for the best.'

I felt so frightened, surrounded by all these tall people in uniform. I felt smaller than ever, as all pairs of eyes turned to me. I was told to get my coat and my belongings. Feeling hot with nerves, I picked up my things and said goodbye to Adam.

'I'll be in touch,' he murmured as he gave me a quick hug. I saw something pass across his face. Disappointment? Anger? He looked different, like he'd lost control. I wanted to tell him that I was sorry, that it wasn't my fault. I didn't want him to be cross with me. Two officers held up search warrants. They wanted to look through his flat before they left. I'd no idea what for. I just hoped that Adam wasn't too angry. I'd say sorry as soon as I got back.

*

I sat in the back of the panda car, next to the WPC, the streets of Stevenage rushing past the window. They were driving fast, as though it were an emergency. I sank down lower in my seat, holding on to my seat belt as we swung around corners, feeling like a criminal. I'd no idea where they were taking me and I wanted to cry. The WPC kept giving me reassuring glances.

'We've found you a lovely place to stay,' she said. Her voice was all soft and caring. But I knew it was her job to sound like that with kids. To try and make me feel more comfortable.

We pulled up outside a lovely big Victorian house with large bay windows. The lights were on and it looked cosy inside. I was taken to the front door step and one of the officers rang the doorbell. A woman answered. She was around forty, quite plump, and wore a pretty, flowery dress. Her hair was piled on top of her head and held firmly with a rainbow-coloured clip at the back. Her lovely warm smile reached her eyes as she looked at me.

'Hello, Terrie,' she said to me, without even being introduced. She leaned over and wrapped me in a huge hug, her arms squeezing firmly.

'I'm Angela.'

TEN

Stolen

Her house smelt sweet and as full of perfume as she did. The smiling faces of two obviously much-loved girls were framed on the hallway walls and a bouquet of fresh flowers sat on a telephone stand. She waved me inside, thanking the police officers and muttering about files and assessments. Then she called two girls, Stacey and Molly, downstairs.

They had the same colour hair and eyes as Angela and looked at me shyly.

'Hello,' they said in unison. I noticed how nice their clothes were, all pretty with perfectly matching colours and their hair shone under the hallway light.

'These are my daughters,' she said, introducing us. 'I am going to be fostering you, Terrie, for the foreseeable future. So you will be part of the family.'

I stared at her. Adults, especially social workers, often talked about 'foreseeable futures' but I didn't really know what that meant. I felt a little excited though. This house and this woman seemed really normal and nice. Compared to Mum's place it was a palace, and I wondered if this Angela lady was as nice as she was making out. I hoped so.

The girls looked me over. Stacey was only nine and just glared at me but Molly was twelve and seemed very friendly, asking what pop music I liked. Angela told me to go and have a shower. Then she handed me some of Molly's clothes to wear 'until we get you a new wardrobe'. Afterwards, she showed me where I would be sleeping – it had been the dining room but she had converted it into a bedroom for me. Then Angela gave me some spaghetti Bolognese she had left over from dinner. She watched me as I ate it. It tasted amazing.

'Glad you like it,' she said, beaming, as I sucked up a string of pasta. 'It's very important to me that you're happy here and that we have a good time together.'

I didn't say much. I was tired and overwhelmed but Angela seemed to understand this and let me go to bed. Already I liked her.

The bed was a proper one and the duvet cover smelt fresh and clean. As I slid under it, I felt the material between my fingers. It felt so soft. I'd never had my own duvet cover before. I'd always slept in the sleeping bag at Mum's house and under a blanket at Liz's. Adam's flat had always seemed luxurious to me, but then I'd had to pay such a big price to experience that. Here I felt comfortable *and* safe.

I snuggled down, listening to the clock ticking on the wall as Angela padded around upstairs. Before she turned off the lights she stuck her head into my room again.

'I hope you'll be happy here, Terrie,' she said. 'It's so wonderful to have you with us.'

'Thank you,' I said. I closed my eyes and drifted off. I felt so relieved not to have to have sex that night and just to be able to fall asleep, even though part of me also missed Adam's cuddle.

The next morning, Angela let me choose which cereal I liked and made me breakfast. She hummed to herself in the kitchen and seemed like a happy sort of person. She told me all about herself as she moved around, clattering bowls and filling the room with smells of fresh coffee and toast. It was all so different to being at Mum's. If I was lucky, there'd be one box of cereal or some stale bread for toast. Usually, Mum would be crying or sitting in silence while the TV was on full blast with Pat and Ron hanging around like bad smells, pushing me out the way while they made their tea. In contrast, Angela's kitchen was so welcoming and I was made to feel like I was part of it all.

'My husband died,' Angela explained in her soft voice. 'So I decided to help other people by fostering nice children like you, Terrie, who need help. I hope you'll enjoy being here. I want to look after you now.'

I didn't know what to say, so I didn't say anything. Just 'please' and 'thank you'. I didn't want her to think I was rude. Angela explained that she had 'rules' and that we had to stick to them, because that's what happened in 'happy households'. I'd have to get up at 7.15 a.m. every morning and go to school every day. She knew this would be hard at first 'but it would only get easier in time'. Then I was to come straight home after school. I was allowed to see friends as long as I was back at 5.15 to do my homework before dinner at 6 p.m. sharp. I would be allowed back out at 6.30 p.m., but had to be back by 8 p.m. Bedtime was any time up to 11 p.m. As Angela spoke her girls stared at me for my reaction. 'Do you understand all of this, Terrie?' she asked, looking at me carefully.

I nodded. I didn't like the idea of having to be any place at any particular time and already I knew I would miss drinking and taking speed and kept wondering what Tasha and Lucy were up to. I wondered how I was going to manage this. As much as I liked Angela's place, I knew that being made to follow a strict routine would be tough. After all, I was used to coming and going whenever I liked. As Angela spoke, I wondered just how much she knew about my life before I'd arrived here.

I decided not to worry and to see how things went. After all, I was sure that once I'd settled in, I'd get away with a few nights out. Thankfully Tasha's place was only a mile or two away, anyway.

I wanted to fit in and really did try to stick it out. But for the first few weeks, my enormous change in circumstances was very hard to deal with. Having a schedule and sticking to Angela's timetable was suffocating. I missed coming and going and eating when I wanted, although having Angela's lovely home-cooked meals to come back to was a treat. Most of all I struggled with having to attend school again. Once or twice a week suited me, but having to go day in, day out, all week and to sit through all the lessons was a lot to handle, even though I liked seeing people like Lee and the other friends I'd made at break times. I also missed my computer games at Adam's and I wondered what he was thinking. I didn't want him to be so angry with me that we wouldn't be friends any more. What would happen if he turned against me? I felt scared to let him go – after all, there wasn't much else outside of Angela's for me, was there? But I still felt that not having to have sex was also such a relief. Now, as an adult, I can see that having me around was probably not easy for Angela's kids. Stacey could be a bit bitchy to me, and while in front of Angela she was all sweetness and light, whenever Angela left the room, she'd turn to me, her eyes glinting.

'That's *my* mum, you don't have one,' she'd snap. Or, while we were doing our homework, she'd not let me use her felt colouring pens. 'That belongs to me and *my* family, not you,' she said, snatching them back.

But as time went by and the days turned into weeks, I started to have a giggle with her, just as I was able to with Molly. One night, Angela bought us face packs and nail varnish. She made popcorn and put on a video, a funny American comedy, something very different to my usual horror films.

'You can all have a spa night now,' she suggested. Molly and I painted each other's nails and put Stacey's hair in plaits. By the end of the evening I'd laughed so much that my face hurt and I hadn't even had to drink any alcohol to have a good time. My old life suddenly felt like a world away. Now I had things I had never dreamed possible – a lovely warm foster mum who cared, cooked and cleaned and made sure I was well looked after; a nice warm bed; a proper uniform; clean clothes for the weekend. Every time I woke up, I knew exactly where I was going and what would happen. Stacey and Molly followed the same routine, so there wasn't any confusion over what you needed to do with your day. For the first time in my life I had a taste of what was 'normal' and it felt quite amazing.

I was starting to settle in, helped by the fact that for weeks and weeks now I hadn't heard from Adam. Then one day as I was walking down the street on the way home from school I bumped into Tasha.

'Hey!' she shouted, running over.

I was thrilled to see her, although I felt a little embarrassed by my new school coat and shiny shoes. I didn't look like the old Terrie and wondered what she'd think.

'You're looking well!' she laughed, lightly pulling at my new coat. 'I've missed you.'

I threw my arms around her anyway. 'Me too,' I said, meaning every word. 'How is everything?'

Tasha's face darkened. 'Well, actually, Adam found out from your mum that you'd been fostered. He's furious you've not been in touch, Terrie.'

Just the sound of his name and the fact that he was angry made me feel slightly sick. Tasha looked a bit scared. 'He's really bloody mad,' she said. 'What have you done to him?'

'What?' I cried. 'I've not done anything!'

'You must've done something,' sighed Tasha. 'He's so upset with you.'

I changed the subject. I didn't want to chat about Adam. Tasha gave me her new mobile number and told me she was moving into a place of her own. Even though she was still just fourteen, Tasha had lied about her age and had managed to get a flat and move out of home. 'Keep in touch, eh!' she said.

I really wanted to. I'd heard that Lucy had moved away from Stevenage now and, apart from Adam, Tasha was the only real friend I felt I had.

I went home to Angela's worrying more than ever about Adam. I wished he wouldn't be angry. I hoped I could change his mind and calm him down. I hoped he didn't hate me now. Tears pricked my eyes. Oh God, if he hated me, what would I do? If Angela decided she didn't want me any more, and that could happen at any moment, who would I have left?

That evening, Mum rang Angela's house. Adam had been calling her, in a terrible temper.

'He says he's going to slice my throat,' she whispered. She sounded half scared to death. I started to tremble. Tasha had once said that Adam had been in prison, but she didn't know what for, and I knew that he had a temper, but I hadn't thought he was capable of doing such things before. He hadn't stopped there, either. He'd started telling people that he was going to burn Mum's and Angela's houses down.

'Try not to worry, Mum,' I said, trying to keep my tone light. 'He's just sounding off.'

Putting the phone down, I blinked back my tears. In my new situation, I felt so much happier and safer. I was sure that Angela would help me. But somehow I didn't dare tell her what Adam had said. After all, what if he did get angry and try to burn her house down? I also didn't want Angela to get involved with him. She was just a nice lady who didn't deserve any trouble.

I didn't know what to do or who to turn to – I felt as though I couldn't keep any more terrible secrets locked inside me. Molly and I had been growing closer over the weeks and the barriers between us were beginning to come down. So, after spending an evening playing on the computer and colouring in after dinner, I found myself on my own with Molly and decided that I would confide in her. I couldn't bring myself to tell her about Adam, or my dad, but somehow Jim's ugly face popped into my head and I felt an overwhelming desire to unburden myself.

'Can I tell you something?' I asked Molly.

'Yes?' she said, putting down her pen.

Her eyes crinkled with concern, just like her mum's. I thought how very lucky she was to have been born to Angela.

'You mustn't tell, though,' I said. I started to feel a bit sick, as though I were making up a terrible lie or about to get told off.

'Tell me,' Molly said.

'There was a friend of my friend's called Jim, who used to put his hand inside my knickers,' I said in one fast sentence.

Molly's eyes widened and immediately I wished I could snatch the words back. But it was too late.

'Urgh,' she said. 'What a horrible thing to do!'

I nodded. We carried on with our colouring in silence. Half an hour later, Molly went to the kitchen to get a drink and she returned with her mother. Straightaway I could see by the look on Angela's face that she'd told her. Ushering Molly out of the room, Angela sat me down.

'Terrie,' she said gently. 'First of all, you shouldn't tell Molly things like that. You should come to me first. But secondly, what this man did was a crime and we need to tell social services.'

She held my hand, and looked at me with watery eyes filled with concern. I let her stroke my hand and I closed my eyes. I couldn't quite believe that I'd told someone. I'd no idea what would happen next, but somehow I knew I'd done the right thing.

'No one is ever going to hurt you again,' Angela continued. 'And don't feel like you have to say it all at once. The rest will come out in time. In your own time.'

I nodded. She was such a lovely woman.

'I also don't think things are quite right with that Adam character the social services told me about,' she muttered, half to herself. 'He shouldn't be hanging around you.'

I said nothing. As much as I wanted to spill everything about Adam, I didn't want him to kill my mum or burn our house down. I knew that Mum was so vulnerable that she couldn't defend herself and, as useless as she was, she was still my mum, and I loved her. I didn't know what to do. I felt so trapped. If I did break my silence, what would he do?

I tried to push Adam's threats and my worries about whether he'd forgive me to the back of my mind, and I threw myself into my new life. As time marched on, I found myself happily living day-to-day at Angela's, with her jolly laughter and delicious home-cooked meals. I really began enjoying school and attended every day. I was good at English and found myself getting good marks for the first time in my life. The social side of school was becoming more fun too. I wasn't judged on being scruffy any more. People liked me just for my sense of fun and personality. I'd grown especially close to Lee. When he asked me on a 'date', I was over the moon. The fact that a boy as nice and normal as he was, someone from a 'posh' family who went skiing on holidays and drove nice cars, might like me was a revelation to me. I just couldn't believe my luck.

'You're really pretty, Terrie,' he told me once in the play-ground. Coming from him it was the best compliment in the world. I felt like I was flying home on my walk back to Angela's that afternoon.

I started to love coming back to her house too. Doing home-work didn't seem so bad, as we could always watch our favourite TV programmes afterwards while snuggling on the sofa. Then we all sat down at the table together for dinner. I'd started to eat all kinds of vegetables and different dishes I'd never heard of, like chilli and casseroles. The way Angela said 'Goodnight, sleep well' always made me smile too. She had such a lovely way about her and even though she wasn't my real mum, I knew she'd look after me. Sometimes, sitting in between Molly and Stacey on the couch while Angela brought in some tea and biscuits, I could almost kid myself that I really was her daughter. Part of me wished so much that she really was my mum. Knowing that her safety net was always there, that she worried about me, gave me a lovely warm, fuzzy feeling. Some mornings, I'd wake up and want to pinch myself. This really was my life now and, somehow, I'd started to think that everything would be all right again. I could put my past and all the sordid things in it behind me.

Four months went by and I was just leaving class one day when Lee caught my arm.

'Hello,' he said. 'Fancy meeting some time over the weekend?'

We'd started hanging around together more and more and had begun to get quite close. We played our favourite ball games together every break. Recently he'd given me his school jumper when I had left mine at home. He'd told me to keep it as his family could afford another one. It was such an innocent relationship; nothing more than hand holding and a couple of brief kisses. But I didn't want more. I liked this. This felt right. I never wanted someone as nice as Lee to know what Adam had done to me. I didn't want him to judge me, or to see me as 'dirty', so I just glossed over the reasons why I was in foster care with Angela and said I'd just had a few problems at home, pretending that, on the whole, everything was normal. And thankfully, in many ways, I didn't need to pretend. This really *was* my life now! Aside from worrying deep down about Adam, I just wanted to enjoy myself again.

I walked with Lee through the playground. His arm was slung over my shoulders. As we said goodbye, he kissed my cheek and

I turned my face to catch his lips. I still couldn't believe someone as cute and lovely as Lee was my boyfriend. Lucky me! Lee smiled and went off through the gates to catch up with a friend as I made my way out myself.

'See you soon, Terrie,' he yelled behind him.

I walked off grinning to myself too. Lee made my heart flutter, for all the right reasons. But as I walked, my smile faded and then I felt a tight sensation in my chest as my heart began to beat like a drum. I was looking at a familiar crop of gingery hair standing right in front of the gates. Immediately Adam caught my eye, his face set like a tight mask.

All of a sudden the shouts and banter of the playground stopped swirling around me and everything seemed to fall silent, like someone had flicked a 'mute' switch. It felt as though Adam and I were the only two people in the world, in a bubble, and I wanted to cry. I thought of my mum, and the threats. Of him torching Angela's house. Of his tongue down my throat. What he did to me. Quickly I looked around me, with desperate thoughts of getting away. But I knew it was useless. I was a rabbit caught in a trap.

'Hello, Terrie,' he said cheerfully, with a steely glint in his eye. 'You're coming home with me.'

I bit my tongue to resist the urge to scream. *Not again*, I thought. *You've only just got away from him!* I wanted to cry and tell him I was sorry and make him believe that none of this was my fault. Then, hopefully, he'd just let me go.

I looked down and he was holding my bike alongside his own. I'd not seen my bike in ages and I thought I'd lost it in the move from Mum's to Liz's. I had no idea how Adam had got his hands on it. Feeling shaky, I looked him in the eye.

'I can't come with you. I have to get back to Angela's,' I said firmly. I wanted to say sorry and to brush past him. As though he didn't matter. I wanted to carry on walking home, home to my new life of delicious dinners, and homework and fun with Stacey and Molly. Now I so badly wanted to run into Angela's arms and tell her everything. I cursed myself for not having told her. She might have been able to help after all.

'Nah, you don't need to be back at Angela's,' Adam said, with confidence. 'She knows I'm picking you up.'

I blinked back tears now. Angela knew? A rising feeling of betrayal and fear started to hurt my tummy. Of course, Angela was probably as scared of Adam as I was. There was no escape. I found myself shrugging, and a sense of going on autopilot took over as I grabbed the handlebars of my bike from his hands and climbed on.

'C'mon, let's go back to mine,' he said grinning.

We cycled the fifteen-minute journey back to his flat together. It felt like the longest ride of my life.

ELEVEN

Imprisoned

I carried my bike up to his flat door and as it clicked behind us, his face twisted into absolute rage. Standing over me he started shouting.

'How could you do this to me?' he screamed. 'Leave me like that?'

He ranted and raved for ages, his spittle landing on the floor by my feet, telling me how he loved me and couldn't live without me. How he wanted to kill my mum to make me sorry. How he was going to make me pay for the rest of my life for trying to get away from him.

I found myself cowering on the sofa. Head bowed, trying not to look at him. I didn't know what to think and was surprised by the strength of his feelings. Now I'd experienced life at Angela's I was even more certain that what he'd made me do was wrong, so surely I should be the one who was angry?

'And I saw you kissing that boy in the playground! You dirty little bitch,' he hissed.

I just looked at him and listened. 'I'm sorry . . . ' I began. But he waved my apology away as though it meant nothing.

'Sorry?' he screamed. 'You little bitch!'

I started weeping. I didn't want him to be so angry, and I wished I could calm him down, but also a growing part of me hated him so much too. Why was he taking me away from my normal life? So many conflicting thoughts were running through my mind as I stood there, shaking with fear. This was a side to Adam that I'd never seen before and it petrified me.

He walked up and down the flat as if he couldn't sit still. Then, as suddenly as the rage had started, it stopped. 'I have to go out,' he cried, running out and slamming the door behind him. I heard a noise as he turned a key in the lock. I ran to the window to watch him cycle off. I had no clue where he was going or when he'd be back. Then I tried the door handle. After shaking it for a few seconds, I realized that it was no good: he'd locked me in like a prisoner.

At first I sat and sobbed for a good hour. I looked at the clock. It was 6 p.m. – Angela would be wondering where I was by now. My dinner would be on the table getting cold. I hated not being there, not being able to apologize for being late. Suddenly I wanted to do everything in my power not to disappoint her. I grabbed Adam's house phone to ring her, but it was silent. I looked at the plastic cable leading from the handset and saw that it had been cut. Not knowing what else to do, I cried for a bit longer, and when I felt that there were no tears left inside me, I switched on the TV and stared blankly at the screen.

The lights and sounds of the soap opera and game shows faded into the background. I couldn't concentrate on anything as my mind whirred with worry and fear. The hours passed, the sky grew dark and Adam still wasn't back. I flicked the lights on, and shivered as it grew colder. Eventually, I nodded off. Waking with a start in the darkness, I fumbled for a light and then looked around. The flat was still silent and empty. Feeling hungry now, I looked in the cupboard for food. There was nothing except bread and butter, so I made toast, but was barely able to swallow it. Then I fell back to sleep. As much as I wanted Adam home, so that I wasn't alone and locked up, I was also scared of his return.

The next morning, the hours ticked by as I watched daytime TV. I'd started to feel very, very scared. I'd no idea when Adam would come back. Maybe he never would? I wondered if he'd leave me to starve in his flat when the bread ran out. There were only a few crumbling, stale slices left. After a while, I must have dozed off as, all of a sudden, I woke with a start. The deathly silence of the flat was broken by the sound of fists banging on the door.

'Open up! Police!' a deep voice yelled through the letter box. Instinctively, I dropped to the floor, my heart racing. Part of me wanted to cry out, but the other part was scared stiff. I didn't know what to do. I wanted them to get me away from here but could I trust the police? They might take me away from Angela's. When I'd arrived at Angela's, she'd told me that if I ran away, they might put me in a 'secure unit', a sort of prison for kids. And it might make Adam even more angry and then what would he do? The police sounded angry too, yelling through the letter box, their deep, heavy voices echoing around the room. So I stayed silent, waiting to hear what they'd do next. I still hadn't made up my mind whether to call out to them when all of a sudden the banging stopped. I ran to the door but they'd gone. I sat slumped on the floor and started crying again.

Three whole days passed. I felt exhausted by the lack of sleep and the stress. I'd eaten the last of the bread that morning and I'd cried so much that my eyes were red and swollen. I bitterly regretted not calling out to the police now. They would have knocked down the door and got me out of there. I also thought about Angela. Would she be so angry with me that she'd never agree to carry on fostering me? Maybe I'd missed my only chance of a normal, safe life? Then, just as I was on the verge of screaming with frustration, the lock turned and in walked Adam.

'The police have been looking for me!' I cried. 'I've got to go!'

'No,' he said, calmly. 'We'll be all right.'

Adam looked at me strangely. He was carrying a bag of shopping and started unpacking. 'We have to go soon, Terrie. We can run away together. No one will accept our relationship. It will have to be just me and you. Then we can be free.'

I stared at him as his voice grew with excitement.

'We can start again. Be together. You know I love you,' he continued.

I tried to smile. I preferred him when he was like this to the way he had been the last time I had seen him, but I didn't trust him any longer. I'd seen him flip too many times now. He made me his usual 'Chinese' from a tin, this time adding in some tinned pineapple too. I was hungry and it was a welcome change from toast, but the food stuck in my throat as I swallowed.

I was sitting curled up on the sofa while Adam did the washing-up when a huge crash at the door made me jump out of my skin.

'Police!' a gravelly voice yelled.

'Come here,' Adam whispered urgently. He grabbed my wrist and dragged me to the cupboard under the sink.

'Here,' he said. 'Get in there!'

Pushing my head down, he shoved my back, and I squished

in among the cleaning products, banging my head on the U-bend. I was so scared, I thought I would wet myself. It smelt of disinfectant and drains.

Then I heard Adam scraping and moving the oven from next to the sink, and putting it in front of the cupboard door. Next, I heard him answer the police.

'Evening,' he said, sounding very calm. 'What can I do for you?'

Sounds of the officers' footsteps filled the flat. 'We have a recovery order for Terrie O'Brian,' said an officer reading from a notepad. 'Is she residing in your premises?'

Adam gave a hollow laugh. 'No!' he snorted. 'Terrie? I've not seen her for a while . . . '

I could hear the officers moving around his flat. Their footsteps were slow and careful, creaking on his floorboards.

'Can we have a look, sir?' one asked.

'Be my guest,' said Adam. He sounded so friendly. So grown-up and in control. I would have trusted him if I were a police officer. Then his voice lowered with genuine concern. 'Terrie's not, er, run away again, has she?' he asked.

An officer huffed a bit. 'That's why we're looking for her,' he said.

Then footsteps approached my cupboard.

'What are you doing behind that cooker?' one asked.

'Oh,' said Adam, making a scraping sound. 'Just some decorating.'

'What's behind the cooker?' asked one. I could hear it being moved. I started to hold on to the U-bend, my neck aching from being held at a funny angle.

'Nothing,' said Adam. 'It's just a cupboard. I've had to move the cooker, you see, to scrape off the tiles. It's a right job, I'm telling you!'

His attempt at lightening the mood fell on deaf ears, as another officer seemed to be helping the first one move the cooker.

I was about to squeeze my eyes shut when light filled my cupboard, making me blink.

'Hello, who have we got in here?' said an officer, looking down at me. He held out his hands to pull me out. I clambered out, my cheeks burning with embarrassment.

'Well! Terrie!' said Adam as if he'd not seen me in months. 'Blimey, what the hell are you doing in there?'

The officers looked at each other as I looked at my feet. I didn't know what to say or do. I didn't know what Adam wanted me to do.

'I'd no idea, officers. Honestly,' said Adam, holding out the palms of his hands. 'But she just won't leave me alone . . .'

They looked at him and said they needed to take me. I wasn't sure if they believed him or not, but it didn't seem to matter. All the focus was on me now.

'Come on, young lady, you need to come with us,' said an officer. He took me by the elbow and led me out of Adam's flat.

Adam glanced at me, then smiled at the police. 'Glad she's been found anyway,' he said. As we drove off in the car, I didn't understand why they weren't arresting Adam. It didn't make sense. But for the time being I had other things to worry about. I knew I would be seen as a runaway and that meant that I would soon be on my way to a secure unit.

They took me to Stevenage police station, where I had to sit in a waiting room. There were two scruffy-looking men there, one of whom reeked of beer and fags, who were handcuffed to their officers. The other one started to shout when he saw his cell door.

'You're all pigs!' he screamed, as they wrestled him past the plastic chair where I was sitting.

A WPC came over and smiled at me kindly.

'Hello, sweetheart, we don't want you waiting out here,' she said. 'Best if you go to bed now.'

Clinking a large bunch of keys at her side, she opened a cell door. It was heavy and she needed both hands and all her weight to open it. She guided me in. She looked so kind, but was ushering me into a grey-walled adult's prison cell, for proper criminals. She looked at her file. 'Ah, you won't be waiting long,' she said. 'Social services will be here soon to take you off.'

I stepped inside. The walls were covered in greying tiles. The only furnishings were a bed with a small, hard mattress and a toilet, all attached to the wall. There were two buttons, one to flush the loo and another for emergencies. The window was a tiny piece of frosted glass high up. I'd seen things like this on TV and films. I started crying.

'You hungry, sweetheart? I'll tell you what, I'll make you a nice dinner and then you'll feel better,' she said.

She slammed the door shut as I sat down on the bed, trying to find a comfortable spot. My feet barely touched the floor. I pulled my knees up to my chest and sobbed. I couldn't believe that I was in a prison cell. A few minutes later, she opened the hatch at the top to look in on me and then opened the door. She'd heated up a 'Hot Pot' and had slopped it on a plate.

'Be careful, as it's very hot,' she said. 'Try and get some sleep afterwards.'

I managed a few mouthfuls, but the salty taste made me want to retch. So I put the plate on the floor half eaten and cried some more. I wanted to call Angela, I wanted to call my mum. Anyone to get me out of there. But I knew that I was caught in the system now. The social services were on to me; they'd have told Angela that I'd been found, and she would have assumed that I'd run away and was bound to be angry. As for Mum . . . what would she do? She'd not want me back. I'd not heard from her since the call about Adam's threats and I guessed she probably wanted to keep out of it. If I could have picked up the phone and begged someone for help, I would have. Even Tasha crossed my mind, but at only fourteen herself, she'd not be able to do much. Once again, I thought there was no point in trying to dig my way out of it. After all, Adam had held me hostage for three days and then I was the one who ended up in a prison cell. It felt like the world had gone mad. And in many ways it had.

I lay awake almost all night, listening to the heavy doors slamming, metal grates being opened and shut, drunk people shouting, ladies screaming. I tried to put the thin pillow over my head but nothing blocked out the din. Then, at 7 a.m., the door flew open again.

'You can leave now, sweetheart,' said an officer. 'Social services have sent their pick-up service to take you.'

Rubbing my eyes, I got up and walked out. My head hurt, and I felt empty with exhaustion. A social worker was waiting outside in a taxi.

'Where am I going?' I asked.

'To Leverton Hall, in Brentwood, Essex,' she replied. 'Don't worry. You're safe now.'

They kept telling me this, but the word 'safe' was meaningless. I'd never felt more vulnerable.

'Does Angela know I'm here?' I asked, my voice breaking a little. I wanted more than anything for her to turn up to take me back to that lovely, warm, safe house of hers.

'Yes,' said the social worker shortly. 'She knows all about it.'

I swallowed. She knew, but she hadn't come to get me. Angrily, I wiped away a tear escaping down the side of my face. I'd just have to forget about Angela now and get used to the fact that I had no one. I stood up straighter. I didn't need anyone anyway.

After driving for an hour or so, the car pulled into a garage. Behind us, the door rolled down and clanked shut, plunging us into darkness for a moment. I felt myself flinch as my eyes adjusted. Two ladies came and opened my side of the car. They were all smiles and looked really pleased to see me. One of them, called Debbie, had long, flowing hair and wore a hippy-style dress.

'Terrie!' she cried, taking my hands. 'Lovely to see you.'

They led me into a square concrete building with orange bricks that looked modern and tidy and with a wide, neatly cut green lawn stretching out in front. I was whisked through the entrance into a side room, where they filled out a few forms. Then I was led into another room. All the rooms echoed a little and smelt of new carpets.

'Now, Terrie, we have to do this with new entrants. We have to strip-search you. So please take all your clothes off, even your vest and pants.'

I felt my eyes fill up again. I didn't want to. I stood there for a few moments as they stared at me.

'Come on now,' said the other lady. 'Whip them off and we can get this done. We've seen it all before.'

Slowly, as they watched me, I pulled off my clothes, my cheeks burning with humiliation. They pulled on rubber gloves and asked me to part my legs as they felt around me. I wanted to be sick. Why were they doing this? What had I done wrong?

'Just looking for drugs and maybe things you shouldn't have,' Debbie muttered.

I hung my head in shame as I turned around when they asked me to. I could feel their eyes boring into my skin like laser beams as I stood there shivering.

'We don't normally do this for eleven-year-olds,' continued Debbie, almost apologetically. 'Usually it's for those who are twelve and above. But we've been asked to in your case.'

I wanted to scream at her to stop, but said nothing. They explained social services had got a court order for me for 'my own protection' as I was 'at risk from myself or others'. I didn't know what it meant. The only person who I could see I was at risk from was Adam and his threats. Why couldn't anyone see that?

When I was allowed to get dressed again, I was taken into the main part of the unit. Doors were locked behind me as we walked down a long corridor with a green carpet and bare walls. There were doors all the way along it, sometimes there were two close together, sometimes it was a while before the next one. Then there was another door just inside each door.

'This place is weird,' I said. 'So many doors.'

Debbie nodded. 'It's so that it's harder for children to escape.' She smiled. All the staff milling around had radios on their belts.

Finally, we arrived at my unit. It consisted of a lounge, a kitchen (either of which we had to ask permission to use), then a bedroom that looked exactly like my police cell, except that there was a shower next to the toilet. The window was made from thick PVC glass, and looked out into a concrete courtyard, which I was told no one was allowed to use.

As I looked into the lounge, some of the kids were eyeing me suspiciously. They all looked much older than me. Some of their stares were cold and accusatory, others were just blank. Most were sitting on the sofa watching the TV, while a couple of them were playing pool.

This really is a prison, I thought.

I was asked to stay inside for the rest of the day, so I just sat down on my bed, crying into my hands.

I don't know how long I'd been sitting there when from somewhere outside my room came the piercing noise of a girl screaming, her cries growing louder and louder like a trapped animal. She sounded wild.

'Get your hands off of me!' I could hear her punching the doors, including mine, as she went along the corridor. 'Fucking get off me!'

Her shrieking was followed by more bangs and then staff shouting 'Time out for Stephanie!' And then there was silence.

What sort of place was this? I lay back on the bed and gave into the sobs again, but soon my throat was raw and I felt emptied of all emotion. Eventually, I sat up, dried my eyes, and took a deep breath.

'Look, Terrie,' I told myself. 'You're here now. You can't go anywhere. You can't do anything except what they tell you to do. Just get on with it.'

In that second, I knew tears were futile. I was facing a good few weeks here at least, so I might as well just make the best of the situation.

Later that afternoon, just as I was beginning to feel hungry after not having eaten since the morning, a key turned in the lock and my door opened. Debbie told me that we were allowed out of our rooms until 7 p.m. and then we were locked in until 7 a.m. But first I could have some dinner.

I sat at a table with five other 'inmates' from my unit. The girl who'd been screaming was Stephanie, and she was fifteen. Then there were Jason and Andy, both sixteen, and both in for 'violent crimes'. Jason was lovely. He was skinny, with dark brown hair in a 'curtains' style, and he was crazy about his Reebok classic trainers. I instantly took a liking to him, as he had gentle eyes and a caring air about him. Then there was Daniel, who was also sixteen, but he looked much older and was on remand for armed robbery, and Carly, a fourteen-year-old who'd run away from care.

Stephanie soon got chatting to me. She was beautiful, with shoulder-length blonde hair and a striking face, but she looked ill. Deathly pale.

'What do you think of Andy?' she asked.

I looked at Andy, who was chatting at the end of the table. He was dark-haired and dark-skinned, and looked very handsome.

'He's nice!' I giggled.

'What?' Stephanie's tone changed. 'So what? You fancy him, then, do you?'

'No! No!' I insisted. I didn't want to upset her. 'I just said he was nice.'

Stephanie seemed to accept this.

'Well, he's mine,' she said pointedly.

'Really, I'm not interested . . . ' I spluttered.

Her face softened.

'I'm Stephanie,' she said, offering me her hand to shake. 'I was a prostitute, that's why I'm in here – "for my own protection".'

Over dinner, Stephanie's story came tumbling out. She was from Somerset and had met an older man a year or two earlier. 'The love of my life,' she said. Her parents were appalled and tried to stop her from seeing him but it wasn't any good. Stephanie soon moved in with him. Very shortly afterwards, her new 'boyfriend' started offering her crack cocaine and asking her to sleep with his friends for money. Within weeks she was a drug addict and a prostitute.

'The crack made me feel less bad about doing it,' she said. She looked sad for a moment. 'I'm still not sure how it all ended up like that.'

Stephanie felt better now, though, as she'd started 'seeing' Andy. 'He's fit, isn't he?' she said, grinning. 'Things are all right in here.' She asked me why I was there.

'They've locked me up instead of my abuser,' I said, as a way of an explanation. It just slipped off my tongue. But after I'd said it, I realized that it was a very good description of the situation. That's exactly what had happened.

TWELVE

A Dark Secret

I soon settled into a routine at Leverton Hall. All the days merged into one. I wasn't happy about being behind locked doors, but at the same time I felt the safest I had ever felt. After all, Adam would never get me in here.

I woke in the mornings, had breakfast, had a few school lessons, then there was a break and then I watched TV or played computer games before dinner. The school lessons were held in a neat side room and I was in a class of six or seven with Stephanie and Andy. The teacher was so enthusiastic. She took us through some maths and English, and seemed genuinely pleased whenever we got anything right.

'I think you'll really enjoy being with us, Terrie,' she said with a warm smile.

We had a bit of homework to do, and I got given some shiny new textbooks and a dictionary. It seemed like no expense was spared on us kids.

Drama was never far from the unit, though. But for once it wasn't happening to me. About a week after I had joined, we were sitting eating chilli and chips for dinner when a member of staff started having a go at Andy.

'It's disrespectful, that's what it is,' he began saying to him. 'You and Stephanie having sex like that in the corridor of all places. It's disgusting . . . '

Apparently, Andy's relationship with Stephanie was common knowledge now and they weren't hiding it from anyone, even the staff. Andy's face twisted from calm to outraged within seconds of Stephanie's name being mentioned. Grabbing his plastic knife, Andy jumped out of his seat like an angry cat and grabbed the male member of staff around the throat, attempting to plunge the knife into his back. Within moments Andy was manhandled to the floor by six members of staff. As they wrestled with him, Stephanie jumped up to try and stop it.

'Andy!' she screamed.

'Stephanie!' he replied, his voice muffled as his face was held down on the carpet. Seconds later he was dragged off, yelling and kicking. Later on we heard that he'd been charged with intent even though the staff member wasn't injured with the plastic butter knife. He was sent to an adult prison.

Stephanie was gutted and, without Andy there, she soon started pouring her heart out to me. We became good friends. She was a lovely, sweet girl. I couldn't understand how she had become a prostitute or how she had fallen into such a rough crowd. Her mum and dad sounded nice and normal and it sounded like she'd grown up in a lovely house. She always wore black, especially long skirts, and we'd listen to music together during the day. She loved Faith Evans and I loved the Spice Girls. I thought they were hugely inspiring as they were all ordinary girls from ordinary backgrounds. Stephanie also made my troubles seem small when she explained what the drug crack was like and how addictive it was.

'It's like heaven in your veins, but once it's got hold of you, you'd kill for it,' she said.

My eyes widened. 'Blimey!' I said. Up until that point I'd never heard of it before, and although it sounded kind of cool, it also sounded very scary.

She explained what life was like on the streets, which seemed a whole world away from the life I'd been living. I couldn't believe that she had allowed men to do this to her, especially for money. It was sick. But then she also felt completely desperate.

'One minute I was enjoying being in love with my boyfriend, the next minute I was doing drugs and standing on a street corner,' she explained. Then she snapped her fingers. 'All in the blink of an eye.'

My problem with Adam seemed tiny in comparison to this seedy underworld of drugs and 'going on the game', as Stephanie explained it was called. Stephanie had eventually plucked up the courage to tell her mum and dad what was going on, but when she called them, they contacted social services who got a court order to have her locked in here. They'd put her in for three months and then they had to apply for another one. My order was for just twenty-eight days. I'd no idea what would happen afterwards.

'Listen, if you need anything, anything at all, just shout,' said Stephanie.

'What, drugs?' I asked. I was a bit shocked. All this time I'd been craving stability and normality and now I was back among temptations!

'No, silly!' laughed Stephanie, gently pushing my shoulder. 'I mean advice, help. If you want to borrow anything, just ask!'

I smiled with relief. 'Oh, sorry,' I giggled. 'Thank you.' And I really did feel grateful.

The days began to roll past quite quickly. But as much as I was liked and looked after by Stephanie, I was hated by Daniel, who soon started to bully me. He'd look at me and leer, asking me to do pervy things to him.

'I want a blow job.' He winked. 'From you Terrie.'

I was stunned, I didn't know what to say. I knew what one was from Adam and his demands. I didn't understand why he was asking me such a thing. Had he heard I was an abuse victim? He made my flesh creep and he knew it. That's when Jason stepped in. I liked Jason. Dark-haired with a big sunny smile, he lit up the room when he walked in. I didn't care that apparently he was in for some violence or another, he was as gentle as a lamb to me.

'Leave her be, Daniel,' he yelled. 'She's only a little girl.'

Once he caught Daniel calling me names and he pushed him out of the way. Jason started hanging around me when we went to the gym or sat watching TV.

'You're like my little sister,' he laughed. And I'd give him a hug. It felt good to have my 'bodyguard' Jason with me. I felt safe. He always had his eye on me, even when I tried to lift a weight that was too heavy for me in the gym one day.

'You're not strong enough, Terrie,' he said, telling me off jokingly. 'You need someone to look after you, don't you!'

I laughed. But inside I thought he was right. I did need someone to watch out for me and it felt good having him to rely on. It made me feel less alone, especially when the days had turned into weeks and I realized that neither Angela nor Mum had any intention of coming to visit me.

But before long, the twenty-eight days were up and it was time for me to leave. I was told by social services that as I hadn't tried to run away since being in the unit I didn't 'fit the criteria' for a young person who needed to be locked up. I was free to go now. But where to?

I said a sad goodbye to Stephanie, and almost cried on to Jason's T-shirt when he gave me one of his big man hugs.

'See you soon,' I promised. But I didn't know when or how. The social services sent their taxi service and I was taken straight back to Angela's again. As she opened the door, she flung her arms around me just like she'd done the first time we'd met. But this time it didn't feel as nice. I didn't feel the same warmth from her – I could sense that she didn't trust me and I knew that she wasn't someone I could rely on. Why didn't she know that Adam had kidnapped me and that I hadn't run away?

'Thank you for bringing her home,' she said to the social services.

I didn't say anything. I went inside as Molly and Stacey stared at me. It felt as though an invisible wall had been built up around us. I wanted to scream and tell them that it had all been Adam's fault, but they looked at me now like *I* had been the bad one. Like it had been my fault for running away and turning my back on them and I hated it. I said nothing as I knew they wouldn't believe me anyway, so I just laid on my bed, staring at the wall.

'I hope you don't try to run away again,' Angela said, perching behind me. 'I just want you to be happy here, Terrie,' she said.

She reached out and laid her hand on my shoulder. I resisted crying as I felt myself welling up at the tenderness of her touch. Instead, I turned over and looked at her. I wanted to tell the truth now. I wanted her to know what Adam had done, how he'd locked me in. How he touched me and made me so scared sometimes. But once again the same fears stopped me from pouring it all out – I was scared of what Adam would do to Angela, my mum and me, knowing that no one was a match for him. Now I was back where I was safe and cared for, so perhaps if I just ignored what had happened it would all go away . . .

But too much had happened to me and I couldn't deal with the accusatory looks on Molly and Stacey's faces over dinner, so at the first opportunity I had after we'd eaten, I made an excuse and went out, running all the way to Tasha's house. She grinned when she opened the door and saw me. I knew Adam popped round sometimes, but Tasha was the only person I had, and it was worth the risk. I just needed to see her, have a drink and forget what my life had become.

'Come in, we've missed you,' she said eagerly. She poured me some wine and gave me a bag of powder. 'You're just in time,' she said.

That evening, I took as much speed as I could and drank until I passed out. I didn't care any more. After all, no one cared about me, did they? Later on, at around midnight, as I came to, Adam was standing over me. He'd heard that I was round at Tasha's. Spying his ginger hair in my haze of drink and drugs I felt sick again. I didn't care; let him do what he wanted. I couldn't stop him; the police couldn't stop him. What was the point?

'Did you get arrested?' I asked him.

'No,' he smirked. 'Just a verbal caution.' I didn't know what that meant exactly, but he looked pleased with it.

'Where did they take you?' he asked.

'Leverton Hall,' I replied. 'I didn't want to come out. I loved it there.'

After a few more drinks, I found myself swaying to some music and, predictably, Adam made his move. That night, he took me back to his flat, then he laid me on the sofa and I watched with detachment as he started having sex with me again. After he finished I just lay limp in his arms, feeling like a used and broken doll.

The following morning I went back to Angela's and said I was sorry for going off like that and tried to get back into the 'routine'. She was obviously worried about me but seemed to be taking it calmly. I think she was afraid of rocking the boat; she just wanted me to be settled. But things felt different, even though, on the surface, she tried to be the same as ever. Stacey and Molly were more guarded too, playing on their own and, once again, seeing me as an outsider. As hard as I tried, I couldn't settle back into school either. Lee couldn't understand why I'd run off like that and I couldn't explain it to him. I didn't want to tell him about Adam. I didn't want him to know the ins and outs of my horrible life. I felt worthless and disgusting and all I wanted to do was to get drunk and take drugs to try and forget. Just a few hours of feeling woozy and giggly was all I craved, the chance to live outside my life.

As the weeks and months went by, Angela started to quiz me about Adam too. Previously she'd been very careful not to 'get involved' but now she had real concern in her eyes when she saw me heading out. She never knew, and neither did I, if I'd be home that night or not.

'Please stay away from Adam,' she begged one evening.

I looked at her. However much I hated him, at least at his flat I could drink, take speed and stay up as late as I wanted. In my mind that was so much better than lying on my bed at Angela's with my mind racing about, dwelling on all the horrible things that had happened. At that point in time I couldn't see another option, another way for my eleven-year-old mind to cope with my life.

'Okay,' I lied.

That evening, I went to Tasha's but when she offered me a drink, I pulled a face.

'What's up?' she asked.

'It's my tummy,' I complained. 'I feel all bloated and weird.'

She gave me a funny look. 'When was your last period?' She frowned.

I looked at the ceiling. I honestly couldn't remember, but then it wasn't something I took much notice of anyway.

'You could be up the duff,' she said casually. 'Get a pregnancy test from the chemist.'

I laughed, even though now she had me worried. Surely I couldn't be?

I hoped that Tasha would take me to get a test, but instead she gave me some money and I went by myself. I brought it back and went into the toilet. As I peed on the stick the lines appeared immediately.

I was eleven years old and I was pregnant. Emotions rushed through me as I stared at the stick in disbelief. But I found myself smiling, with a surge of real, pure joy. Wow! I'd always dreamed of having kids. Of having someone to love unconditionally and someone to love me. And my dream had come true. A baby! But my excitement was also tinged with fear. What would Adam say? My mind was racing ahead and I knew I'd need him to help pay to look after my baby so, in complete shock, I went straight to his flat to tell him. I held my breath as I knocked on the door. As soon as he opened the door I blurted out the news. He picked me up and spun me around.

'That's amazing,' he cried. 'We can go away and live somewhere, be a proper family! We can make this work for the baby's sake.'

My fear disappeared, replaced by a surge of relief and then a wave of happiness as I pictured life with my baby. This was it. Everything was about to change. Surely if he's got a baby to look after, Adam would suppress his violent streak, stop scaring me and threatening Mum and Angela, and do everything he could to help us live as a happy family? He certainly seemed pleased enough. That night I fell asleep in his arms and pushed all thoughts of his threats from my mind. I was having a baby. I couldn't believe it.

The next day, we went for a walk in town and in front of his friends, he exclaimed again how he was going to marry me.

'We're going to be together for ever,' he told people. 'We're having a baby.'

Looking back, I wonder who on earth could take this claim seriously. A thirty-three-year-old man telling his friends that he was having a baby with an eleven-year-old? It's so sick it sounds unbelievable. But many of his friends were deviants or criminals themselves. They didn't know right from wrong any more than he did. Plus, many were scared of him. His reputation was of someone not to be messed with.

Adam still frightened me, but I believed with my whole being that things were going to change for the better. I also needed him as I was pregnant and was dependent upon him for somewhere to live, although that night I knew I had to get back to Angela's.

'She'll be ringing the police if I'm gone for too long,' I explained.

'No, let's run away,' said Adam. 'We can just pack our stuff and go.'

But I didn't want the stress. I wanted him to find a proper flat for us to live in and do things properly, like he'd said he would.

'Let me go back just for tonight,' I begged. 'I promise I'll come back soon.'

When I arrived at the house, Angela opened the door, her mouth fixed in a grim line. I wanted so much to talk to her, but I knew I couldn't, and anyway I was so exhausted I could barely think straight. Angela went to speak but I cut her off.

'Please, Angela. I just need to go to bed. I'm so tired.'

'All right then,' she said. 'But we've got a lot to discuss in the morning.'

All sorts of thoughts were running through my mind as I slipped under the duvet, but I immediately fell into a deep sleep.

The next morning Stacey and Molly had already left for school by the time I woke up, and as I ventured downstairs I saw Angela washing the breakfast things at the kitchen sink. She saw me and dried her hands, ushering me silently into the living room. 'I am very disappointed in you, Terrie,' she said, slowly.

I looked at her, and felt my heart swell with pain. Her eyebrows were knotted, and her gaze steady. 'Very disappointed indeed,' she repeated slowly. She'd never used that word 'disappointed' before. It hurt me somewhere deep inside. I hated the way I'd disappointed this lovely, caring foster mum, someone who'd cooked and cleaned for me for the past eight months, who'd tried to care, even if I struggled to trust her like I used to. I started to cry. I didn't want to her to think that badly of me. I felt crushed. So without thinking I blurted out the truth.

'I'm pregnant,' I sobbed. 'Adam is the father.'

She gasped, a sharp intake of breath, as she reached out and took my hands in hers.

'Oh my goodness,' she exclaimed. 'Oh no!'

For the next fifteen minutes she explained how bad a pregnancy was for my young body and how it was impossible for me to have a baby and be a proper mum. And how any dream I had of being with Adam and creating a home with him was very, very wrong.

'You are living a fantasy as you are so desperate for a family that isn't broken,' she said softly.

I nodded, sniffing and crying as she spoke. I clutched my belly as the trapped wind feeling was worse than ever today.

Angela got up, made me a drink and told me to stay there while she called social services. Literally ten minutes later I was on my way to Lister Hospital, with Angela. Whatever phone call she'd made meant a fast-track hospital appointment. Without even waiting I was taken straight into a scanning room.

'Do you want me to come in?' Angela asked.

'No, thanks,' I said. Strangely, I felt embarrassed by all the fuss.

The nurse pulled up my top and put gel on my tummy and ran something that looked like a microphone across my skin. I shivered with the cold. As the black and green screen flicked into life I could see the shape of a baby jumping and moving on-screen, just as another trapped wind feeling occurred: it was my baby moving!

'Wow,' I said, trying to sit up for a better view. I could make out a baby's foot very clearly. I was so skinny, my tummy was already protruding like a pregnant lady's. I thought how strange it was that I'd not noticed before. The nurse told me that I was about twelve weeks gone and how an abortion was booked for the next day. I stared at her. I hadn't even been asked my opinion. But earlier Angela had told me how damaging having a baby was. So I just nodded. I was so tired. Who was I to argue anyway? Adults were taking control now.

I was taken to another room, where Angela had to sign lots of paperwork. Then someone called my mum and she came down to sign something too. She didn't look at me or say anything. I don't think she even fully understood what was going on.

'You're too young for babies, Terrie,' she said simply before she left.

That evening, I was taken home to Angela's where I went to bed early. I fell asleep with my hand on my belly, feeling the little baby kicking and jumping around and silently I said 'goodbye'.

The following day Angela drove me to the hospital and I was put into a bed. Briskly the nurse explained that I would be put to sleep and would not feel a thing. Beforehand, though, they hooked me up to a drip with drugs to make my cervix dilate. It wasn't long before they started working and I began to wince with the pain.

'Can I have something to help?' I stammered to the nurse.

'You'll be put to sleep soon,' she said abruptly. So I just turned my head into my pillow and bit my lip. Somehow this pain felt like a punishment and I'd no right to complain. Then I overheard them saying that it wasn't going to be an easy operation. Someone else muttered that I was 'sixteen weeks gone' and it would 'take some time'.

The contractions grew stronger and I found myself wincing and moaning. For three hours I sat in the bed, gripping the side bars until my knuckles turned white. No one came to see me.

Angela had gone home. She needed to be there to see her daughters home from school. Finally, I was given another injection and everything went dark.

THIRTEEN

Take Me Away

I woke up to see a nurse hovering above me, her face full of warmth. 'Wakey, wakey, Terrie, time to wake up.'

I felt as though my insides had been taken out, screwed up and restitched back in, which, in a way, they had been.

'Hi,' I said, weakly.

The world felt empty, flat. I clutched my tummy. No more trapped wind. I twisted my head and the wet feeling next to my cheeks told me that I was crying. I just wanted to sleep, to shut everything out.

The nurse nodded. 'We'll take you to a ward now. We won't put you in the maternity wing as you'd see other babies and that wouldn't be fair.'

I nodded. When I arrived, Angela was waiting for me. She was holding a teddy bear and handed it to me as I tried to sit up.

'Thank you,' I said weakly. I wasn't sure why she was giving me a cuddly toy. She looked a bit awkward. We sat and chatted as we waited for the anesthetic to wear off. Then, when I had woken up a bit more, Angela was allowed to take me home. We drove in silence for a bit, then words poured from her mouth.

'It was for the best . . . you won't regret it . . . you're just too young to think about babies, Terrie. You're still a baby yourself. You have to stay away from Adam now. I don't think the police can press charges without a statement from you, as a conviction then is unlikely. Terrie, you've got to give them a statement. He's got to pay for what he's put you through . . . '

I could hear her voice but I only took in half the words. I just kept thinking about my dead baby. Doctors had killed my baby and I'd just sat back and let them.

Back at Angela's she asked if I wanted to watch anything on TV. Stacey and Molly were staring at me as though I was an exhibit from the zoo and I felt so uncomfortable down below. My tummy hurt and I was bleeding heavily. As Angela was chatting about dinner, TV and school, I started to zone out. I wanted to get out. And to get out now. I looked at the front door and as if she had read my mind, her face grew dark.

'No, Terrie, not tonight. You need to recover. Do you understand? You need to lie down, you've been through a real ordeal,' she said.

I started to feel sick. I looked at Angela with her mumsy flowery dress and her fussy manner and started to feel anger towards her, pure white, hot rage.

You just made me kill my baby, I thought, as she started clattering the dishes to get dinner on. *You've got kids of your own who love you but you made me kill mine . . .*

Later, I started to sidle out towards the door as Angela's back was turned while she was peeling vegetables at the sink. I wanted to go and tell Adam. It was the least I could do. It was his baby as well. I wanted to tell him that the dream of our flat and our family was over. I pushed open the door.

'Where are you going?' cried Angela. She was angry. I had rarely seen her angry.

'To get some batteries for my Walkman,' I lied. Before she could answer I ran out of the door. Tears streaming down my face, I could now set my emotions free. I hated Angela right at that moment. I hated the doctors. I hated my life. I wanted, needed, someone but had no one. I arrived at Adam's flat, gasping for breath.

'Whoa, Treacle!' he said, grabbing me by the shoulders. 'What's happened to you?'

'They made me have an abortion,' I sobbed. 'They made me do it!'

He held me in his arms and soothed me. 'It's okay,' he murmured. 'It's probably for the best.'

I stared at him. I couldn't believe what he was saying. His comment tore at my insides and I wanted to throw up and run away, far away from all this terrible pain but, instead, I managed to control my voice. 'I . . . I . . . I have to go back,' I whispered. 'Otherwise she'll get the police out.'

I left, feeling so empty and alone. When I arrived back at Angela's, the smell of roast chicken greeted me as I opened the door, but so did Angela, standing in the hallway, tears in her eyes, looking absolutely furious.

'You lied to me, didn't you?' she cried. 'You didn't go and get batteries! Where the hell have you been?'

'To Adam's,' I shouted back. 'I wanted to tell him about his baby.'

Her face went almost beetroot as her mouth trembled to get the words out.

'You stupid, stupid girl,' she hissed. 'Not him! Not now! Don't you realize what he has done?'

I put my hands over my ears. I couldn't cope with it all, with all the conflicting emotions running through me. I knew I could never trust Angela again – instead of coming to find me when Adam kidnapped me, she just assumed I'd run away. Why didn't she come to the police station, tell them I didn't need to go to Leverton, that she'd take me home and look after me? Instead she'd jumped to the conclusion that I'd brought it all on myself, that I was the one to blame. Then there was Adam. I knew he was dangerous, I knew I should have nothing to do with him, but I was too scared to give a statement against him – what if it came to nothing? The police had done nothing to help me so far so why would it be any different if I just signed my name to a piece of paper? I wasn't sure I wanted to speak out against him anyway; after all, he was the only person I believed really cared for me. And what did any of it matter? I'd been made to kill my baby. The only good thing in my life had been cruelly snatched away from me.

'Go to hell!' I screamed. Before she could grab me, I ran for the door. Then into the street, tears dripping off my chin. Ignoring the pain I felt down below, I ran and ran until I'd reached Adam's flat door again. I stood there for a moment, feeling dizzy. I hesitated before I buzzed the doorbell. I didn't want to go in. Not really. But I had nowhere else to go. There was Tasha's, but she was always with her new boyfriend, who I didn't like. My own mum didn't want me. I had no one, and no one wanted me – except, of course, Adam.

I pressed the bell. Instantly the door opened, as if he'd been expecting me.

'Back so soon?' he said, smiling.

'You know you were talking about us moving away and getting a flat together?' I said, breathlessly. 'Well, I want you to help me get one. Just for me, though. I need help, Adam. I've got nowhere else to go.'

'Oh, the flat,' he replied. 'Well, that was only if we had a baby together. But there isn't a baby now, is there, because you got rid of it. So no flat.'

I felt sick. He ushered me inside, asking me what I'd like to drink. I realized suddenly that I was still bleeding; I felt a warm trickle down my leg, reaching my ankle and soaking my sock. The pain of my operation was catching up with me. Sharp, stabbing pains like knives were throbbing inside my tummy. I held my head in my hands. 'No,' I sobbed in agreement. 'There's no baby.'

Now I was crying from the emotional as well as the physical pain.

Adam ruffled my hair and passed me a drink. A vodka and coke.

'Here, get this down you. It'll make you feel better. Don't worry. You can stay here with me.'

I looked at him. I took a large slug and then switched on the TV. I needed something, anything, to take it all away. Adam sat down with me, his arm around me like any man would sit with a girlfriend. When a few minutes had gone by and I'd managed to calm down a bit, he looked at me.

'You up for some sex, Terrie?' he asked.

I looked at him, thinking I'd misheard what he'd said. 'No, I've just had an abortion. No,' I said.

'Please, babe?' he said.

'I'm still bleeding,' I said, turning back to the TV. 'I feel horrible.'

'Please, babe?' he persisted. 'I'll only be quick.'

I hugged myself, feeling the blood sticking in my knickers.

'No, Adam,' I said. A horrible sick feeling started to creep over me, as he began playing with my hair.

'Go on,' he said. 'I really need some. It won't take a minute.'

As I turned to him, I saw a determined look pass across his face. He picked me up with one, swift movement. He marched into his bedroom and, with full force, threw me on the bed.

'I won't be long,' he snapped, pulling down my jeans and knickers. He pushed himself into me as I let out a blood-curdling scream. The pain was horrific. It hurt so much that I thought I was going to die then and there. Luckily it was over quickly. As he got up, I could see that my sticky blood covered my legs, the sheets and his torso. I lay sobbing. I felt so disgusting, and the metallic smell of blood all around me made me feel sick. And my tummy burned with pain. Then I heard the front door click and Adam left. After half an hour or so, I got up and ran a shower. Washing away the blood, I watched it swirl down the plughole, feeling as though it was my life that was draining away. I wanted to die. I felt so ill. I was so scared. But even though I didn't want to be here with Adam, I had absolutely nowhere else to go. I dried myself and got changed into some clothes I'd left in Adam's flat from a time before. Then I sat down and continued crying. Adam got back several hours later, looking very upset. He sunk to his knees to sit on the floor by me.

'I am so sorry,' he said, burying his head in my lap. 'I am so, so sorry, Terrie. I didn't mean to do that. I just wanted to be close to you . . .'

I refused to look at him. I felt so sick, and didn't want him to touch me. But he held my hand tightly anyway. I was too scared to snatch it away.

'Terrie, babe, we'll have to go. You do realize that?' he continued. 'We can't stay here. The police will be on their way soon. You know they'll take you back to the detention centre.'

I sniffed. He was right, they would do. Maybe that would be a good thing? But Adam's face told me that he wasn't going to let me go that easily.

'Right,' he said, suddenly full of energy. 'We need to get going.'

Frantically, he ran around the flat, opening his wardrobes and drawers, flinging clothes into a holdall. Then he grabbed my wrist. 'We'll go somewhere, anywhere, tonight and then find somewhere more permanent afterwards.'

I stared at him. He looked and sounded like a madman. But who was I to argue? I was so tired and frightened, so I went along with it.

We turned off the lights and left the flat. Then we started walking. We walked for miles, going from house to house, knocking on the doors of all Adam's friends. They all turned us down, some making polite excuses, some being less polite.

'We're not taking you in if you're on the run with Terrie,' said one. 'The cops will be at our door.'

Clutching my hand tightly, Adam dragged me along, stopping to stand in the shadows if he spotted a police car. Eventually, around midnight, both of us were exhausted and we'd still not found anywhere for the night.

'Damn it!' cried Adam. 'Where are friends when you need them, eh?'

We carried on walking for a little longer, then Adam suddenly stopped. I was so exhausted and in incredible pain, and I allowed myself to hope for a second that he was about to say we should turn around and head back to his flat.

'This will just have to do,' he said.

I followed his line of vision but all I could see was a Somerfield car park. 'Where?' I asked.

'There.' He nodded and pointed towards the outside brick building that held the bins.

I started crying. 'Adam,' I sobbed. 'I can't sleep there.'

Not listening, he grabbed my wrist and marched me over to it. Standing over me, he pointed to a dark, dank corner by the metal bins.

'This will do. At least the police won't find you,' he said.

Terrified at the look he gave me, I sank to my knees and then curled into a ball, lying on a piece of ripped cardboard from a discarded frozen food box. Then, rocking myself, I tried to snuggle into my coat as the cold hard floor made my bones ache. Adam didn't lie down himself. He sat on the kerb nearby and said he'd 'keep watch'.

I looked at him. His face was lit by the orange light from the lamp post. I hated him. I thought how much he'd hurt me, this man who kept telling me he loved me. And now he was forcing me to sleep in a bin? Was this all I deserved? In many ways it felt like it. I already felt like a piece of discarded rubbish. All night I lay awake, feeling myself bleeding still, wondering what on earth was going to happen next, until I heard the sound of the bin men arriving.

'Come on,' hissed Adam. 'Time to move, babe.'

I stood up, aching all over as though I had flu. Adam looked wired.

'Right,' he said. 'You're on the run, so you just go somewhere, like your mum's, okay? And we can catch up later.'

And then, in the morning light, he walked off quickly, hands in his pockets looking like an ordinary man, rushing to work.

Drying my eyes again, I arrived at Mum's house. I was exhausted and had never felt so low. As usual, Mum barely raised her eyes from the TV as I came in. She didn't ask what was wrong or where I'd been. I ran myself a bath. Easing myself into the hot water, I felt pain everywhere. I was still bleeding profusely from the abortion. It stung down below when I got in the water. Part of me wanted to submerge myself and never come out. I knew the police would be after me again. I knew that Adam was never going to leave me be. I felt I had no escape whatsoever. I sank into the water for a bit and then dried myself roughly with a towel, hating my body, hating everything. I went and lay on my bed to cry again, then the phone rang.

Mum called me down. 'It's Tasha on the phone,' she said.

I wondered what she wanted. Sometimes I wished that Tasha wasn't friends with Adam; she was always telling him where I was, or what I was doing

'Hello?' I said.

'You have to come, Terrie,' she said. 'It's Adam . . .'

'Why, what's he done?' I asked.

'He's bleeding everywhere. He's tried to cut his own heart out . . . he says you've broken his heart and he wanted to cut it out to stop himself from loving you.'

My teeth gritted. What was he playing at? Tasha explained how one of Adam's friends had turned up and helped clean the wound. I didn't know what to say. After everything Adam had done, he was still making me feel as though it was my fault. And as much as I hated him, I also felt very guilty.

'Okay, I'll go and see him,' I said.

Mum overheard me. 'I don't think you should go,' she said suddenly. I looked at her in surprise. Mum never said much about anything.

'Why?' I asked her.

'You hanging around with Adam. It's not right,' she said. 'If you go, I am calling social services.'

I shrugged. In some ways I wanted her to; at least it would prove that she cared about me. I threw on some clothes and went back to Adam's flat. I found him crouching on the kitchen floor, clutching his chest, pieces of swab with blood on them were stuck all him over. His friend Danny was standing next to him.

'You're a little slut,' said Danny. 'A horrible slag. Look what you've done to him.'

I didn't know what to say, so I just sat with Adam until he stopped crying. Then I went to Tasha's house. More than anything now I just wanted to have a drink to stop me from thinking.

Within half an hour of me being there, though, the street was filled with the sound of sirens. The police had arrived with a court order to take me back to the detention centre. And, this time, I couldn't have been happier to see them. For once I didn't want control over my life. I wanted someone else to take over. Even if they were going to lock me up again.

Tasha's face dropped and she went pale as fists pounded on the door.

'Open up!' one yelled. 'We're here for Terrie O'Brian.'

As though she'd had an electric shock, Tasha sprang from the sofa and opened the door. Instantly three officers, including a WPC, were in the room.

She explained that they had a three-night control order and I was to go back to Leverton Hall until they got a residency order. I nodded and Tasha hugged me.

'How did they know you were here?' she whispered.

'Adam?' I guessed.

Tasha squeezed me tight for a moment and I felt tears welling up, so I pushed her away.

'Bye,' I said abruptly, turning without looking at her face.

I was hungry and tired and was quite happy to be going to see Stephanie and Jason again, but at the same time I wanted to cry. I'd only been away from there for a matter of weeks, yet so much had happened in that time.

First, though, the car took me to Watford County Court where I was introduced to my own solicitor. I liked her. She told it to me straight, just like it was. She said her job was to reduce my court order and detention.

'But I want to go back in there,' I explained. 'There's nowhere for me to go out here, you know.'

She looked puzzled and then smiled. 'Everyone's situation is different, I suppose,' she said. 'Well, social services are going for a six-month order as they want to do psychological tests on you and to offer you counselling. I was going to ask for a one-month order, but I can ask for three months instead?'

I nodded. Three months sounded like a long enough time to me. I also thought that maybe counselling might help. I didn't really know what it involved, but if someone wanted to talk to me about everything that had happened, maybe they could help me.

*

I was terrified when the judge took his position. It all seemed so serious. Mum turned up, looking as confused as ever, but muttering something about it 'being for my own good'. During the proceedings, the judge called Adam 'a forbidden fruit' and said that if a fruit was no longer forbidden, people tended to lose their desire for it, so I should still be allowed contact with him. Even then, I knew this was wrong; I couldn't understand why no one truly wanted to protect me from Adam. He wasn't a good man. After the hearing I was told to return to the detention centre for three months. And it was nothing but a relief.

I went back to Leverton Hall, had my strip-search, which I found just as humiliating the second time around, and then found myself back in the unit, with the guys I'd become friends with before. I threw my arms around Stephanie when I saw her. Her hair had grown a little longer but she still looked pale as death.

'So good you're back,' she said, grinning.

Jason was made up too. 'You've got your big brother back now,' he said.

Another girl, Lisa, had joined the unit. She'd just had a baby who'd been adopted as she was only fourteen. Her boyfriend was sixteen, but when he found out that she was pregnant, he left her. As seemed to be the case with all of us, social services wanted her to be locked up afterwards 'for her own protection'.

'What are you in here for?' she asked.

'Because they prefer to lock me up rather than my abuser,' I repeated. Even my solicitor had said she couldn't understand from all the reports why Adam hadn't been arrested.

I'd listened carefully to Lisa's story over dinner that night. I was starting to become obsessed with the idea of having another baby. The empty feeling after my abortion was growing and all I could think about was babies. At night I even dreamed of holding one. It was like a physical ache as my body missed being pregnant.

I imagined how I'd feel holding a perfect little person in my arms, and how much love I would give the baby. I couldn't help but think of the flat Adam had promised me I could have if I had a baby. I kept imagining how perfect life would be if I had a baby and a flat to myself. It seemed like heaven.

It didn't take long to settle back into detention centre life. Stephanie and I started swapping our favourite music again. I hung around playing games with Jason and, of course, Daniel carried on trying to bully me.

'Do you want some?' Daniel ribbed one day over dinner. 'Go on, Terrie. Get on your knees, girl, for a BJ.'

Just as previously, Jason overheard and stood up. 'Shut up, Daniel,' he snapped again. 'She's only a little girl,' he shouted. Daniel quietened down. I was so grateful to Jason for being there. Little did he know, I'd both heard and experienced far worse. I liked the idea that he thought I was innocent; that's what I wanted to be.

After three months, my stay was extended by another month by social services. It was around then that Jason was moved to the open section of the detention centre. He was gearing up to be released and he couldn't wait. I wasn't looking forward to him going, though. We'd grown so close. We would spend almost every day together, playing *Mario Cars*, going to the gym, and we always sat together for meals. I never once thought about telling him about Adam, although he must have suspected or heard why I was inside. Gradually, he was allowed out at weekends to see his parents, before he would eventually be let out completely. We never said goodbye properly when he left the secure section, as he was in the open prison at first and I saw him regularly in the grounds outside, or he'd pop by during our leisure time. He seemed calmer now, more grown up, but at the same time still the caring boy who just wanted to know everyone was okay.

The last time I saw him he was laughing and messing about as usual. 'Bye, Terrie, see you next week,' he shouted over to me. 'I'm off home for the weekend.'

But he didn't appear back at Leverton the following week, and when a local radio station released a story about a seventeen-year-old who'd been stabbed to death in the Pink Toothbrush Nightclub in Basildon, someone said the victim sounded like Jason.

At first the rumour that it was Jason was denied by staff. Then, as people got more upset, they admitted it was him. I was completely devastated. He was such a lovely boy. Maybe from the wrong side of the tracks, but he wanted to live a good life. But now he'd never get the chance. We weren't allowed to attend his funeral or contact his family. It was as though he had just disappeared. We weren't even allowed to say a proper goodbye.

Recently, after somehow getting my number, Tasha had started calling me in the centre. I wasn't thrilled that she'd been given it. I liked being away from Adam and I didn't want her to pass on the number to him. Then, one day, lo and behold, she passed the phone to Adam. 'He's just dropped in, Terrie,' she insisted. 'Go on, have a quick chat with him.'

My heart started banging. I didn't want to speak to him, but I daren't put the phone down.

'Hello, babe,' he said. 'Now I really need to talk to you about visiting orders, don't I?'

I took a deep breath. 'No, Adam, I don't want you here,' I replied. He fell silent. Then his tone turned menacing.

'You're in there all safe, while I'm picking up the pieces!' he spat. 'You've got it so cushy . . .'

I felt sick as he went on to tell me how he was going to 'carve himself up'.

'Stop it,' I finally said. 'Please, please, just leave me alone.'

I put the phone down and started sobbing again. I wished so badly that Jason was there to give me a hug, to make me feel protected like he had always been able to. Because no matter how far away from Adam I managed to get, I never seemed to be able to break free of his clutches.

FOURTEEN

Oblivion

Adam started ringing the unit about three times a week. I was only allowed phone calls between 4 p.m. and 7 p.m., and they were taken privately in the box room, a bare room with yellow walls, a desk and a phone. I knew that sometimes staff recorded the calls, and I longed for them to listen in to him, then they'd put a stop to it. But no one did, not until much later. I felt that taking his calls was the best option. After all, I didn't want him to get even more upset and to start threatening Mum again. I didn't want to make him angry. He often rang 'for a chat' and I'd just answer 'yes' or 'no' to his brief questions. I thought it was an easy way of keeping him happy. His moods were all over the place; one minute he'd be happily telling me about a decorating job, and the next he'd start snapping at me: 'You miss me, eh? Do you? I hope you fucking do.' Not once did I hang up, though. Although I was safely locked up, I knew that if I did hang up, he'd probably call me more often, or take it out on Mum.

One day, his tone of voice turned especially nasty. 'Guess what?' he spat. 'I'm seeing someone else now.'

My stomach turned over. I didn't know whether to feel relieved or what.

179

'Who?' I asked, trying to keep my tone light.

The answer came as a complete blow. 'Your. Own. Mum.'

I felt bile rise in my throat as I clutched the phone. Mum? My mum? What was he playing at?

'Really?' I said, again trying to control my voice. I so badly didn't want him to know how I was feeling inside, as my guts twisted into a knot. Oh God, not Mum. She wouldn't know how to defend herself against him. She was so naïve, childlike in many ways. The thought of her and him made me want to scream. I swallowed hard to control my voice. My hand started shaking with absolute terror. But I opened my mouth and forced out a sound.

'Ha ha ha!' I laughed. 'Ha! Ha! Ha!'

Laughing was the last thing I felt like doing, but I suddenly felt very determined not to give Adam what he wanted.

'Yeah, and it feels so good fucking her instead of you,' he spat.

After that phone call, I went back to my room and felt more disgusting than ever before. I knew he was just trying to upset me, so I shouldn't let him win, but the thought of Adam with his hands on my own mother made me want to vomit.

The following day, Mum rang. She didn't often call, but I was glad she did. I wanted to check to see if Adam was telling the truth.

'Mum, are you in a relationship with Adam?' I asked.

'Oh?' she said, as if I'd asked her if she liked chocolate. 'Yes I am.'

I wasn't sure if I believed her. Sometimes Mum just said yes when you asked her things to try and be helpful, even if it wasn't true.

'Are you having sex with him?' I asked, my chest tightening at the thought.

'Oh yes, he comes round, picks me up, takes me upstairs, and he does it to me on the bed,' she said, as if she was discussing picking up some shopping. Then she carried on, giving a very graphic description of what he did to her. Tears fell silently down my chin as I squeezed my eyes shut, trying to block out the image of my abuser, the man I hated, having sex with my mum now.

'Okay, okay,' I said. 'That's enough. I don't need to know any more. Please.'

She fell silent. 'Sorry, Terrie,' she said. I don't know why she said it. Usually she never acknowledged anything that hurt or upset me.

'That's okay,' I said, quietly sobbing. 'It's not right, but I know you can't help it.'

That night when I went to bed, the familiar feeling of betrayal once again washed over me, making me want to scream. Mum was now sleeping with the man who abused me. I know I had never told her the full story, but she knew something had been going on, I was convinced. How else did she think I had got pregnant? Why else did she complain to social services that I was always at Adam's? And, goodness knows, I believed that Adam must have told her. As much as I hated him, I hated the fact that he was sleeping with my mother even more. I had been betrayed by an adult yet again – and this time it was my own mother.

A few weeks later, it was my twelfth birthday – and I was celebrating it locked up in a detention centre. But for the first time in my life, I was given a proper iced birthday cake with lit candles. Sitting at dinner, I wasn't expecting anything when, suddenly, the staff walked in with a plain white cake with Happy Birthday in baby-pink piped icing over the top. The candles flickered and, as they walked in, everyone burst into song. I couldn't help smiling as all eyes turned to me. I felt a mixture of shyness and pleasure as everyone cheered, urging me to blow them out. I took a deep breath and blasted them all out at once as everyone clapped through the smoke. I looked around me. I'd dreamed of having a birthday cake all my life, and now finally I had one. The circumstances were far from ideal, I thought, but better than I ever imagined I'd get.

After a four-month stint inside this time, I was found another foster placement, this time with two ladies, Nicki and Anna. Once again, a social services taxi drove me to their house. It was a big old Victorian-style house on the edge of Stevenage. But the reception I got was very different from that I had received when I had arrived at Angela's place. Nicki, a woman in her late forties with short hair and an unsmiling face, opened the door. After a swift introduction, Nicki waved the social worker off and turned to me.

'Right,' she said, eyeing me suspiciously. She indicated to me to hold out my hand and then poured a pile of twenty-pence pieces into it.

'If you want to use the phone, there is a pay phone in our house,' she said. 'I'm not paying for your calls beyond that, okay? We have our own landline.'

I glared at her. I knew foster carers got paid. Some did it for love, some did it for the money. Already I knew what her game was and that she hadn't taken me in from the goodness of her heart.

'And I've been told to drop you off and pick you up from school,' she sighed. 'Which I will do, but you have to realize that I am not your personal taxi service.'

Then I was shown to my room: a basic bedroom, with a small, single bed, a small bookshelf with a few dusty books, a small desk and lamp, and a wardrobe. It looked like a neglected spare room. I was told to expect dinner in an hour. I soon realized that Nicki didn't cook. She showed me how to use the microwave and told me to choose a ready meal from the fridge or freezer. I went to have a look and it felt so weird, rummaging through some woman's freezer. I know she was fostering me, but the 'welcome' she gave was anything but. I was a stranger in a stranger's house, helping myself to her food. There was hardly anything that looked nice but eventually I found a spag Bol microwave meal that only needed three minutes' cooking.

That evening, after dinner, I was watching TV when Anna, another short-haired lady, came home. She said a brief hello to me, but didn't wait to hear my response, then marched up to Nicki smiling, planting a long, hard kiss on her mouth. I stared in shock. I'd never seen lesbians before. It didn't bother me, but it was a bit of an eye-opener. The evening was spent watching a wildlife programme that they seemed to be enjoying, but not once did either of them try and start a conversation, so I couldn't be bothered to either. Hugging a cushion, I wondered how long it would be before I could get out and see Tasha.

The following day I found myself back at Barnwell. Nothing had changed and my classmates seemed pleased to see me. Lee had another girlfriend by now. I didn't care, however. After everything that had gone on I realized that he was never going to go for a girl like me. He was too good for me, and I resigned myself to thinking that there was no point in even hankering after a 'normal' life with a nice boyfriend. After all, I was never going to get it.

I tried to settle down at Nicki and Anna's place, but nowhere had felt less like home. Yes I was fed, clothed and kept clean, but I don't ever remember actually having a conversation with Nicki. She soon stopped her 'taxi' service to school, too. One morning she slung a fiver at me and told me to get the bus that week. That Monday, I decided not to catch the bus back home. I was feeling quite lonely and miserable so I decided to hook up with Tasha and Lucy again. Tasha had yet another new boyfriend now and she'd told me she didn't see much of Adam these days. She was still the best friend I had in the outside world and, most importantly, she had somewhere where I could go and stay.

Soon I was back drinking and taking speed, and occasionally I even took cocaine. It helped me to forget about my baby, about Mum and Adam, about everything. I just craved oblivion. After all, what did the real world have to offer? I think Tasha liked having me around to be her skivvy. She'd just got a place from the council, so I helped her with errands and housework, and gave her some of the allowance I was given by social services for boozing. I made sure I showed my face at school and back at Nicki's house every other day to stop them from calling the police, but I would happily bunk off school or disappear for the odd night. I only saw Mum when I wanted money from her. Every fortnight, when she received her benefits, I'd ask her for some of it and she'd hand me between £50 and £100 in notes. She wasn't capable of saying 'no' to me, although sometimes she'd spent it all before I got to her. Then I'd go straight out and spend it on drink and drugs, mainly Mad Dog and ouzo from a dodgy off-licence where they turned a blind eye to my age, and speed. I never saw Mum and Adam together and she never mentioned their relationship, so I just ignored it. I hated him for taking advantage of her and hated her for the betrayal.

Most of the time I was with Tasha. It seems crazy but social services were more inclined to chase me when I was staying with her than when I was at Adam's. A few times Tasha had a phone call from them telling her that she was breaking the law by allowing me to stay at her place.

'You're harbouring a young person in care and that is an offence,' they told her. But they never called the police and Tasha laughed it off.

'You'll be all right, Terrie,' she used to joke. 'You always are, ain't you!'

Meanwhile, Adam had moved into a new flat, possibly one of the reasons I'd not heard from him for a few months. But as suddenly as he'd left my life, he reappeared again. One evening, I was sitting at Tasha's, and her boyfriend Mike was there. As usual, we were drinking while watching TV and talking about which drugs to take that night when a loud banging started at the door.

Tasha's eyes widened as Mike jumped up.

'Mike!' screamed a man's voice. 'Let us in!'

'Get yourself out here!' shouted Adam.

I jumped up myself. Then, before any of us had time to react, the first man's foot came crashing through the door and the pair of them were inside.

Rooted to the spot, Mike looked terrified as the man grabbed him and dragged him into the bathroom. We listened as Mike screamed, while the man kicked and punched him like a madman.

'Do something!' I shouted at Adam. But he just stood there, rolling a fag.

Eventually, Mike emerged, his face bleeding, his eyes swollen. He groaned and staggered into the bedroom where he shut the door. The other man left quickly. The whole scene was so shocking, I just sat there, feeling as though I was in a dreadful film. Tasha was crying and ran to see Mike. No one said anything, but I knew it was probably something to do with drugs and money.

'How are you, babe?' asked Adam, a smirk appearing across his face. 'So, do the police know you're here, then? Might have to tell them, eh,' he said with a wink.

Tasha had helped Mike out of the bedroom by that point and had a look of concern on her face when she heard what Adam had threatened. Mike looked at me but didn't say anything. Adam ignored him completely. I didn't always feel entirely welcome when Mike was around. I felt a bit of a gooseberry sometimes.

'Tasha, I can stay here, can't I?' I asked her.

She shook her head. 'Listen,' she said. 'The police haven't been yet, but I don't want them on my back.'

'Come with me, then,' said Adam. 'I've got a place now that the police don't know about.'

'Yeah,' said Tasha. 'Go to his.'

I wiped a tear from my face, as Adam slipped his arm around my shoulders. So I was back to square one again, with Adam being the only person who actually wanted me in his life. From that moment, he acted like we were back together and that was that.

'Can I not stay another night, Tash?' I began. I started to feel quite desperate inside, like I wanted to beg. But the look on her face told me not to. She and Mike were pretty serious now and he shook his head too. 'Not enough room here,' he said.

'I'm so happy you're back, babe.' Adam smiled. He squeezed my shoulders. I wanted to shrug him away, but at the same time, a small part of me remembered how nice he could make me feel, sometimes.

'C'mon,' Adam murmured in my ear. 'Me and your mum are finished. You're the only one I want. You know that. Come on!'

I wiped more tears. I didn't have anywhere to go. I didn't know what to do. To hear that he wasn't seeing Mum any more was at least a relief. At least she was out of it now.

'It's late,' Tasha sighed, opening her front door. 'Sorry, Terrie.'

Like a lamb to the slaughter, I resigned myself to being back with Adam. He looked so happy when we walked to his car, holding my hand tightly. 'We need to keep you out of that kids' prison,' he said. 'I want you to make sure you go to Nicki's and school a few times a week, come what may . . . keep them off our backs. ' His words came rushing out. He was already making plans. I nodded dumbly. I felt like a robot. One who had little or no choice. I knew I'd have to do as he said.

In his new flat, everything looked very similar to the last place. So neat and tidy. Adam sank down on his knees while I sat on the sofa.

'Don't be sad, Terrie!' he said, smiling kindly. 'I'm here for you, only you. I'll look after you. You know that. And let's face it, I'm all you've got.'

I nodded dumbly. I knew he was right. He handed me a vodka and coke. 'Get that down you,' he said. 'That'll put a smile on your face.'

Within two hours he'd picked me up and taken me to bed, where I was having sex again. I was glad to be drunk.

Avoiding another court order proved easy. All I had to do was to make sure that I went to Nicki's every other day for dinner and bedtime. She never told me off. She seemed satisfied if I went to school a few times a week. There were no complaints, and I didn't turn up at hers drunk. Social services had also stopped asking about my school attendance. I was doing enough to keep everyone happy, especially Adam. He always seemed to be in a good mood if I did what I was told.

Once again, I was firmly in Adam's clutches. And as the time went by, despite hating him, I also began to feel that I 'needed' him – like a prisoner who becomes dependent on their jailer, I couldn't imagine life without him. He gave me money when Mum didn't have much. He bought me clothes so, for once, I looked 'cool' when I did actually did go to school. Now I always had the best trainers and jeans. He cooked me dinners, as now usually Tasha was with Mike, not wanting me to hang about. But most of all, he told me that he loved me, all the time. To the point where I actually started liking myself. Well, at least a little bit.

'You're the most amazing person, Terrie,' he told me once after sex. 'I love you so very much and you'll always be safe with me. Other adults won't understand that, though.' I still hated kissing him and having sex, but his words made me feel good, so I began to believe that the pay-off was worth it. I would still try to make excuses to put him off. 'I've not cleaned my teeth,' I'd say sometimes, as he tried to push his tongue into my mouth. Sometimes it worked and he left me alone, or we had sex but he didn't kiss me. I'd close my eyes and imagine myself far away, anywhere but on his sofa or in his bed. Then when it was over, he'd snuggle up to me, and stroke my hair.

'I love you so much,' he'd say, over and over.

Soon it was Christmas again, and up until now, I had gone home every Christmas to see Mum, as I didn't have anywhere else to go. The foster families spent it with their own families and I was told to go back to mine. This Christmas, though, Adam cheerfully told me that he'd be joining me and Mum in her council house.

'I'll get you something nice this year,' he promised me. I forced a smile. I didn't fancy the idea of spending the day with Mum and Adam, especially after what had happened between them, but I told myself that it was 'only for one day'.

It was the worst Christmas I can remember. It started well, with Mum acting as though nothing had happened with Adam and a couple of good films on the telly. All Mum did was sit quietly in her chair, drinking tea. I knew she must know something was going on between me and Adam, but she seemed to have resigned herself and was ignoring it. As usual, we had no dinner, decorations or any of the normal Christmassy things. But then Adam handed me a wrapped box. It was a watch, a grown-up lady's watch, with a leather strap and a small, pretty clock face. I'd never had a watch before and it looked rather posh.

'Thank you,' I whispered. I loved it. But I hated him for making me feel even more indebted to him. My emotions were all over the place. That night Mum went to bed early and I was left watching late-night TV with Adam, alone on the sofa. Before long his arm crept around my shoulders and he was nuzzling my ear.

'Give me a blow job,' he ordered.

So, while a TV audience clapped in the background, and festive music was heard from outside, I sank to my knees as Adam lay back, his eyes closed, a smirk of contentment across his lips. I just closed my eyes and tried to think of it being over. Even though I'd been having sexual contact now with him for years, I still hated doing it. I tried to think of something else, anything else, and to make it as quick as possible.

As I was carrying on, Pervy Pat came downstairs for a glass of water. I looked up and for a few seconds our eyes met. He stopped dead. Not wanting to cause a scene or to disturb Adam, I just carried on, feeling sick to my stomach. Part of me, though, felt so relieved that Pervy Pat had caught Adam forcing me to do this. Surely he'd say something? He might have been a pervert, but he was also my great-uncle, wasn't he? But as I continued, I could see him in the corner of my eye, just standing there, staring. Slowly, drool from his lips started dribbling down his chin, as he stood stock-still like a lamp post. Then, as though nothing had happened, he turned and walked off back upstairs without a second glance. Hot tears stung my eyes as I squeezed them shut. Once again, an adult I knew wasn't going to save me from this. I knew yet again that nobody cared.

As the months passed, Adam's determination to see me slip under the radar of the authorities seemed to be working. I'd found a way to keep everyone happy just by turning up to school as often as I had to. I used to enjoy some of my lessons, including English but, by now, I'd fallen so far behind that I'd started hating it. I was always caught messing about in French, as I had no clue what anyone was on about.

'*Bonjouuur!*' I'd cry to the French teacher when I walked in.

She must have thought that I was a pupil from Hell, but I didn't care. I didn't see the point of my even being there. After all, what was the point of someone like me learning another language? I doubted that I'd even be able to get a job or do very much with my life, let alone travel abroad. I couldn't even imagine growing up, being an adult. Just getting through each day and week was as far as I took life. But in my eyes, as long as I turned up at school, got that tick by my name on the register, no one could complain. And I was keeping Adam content.

Soon enough, it was my birthday again. I was to be thirteen. A teenager at last, even though I'd spent the past year or so acting like an older teen anyway. Adam was especially excited about this birthday. He seemed to view it as a 'coming of age'. He bought me a little miniskirt and a pair of enormous heels and told me to dress up.

'I'm taking you out for some fun tonight,' he said. 'Out for a nice meal.'

I put on the outfit, and a leather jacket that Adam had bought me on another occasion. Then I plastered my face with make-up. I'd started to wear lipstick more often now, after Tasha had shown me what colours suited me. I looked in the mirror and swivelled my hips as I admired myself. The heels were enormous and added several inches to my four feet nine inches. I still looked tiny, though, as the jacket hung off my shoulders. The image staring back at me reminded me of a beauty-pageant girl from America whom I'd seen on TV. A little girl pretending to be a woman. Adam's plan was to take me to Stevenage leisure park. There was a bowling alley, cinema, nightclub and restaurants there, and I couldn't wait. He drove me down in a car he was borrowing.

'What do you fancy eating, babe?' he asked. I couldn't decide. I wasn't used to having such a big choice.

As we arrived in the car park, Adam's mobile rang. 'Yep, yep,' he said, quickly. 'Right, I'm on my way.'

He peeled £20 from his wallet and handed it to me.

'You'll have to get yourself home, Treacle,' he said. 'A job has come up. See you later.'

He pushed open the car door for me to step out and then drove off at speed.

I stood there, alone, barely able to walk in the heels, watching his car disappear in a cloud of exhaust fumes. It was very dark now, and it had started to spit with rain. I'd no idea what he was dashing off for, but he was probably up to no good, whatever it was.

I turned to look for the way out of the car park. Just as I did, another car pulled up, its headlights dazzling me. Out climbed an older teenager and her boyfriend. She looked so happy as he grabbed her hand and they walked off together, her high heels clip-clopping to a restaurant for a romantic night out. As she walked past she looked me up and down, making me feel so small. Once again I felt like an unwanted outsider while all around me people led normal lives. Miserably, I trudged to a phone box where I called a cab from a number in the booth. Then I went to Tasha's house to get drunk and snort coke; she'd rung me earlier on the mobile phone Mum had given me, to say that Mike was out. I'd been shocked when Mum gave me the phone; she said I might need it if I ever was on the run. A rare act that showed me she may at least care a little.

Within an hour I was spewing up in Tasha's kitchen sink. I felt wretched and craved the usual buzz from drugs but that night it wasn't happening. So I fell on the sofa and tried to sleep it off.

'Happy Birthday,' Tasha muttered, ruffling my hair as she staggered past.

Despite the chaotic life I led, there was one nagging feeling I couldn't shake off – I wanted a baby. I couldn't help but notice pregnant women everywhere and every time I had a period I felt a bit sad that I wasn't pregnant again. It sounds crazy, as I was only a child myself, but, in my childish way, I still thought that having a baby to love and love me back was all I needed to be happy. I knew a baby would love me as its mother whatever happened. After all, despite my own mum never properly looking after me, I still loved her, didn't I? And I was sure I'd be a better mum than my own. I often found myself rubbing my tummy, daydreaming, imagining the fluttering feeling again of something so innocent growing inside me. Even if Adam was the father, a man I sometimes hated, it was better than nothing. Then Tasha told me that she was two months pregnant. She'd been seeing someone behind Mike's back, a guy called Tony, and she'd fallen pregnant by him and now she'd split with Mike and they were together.

I pretended to be happy, but inside I was seething with jealousy. It wasn't fair. I started to avoid her, as I felt so envious. But it also made me more determined to get pregnant myself. I never came on to Adam, but when he asked to kiss me, I never turned my head anymore or made excuses about not kissing, or claiming I was having my period.

Around this time, social services paid me an impromptu visit at Adam's flat. I was eating a cheese sandwich and watching a lunchtime TV show when the doorbell rang.

Adam leapt up to answer it. The social services were unsure as to whether or not they had the correct address at first.

'Adam?' they asked, showing ID.

'Yes?' he said, hesitantly.

'We got your address from a forwarding address at your old property,' one explained. 'Is Terrie here?'

He waved them in, a flash of anger momentarily passing on his face behind their backs. 'Terrie,' he said, putting on a smile. 'Someone to see you.'

They sat down and pulled out two files with Post-it notes all over them. I started to feel quite ill. I could sense that Adam wasn't pleased. He thought we'd been keeping them happy. He thought his plan had worked. Now his knee was jiggling impatiently and I felt scared.

'We've spoken to Nicki and she mentioned that you some-times disappear for whole nights at a time,' said one. 'We've had a meeting and decided that it might be best to send you back to Angela's house. After all, you got on quite well there, didn't you?'

I looked at Adam. The frown on his face had deepened.

'Would you prefer Angela's to Nicki's?' asked the other one.

The thought of being back at Angela's sent a lovely feeling through me, making me feel safe and warm. However, the thought of saying this in front of Adam petrified me so, instead, I just nodded. It was true, I did want to go back there. He was staring at me.

'That's sorted, then,' said the social worker. They asked a few other questions and snapped their files shut. 'We'll send a taxi to pick you up.' By the time they left, Adam looked like he was going to explode.

'You might be going back to Angela's,' he said in a low voice, 'but you cannot escape me completely. I'll never let you go.'

He sat silently in a sulk, watching TV as I packed my things. Then the taxi arrived and once again I was moving on. 'I'm sorry,' I spluttered as I walked past him while he held the door open.

'You fucking will be,' he snarled.

Angela welcomed me with open arms again, despite the way we'd parted.

'I'm so thrilled you're back, Terrie,' she cooed, as she smothered me in one of her big motherly hugs. I had to admit, it was nice to be back. Stacey and Molly seemed pleased to see me too, at least on the surface, and straightaway offered to do my hair. I felt as though they were probably still judging me from last time, but I smiled and went along with it.

Later that evening, I didn't go to Adam's. I didn't want to. It felt good to be back within that nice, normal house again. I'd forgotten how it felt to be there, being looked after by someone who didn't want something terrible from me, and eating proper home-cooked meals. I'd grown very tired of Adam's tinned meals. And just the thought of having my clean bed, to sleep in alone, without Adam pawing at me, trying to have sex with me, was such a relief. It was like I'd blanked all this out when I was with him. Now I was back, I could just relax a little again. Of course, at the back of my mind, I wondered what Adam was going to do next. I was frightened of his temper. But, for tonight at least, I could just be a child again.

*

Angela seemed keen to chat about 'what happened last time'. She looked sad when she spoke about the abortion.

'I think you should have had some counselling, Terrie,' she said. 'I'm sorry it wasn't on offer. I wish things had been handled differently.'

I bit my lip and willed myself not to cry. I didn't feel I could stop if I did. Just hearing the mention of the baby made my tummy throb a little, in memory of the pain.

'That's okay,' I found myself replying. I didn't want Angela to feel bad. After all, she was a good person deep down. I didn't want her to carry on talking, though. I wanted to put my hands over my ears and to tell her to shut up.

'Everything will be okay,' she continued softly. 'You just need time to recover, and to put this terrible event behind you.'

I nodded, like a robot. I wanted her to think that I was okay, and in many ways I wanted to pretend to myself. But I knew that everything was far from okay. Adam would be sitting in front of the telly now on his own, full of rage that I'd been taken away again, plus, we'd been having sex so often that I sometimes wondered whether I could be pregnant again. And as much as this Adam situation wasn't right, I wished it could be.

'I'm glad you're back here, anyway, and I'll always be here for you,' she said.

And if I wanted to find out whether or not she meant it, I soon would. Shortly after moving in, I found out that I was pregnant again. Angela was the first person I told.

I could see a sense of horror pass over her face momentarily.

'Oh, Terrie!' she said. Then she controlled her features and sat me down.

'You know you're still too young. Your body hasn't developed properly yet,' she began.

I nodded. 'But I want this one,' I said firmly.

'Yes,' she sighed, looking as though she might cry. 'Well, this time it should be your decision. Who is the father?'

'Adam,' I said.

She took a deep breath. 'Terrie, I'm going to tell the police. He mustn't be allowed to get away with this.'

I nodded. I knew she was right. By now I knew that what he was doing was illegal, as you weren't supposed to have sex until you were sixteen. But at the same time, the idea of getting Adam into trouble horrified me. I feared that he might start threatening to burn Mum's house down again, or worse. I didn't know what else he was capable of. And, yes, still deep within me was a part of me that wanted to please him.

That evening several police officers came to the house and, together with Angela, I was helped to write a statement. I told them all about how he'd been having sex with me for years and how I felt I couldn't get away from him. All the while, Angela dabbed at her eyes and twisted a tissue in her hands. I was very matter of fact, but I could see how shocked she was, even if she didn't say it.

Afterwards, the police said that they were taking my words away to type up as a proper statement for me to sign. It would take around thirty days, they said, to type it up and sort it out. Then it would be up to me to sign it and they could arrest Adam. I didn't care by now. I felt safe. I was at Angela's, she was helping me and I was going to have a baby. I hoped that I would be given my own flat as well. Everything was going to work out for the best after all.

FIFTEEN

The Visitor

Straightaway I stopped drinking and taking drugs because I knew they were no good for my baby. I don't think Angela ever knew the extent of what I did, although she'd smelt alcohol on my breath a few times when I'd got home from Tasha's or Adam's. I was determined now to turn over a new leaf and, with Angela's help, it was finally possible. The relief was huge. I was going to try and live a normal life for the sake of my baby. Well, that was the idea – until out of the blue I got a phone call at Angela's house.

It was Tasha. I'd texted her the number in case she ever wanted to ring. 'Adam misses you,' she said. 'He needs you, Terrie.'

I felt my body stiffen. 'I don't want to see him, Tasha,' I cried. 'I'm pregnant.'

As soon as the words had left my lips, I wanted to snatch them back. I'd wanted to get used to the idea myself first, before telling other people. Especially Tasha, who I didn't trust not to tell anyone – particularly Adam.

'Wow, congrats, Terrie!' she said. 'Whose is it?'

'I don't want to say,' I said, miserably. I knew exactly where this was leading.

'Well, you've got to tell him!' she cried. 'The father! Otherwise it's not fair, is it?'

I hoped she'd guess it was Adam's baby. But I didn't want to tell her either.

After a bit of a think, I decided that Tasha was right. I had to tell Adam. However unfair he'd been to me, it was only right and maybe he'd decide not to come after me and threaten or hurt me then.

So a few weeks later, one afternoon after school, instead of going back to Angela's I popped into his flat to tell him. I only wanted to stay five minutes. After all, Angela was doing an amazing job of looking after me, taking me to see doctors, sorting out scans, and generally being very supportive. I didn't need him any more.

'Oh my God, that's great!' he yelled. 'We can do it all properly this time!'

He picked me up and twirled me around, just like last time. Except that, this time, I was actually going to keep my baby.

'Does anyone know I'm the dad, though?' he said, suddenly serious.

I lied and said no. 'I have to go,' I said, not wanting to stay. 'I've got to be back at Angela's for five.'

Adam glanced at the clock. Then he went into a five-minute rant about how much he wanted me and this baby. How he was going to 'sort himself out', 'be a proper dad'. How, finally, he could get a bigger flat and we could live a happy life.

'Isn't that what you've always wanted?' he said, looking me in the eye. 'A happy family? Well, I know we've had our ups and downs. But I could do that for you now, Terrie. I promise.'

Despite everything, I found myself sucked in by his promises.

The way his face was lit up, as though he truly believed it, made me sit back down on the sofa and listen some more. He was so persuasive. I hated myself for falling for it, and yet here I was doing so. How could I hate him so much but want him to love me at the same time? It was all so confusing.

'I have to go,' I said.

'But you'll come back?' he asked.

'Yes,' I promised.

Back at Angela's, I started to see things differently as she fussed over me, telling me how I could have the bigger spare room when the baby arrived. This would never be my own place. I could never come and go as I pleased. Not like with Adam. And surely this baby would need a dad, too?

The following day, I got up and dressed as usual and ate the breakfast Angela made me. As she chattered away, I heard nothing; my mind was whirring away at what to do next. Now I was pregnant, I couldn't just go off to school as though nothing had happened. I couldn't ignore this situation. And now that Adam knew, he'd be on my case by this evening. Once again, I hated myself for it but I bunked off school and went to Adam's flat. He was fizzing with excitement about the baby and started making plans for our own flat. He even started talking about colour schemes for the nursery. It felt so grown-up and good, talking about my future. I started to feel happy. But by the afternoon, Angela was on the phone. She'd tracked me down to Adam's flat. Her voice was cracking with emotion when I came on the phone.

'Please come back, Terrie,' she begged. 'Please stay away from that man.'

I felt tears sparking in my eyes. I realized at that moment just how much she cared.

'Just say goodbye and I will come and pick you up. Please get away from Adam. Please.'

The desperation in her voice made me wince. And as Adam looked on, a horrible glare crossed his face. I didn't want this. I felt torn. I wanted to please Angela, but now Adam was getting cross, wasn't he? And I so badly wanted to keep him happy too.

By now Angela was sobbing down the phone. 'Please, please just come home,' she begged.

'Sorry, I can't,' I said, as I watched Adam make a 'slashing' movement to his neck.

I put the phone down and started crying. I wanted to go back home to Angela's but also I wanted a flat and a normal life with my baby. Of course, in the back of my mind, I knew social workers would be involved. There'd be questions over my age and over whether I could look after my baby. But I would prove that I could. I was definitely not going to let them take my baby away. I knew it was all messed up, being with a man so much older, but hey, beggars can't be choosers, I thought to myself. This was as close to a normal life as someone like me would get.

'Don't cry, Treacle,' Adam soothed. 'You've made the right choice.'

Two days later, the police were on Adam's doorstep. They were waving another recovery order in my face.

'You have to come with us, Terrie,' they said. Another officer took Adam into his living room and on the spot gave him a caution for harbouring a minor in care. And then, once again, I was taken off in a police car. They explained they'd got a twenty-eight-day order for me now but they weren't going to take me to a police station as they couldn't 'run the risk of you running away again'.

So, instead, we drove around for a bit until the news of where I was to be taken came through on the radio. I was petrified. Once again, I'd totally lost all control and had no idea where I'd end up. I clutched my belly, which was just starting to grow, and closed my eyes as the car meandered down the streets. At least I had my baby.

After fifteen minutes, the police asked me if I was peckish. They pulled into a McDonald's drive-through. I ordered my favourite Quarter Pounder with Cheese and we all ate in the car park, as they chatted to me, putting me at ease. Then the radio crackled again and the orders were sent through. I was to be taken to Aycliffe Detention Centre. Hundreds of miles away in a place I'd never heard of – County Durham.

After a four-hour journey, we finally stopped at the detention centre on the outskirts of a town. It wasn't like Leverton Hall; there was no lockable garage to drive into. Instead, the car stopped outside a low-rise modern-looking building with small windows and wooden slats at the front. It was already dark outside and was starting to get chilly, so I was grateful to step into the warmth of the sliding-door entrance, even if my heart was beating so fast that I was finding it hard to breathe.

The staff were all smiling and friendly-looking. One of them, Sam, held out his hand for me to shake.

'I'm a decorator,' he said in a funny accent. I looked at him, completely puzzled. Why was he saying that to me? Then he repeated it and I realized he was saying, 'I am your key worker.' But I couldn't make out head nor tail of what he was saying, as his northern accent was so thick.

He carried on talking, but I still couldn't understand, so I just nodded and pretended that I did. As I was rapidly taken around the unit, my knees started shaking. It was all so different from the last place: the rooms had no toilets and the beds were just crash mats. We all had to share showers and sinks at the end of the corridor. There were long, thin windows at the sides of every room, so that the staff could peer in from the corridor at any moment. There was no privacy whatsoever. We had access to a kitchen and a living room, where there was a pool table. And we were to be locked in our rooms from 8.45 p.m. until 6.45 a.m.

We arrived at a toilet where I was told I was to be strip-searched. I hated it as much as before, covering my bare chest with folded arms and wincing as they pawed at my private parts. I felt self-conscious of my skinny body and growing bump.

Finally, I was showered, given a new set of clothes – a pair of simple jeans and a plain blue jumper – and introduced to the other residents. First I met Cindy, a lovely fifteen-year-old girl from Brixton in London, who was being held for armed robbery. Straightaway we clicked. She was so funny, full of life, and the only person whose accent I could understand.

Dwight was an arsonist who kept himself to himself. Neil was in for some criminal offence or other and the first thing he said was, 'Hey, you must be a little slag, pregnant already!'

Another lad was nicknamed 'Dopey'; I never found out his proper name. He was a soft-looking lad, who couldn't read or write and so ended up with the nickname. But he was absolutely lovely, so gentle and kind, and very popular with everyone.

Within weeks I had settled in. I became best mates with Cindy and Dopey. We did everything together, including going to our school lessons. Soon after joining the English group, the teacher told me that she wanted to put me forward for my GCSE early. 'You've got a talent,' she said.

I couldn't help but beam with pride. This was the first time any teacher had told me I was good at something. I wanted to prove her right as well. So I started getting new textbooks, and reading Shakespeare plays and other classics, like *Lord of the Flies*. There was a small library where we could help ourselves to whatever books we wanted. Soon I was always found with my nose buried in a book, absorbing whole new worlds and escaping from the one that was my reality. Cindy loved English too and, between us, we'd sit and work through the GCSE notes guides, laughing and joking as we went. I never knew school could be so much fun. Dopey was also occasionally in our lessons and, bless him, he couldn't read or write and didn't have a clue what was going on. They gave him easier lessons to learn, but even those he struggled with. I didn't care how clever or not at school work he was; he was such a lovely boy. He loved sharing any sweets or chocolates he had, and was always asking me how I was, how I was feeling. The kindness in his eyes proved to me that he was genuine with it.

Cindy and I developed our own 'attitude' with the boys in our unit. We got weekly pocket money and could ask the staff to buy us clothes. I already had a few things I'd grabbed when I was picked up from Adam's. My favourite outfit was a miniskirt with a low-cut top. I'd realized what an effect this could have on boys and I liked the feeling of power. Whenever we could, Cindy joined in and we'd strut down the corridors in high heels, wiggling our bums and smiling at any boy who passed us. For once I was the one in control.

As the weeks turned into months and Adam still hadn't been in touch, I began to relax. Once again, I was safely locked away, and as much as I hated the clank of the doors, I knew he could never get me here.

My stay was extended to six months, until after I'd given birth, so I knew that I'd be away from him until then. My mix of emotions for him was extreme. In the outside world it felt as though I had no choice but to be with him. Inside a locked unit, I could be myself again and allow myself to feel 'safe'.

The subject of my statement against Adam was brought up by my social worker during one meeting. It was ready now, after having being typed up by an officer.

'We can only press charges against Adam if you sign it,' they insisted. They pulled it out and put it in front of me. The words on the page seemed to blur into one, and then I realized that my eyes had filled with tears. Adam's words, 'You'll never escape me,' echoed around my head.

'Here's a pen,' said a social worker. 'You need to sign it.'

I stared at the blank space. I knew that if I put ink to paper, Adam would be arrested, taken to court, and I'd have to testify against him. As much as I wanted him punished for what he had done, I didn't want to be the one to do it. What if he wasn't found guilty? Then he would be free to hurt me, my mum, maybe even my baby. I felt a shiver of fear run down my spine. No one had ever protected me from him before, so why should I think they would now?

I shook my head.

'I just want to leave it alone,' I said, pushing the paper away.

The social workers glanced at each other. 'This is your decision,' one said bluntly.

I wanted to cry. I wanted it to be someone else's decision so that I didn't have to take the blame. I had no idea where I'd be after the baby was born, how long I could stay at Aycliffe. There was talk of me being sent to an experimental 'baby unit', specially set up for under-age mums and their babies, but it hadn't been opened yet. I'd no idea what Adam would do. He got angry so fast, I couldn't stand it. I didn't know what he was capable of. He was the one who always spoke of us running away – well, actually, I just wanted to run away myself. Whatever happened after my time in the secure unit, I'd just have to deal with it then. But I knew I wasn't going to sign that piece of paper that would mean my baby and I would have to live in fear day after day.

One day, another boy appeared on the unit. His name was Carl. He was very troubled, and seemed to have severe mental problems. He was always rocking himself and making weird noises. As my bump grew he started to take more notice of it. Once I was lying on the sofa, watching a soap, when he ran over to me and put his head on my belly.

'I can hear the baby crying,' he laughed. 'It's crying, you know!'

I gently pushed him off. I didn't want to make him feel bad, but also I felt protective of my bump.

'Yes, Carl,' I said. Deep down I was pleased that he'd said something about my baby. No one else, except for Cindy and

Dopey, were even remotely interested. The staff never said anything about it and I'd not heard from Mum or Tasha for a while.

A few days later, Carl started messing around at dinner time. Grabbing the knives and forks, he started clanking them together; then, as staff told him off, he lunged for the ketchup bottle and lobbed it hard through the air. I saw it coming straight towards me but had no time to duck. It landed squarely on my bump.

'Owwwwww,' I winced, gasping for a breath. I clutched my tummy as pains shot across my abdomen. 'Someone help me!'

Dopey and a member of staff, who pressed an emergency buzzer, came rushing over. Someone called an ambulance and I was taken to hospital as a precaution. Luckily nothing was wrong except some bruising and I felt fine.

My due date, 6 June, was approaching rapidly. During my meetings with the social workers they kept asking me if I wanted to keep the baby and I kept saying that I did. Then I was told that the new baby unit would definitely be ready for when my baby was born. This was a small self-contained house within the grounds of the secure unit, where I could live with my newborn baby under the surveillance of social workers. 'It's a place where you can feel safe while you learn to be a new parent,' my social worker said. I would be the first person in the unit to try out the new house. Full of baby monitors and with two live-in social workers, it was designed to be a 'real house' for teenage girls to try and learn to be a mum in a safe environment.

I was so excited. This time it was real. I was really going to be a mum. I imagined how wonderful it was going to feel, holding the baby in my arms and being able to live on my own.

Then, once I'd proved I could cope in the detention centre, the authorities were bound to let me out and give me my own place. I was thrilled. A youth worker called Jan Spellman had set up the house, and when I met her, I couldn't thank her enough.

Every two weeks I had meetings with social workers in the build-up to the birth. They told me nothing about what to expect, but talked about me getting a plastic doll that mimicked the sounds of a baby crying to practise on.

'That sounds great!' I said. But in the end they couldn't get funding for it. They started buying me baby things as well. No one ever talked to me about it and I wasn't allowed out to shops myself, so I just watched as bags from Mothercare appeared in my room. Picking up tiny cardigans and babygros filled me with excitement. This time no one could take my baby away. Every now and then, Mum started phoning me too. But she never had a good word to say.

'You're going to ruin your life, having this baby so young,' she said. 'If you'd had an abortion, you could start again and meet a nice man.'

I just laughed at her. What did she know anyway? I'd had an abortion before, but I hadn't seen any nice men turn up.

Sometimes the social worker meetings took on a more serious note, as they talked about Adam. 'Do you think you will feel hatred towards the baby due to Adam being the father?' they asked.

I shook my head. I was determined not to let Adam ruin anything this time.

I was also warned that I might need a 'C-section'. 'What's that, exactly?' I asked. I'd seen a bit on TV, but didn't quite understand it.

'It's where they cut your belly open,' they said, 'to pull the baby out. Your body may be too small to give birth naturally.'

I nodded. I felt scared now, but decided not to think about it. I had no choice and would worry about it at the time. During one of my scans I discovered that I was expecting a baby girl, just like I'd had before. I welled up with happiness when I found out. She could never replace the one I'd lost, but she would love me and I would love her more than anything. I began to think of names. I loved Louise, Shannon and Tamara.

Then, just as I had started to totally fix my eye on the future and my baby, one of the workers knocked on my door. 'You have a phone call,' he said.

I picked up the phone, expecting it to be Mum, when a familiar voice said: 'Hello, it's your uncle.'

My heart pounded as Adam's voice boomed out.

'Tasha has just had a baby girl,' he said. 'Thought you'd like to know.'

'Thank you,' I said brightly, but inside I felt sick again at the sound of his voice. 'That's all,' he said. 'For now.' Then the receiver clicked.

A few weeks later, a member of staff told me that Adam was coming to visit me in the detention centre. To this day I cannot explain why the decision was reached to allow him to visit me. I'd been in the process of writing a statement against him, I'd openly told people he was my baby's father. And yet, social workers saw fit to allow the man who'd repeatedly abused me to come and sit down and talk to me.

'Do you want a visit?' one member of staff asked me.

I shrugged. I didn't dare turn him down, in case he grew angry and did something to Mum. I wanted, in some ways, for the social worker to recognize the fact that I was frightened, even though I was holding it inside.

'Well, don't worry,' the staff member continued. 'We'll make sure someone sits in with you. He says he wants to come and help you.'

The night before the visit, I tossed and turned, barely able to sleep. What did he want? What did he mean by wanting to 'help'? I only dropped off at 5 a.m., and woke at 7.30 p.m., exhausted and dreading seeing him.

Adam was late for his visit and I hoped against hope that he wasn't going to turn up after all. I was messing around in the courtyard with one of the lads when finally he did show up. One of them was giving me a cuddle as I teased him gently about something or other. Just as I turned around I saw Adam's ginger hair flitting down the corridor. Somehow I just knew he'd seen me.

Walking into the meeting room, I felt the room spinning. I saw him scan my face, then briefly glance at my bump. Sitting just behind him was my key worker, Sam. He looked bored and as though he'd rather be anywhere else.

'Hello,' Adam said, standing up as I walked in. He didn't try and kiss or touch me. He just waited until I sat down, and then sat down himself.

He spoke quickly, cheerfully, as if he was nervous. I could see the small windows behind me reflected in his eyes, making them glint. He talked about anything, his flat, his job, then about his neighbours, like a stream of thoughts without any need for me to reply. I wondered when he'd mention my bump, but he seemed more interested in telling me how his neighbours were hassling him for something or other.

'They were knocking at my door,' he said. 'Knock, knock, knock.'

With each 'knock' he banged my knee under the table, so that Sam wouldn't notice.

I stared at him. I wanted to run out, but, as usual, his steely gaze on me held mine steadily, daring me to.

Then he switched the conversation to how I was doing at school and what the unit was like. 'And do you have a boyfriend?' he asked, his eyes briefly flitting to the courtyard where I'd been messing with a lad.

'No,' I said quietly, staring at my hands.

'OK, time is up,' said Sam.

Adam stood up, beaming at me, as though the visit had been a huge success.

'No need to thank me for coming all this way,' he said, smiling.

I tried to smile back, but found tears stinging my eyes instead. I turned around and walked away quickly. This visit from Adam told me that I would never be free of him.

SIXTEEN

The Harder I Try

Just a couple of weeks later, I was told he was visiting again. This time, I wanted to say no, but again, I didn't want to make a fuss. I was scared. It felt easier to go along with it, to keep Adam happy, to keep the peace. I was simply too frightened to sign the statement and just wanted it all to go away, so I thought that the easiest thing to do would be simply to get through the visit. With a member of staff in the room, Adam couldn't do or say anything inappropriate anyway.

But as I walked in, Sam stayed out in the corridor this time. He could see us through the glass window, but he wouldn't be able to hear us or, more importantly, what Adam was saying to me. This time Adam looked harassed. He said hello perfectly politely and then leaned right across the table.

'If you write a statement against me,' he hissed in a low whisper, 'I'll get into a lot of trouble. You'll never ever see me again but, before that happens, I will make life very, very hard for your mum.'

I closed my eyes briefly, willing him to go away. My knees were trembling under the table.

'Do you know how I got here?' he said, suddenly changing

his tone to a bright one. He pulled out a train ticket with a slip of paper attached and waved it in front of my face.

I recognized it as one that social services had issued and paid for.

'Your own social worker paid me to come and visit you,' he laughed. 'Paid me! So don't worry. I haven't come here under my own steam.'

He sniggered to himself for a bit before turning to me again. 'Remember what I said about the statement . . .'

He talked rubbish at me for the next ten minutes, about his flat and job and other stuff I wasn't interested in. Then he got up to leave. He'd booked in a two-hour visit, but left after twenty minutes. Not once did he mention the baby.

I was so relieved he'd gone that I couldn't help myself and sat at the table silently sobbing. But I was also very relieved that I'd ended up not signing the statement. Once again he'd reinforced the idea that it was far too dangerous.

Later on, I saw Cindy and she spotted my red, puffy eyes.

'What's up, doll?' she asked.

If there was anyone I could talk to it was Cindy, but I still couldn't bring myself to tell her. It felt as though talking about it would just make everything worse, so I just let her hug me tight and tell me that everything would be all right. I wished with all my might that she was right, that when the baby arrived things would finally fall into place.

As I got closer to the day of my baby's arrival, I was told that she was in a breech position so would need turning. I didn't really understand what that meant. I didn't know what to expect from the birth, either, as I hadn't been given any books or magazines, and no one had sat down with me to talk me through it. All I knew was that it would hurt and I was planning to ask for as many painkillers as possible. But, other than that, it was all a bit of a mystery to me, one that was scary and exciting all at the same time.

I had been told that I might need a Caesarean section but that they would wait for my contractions to start naturally first to see how things progressed. I was also repeatedly told that the baby probably wouldn't arrive on the due date but, in the early hours of 6 June, I woke up feeling unbearable pain. It was still dark, but I could hear the sounds of a few birds chirping in the trees outside. I glanced at my watch to see that it was just 3 a.m.

Straightaway, I leapt up to press the buzzer. But no one came. The pain was making me wince and groan, so I tried again, and again and again. Still no one came, so I rattled my door handle and started banging.

'Help! Someone, please! I think the baby is coming!'

Still I was greeted with silence. So I yelled again and this time Cindy called back.

'I'm hearing you, Terrie!' she cried. 'Hang in there!'

Then, at the top of her lungs, she started screaming. 'Someone, get the staff! Terrie's in labour!'

But still, after half an hour of screaming, no one came. I started to pour with sweat in panic. Silently I prayed that everything would be okay, as my pains gripped my stomach like a vice, making me drop to the floor. Clenching my blanket on my crash mat, I thought I'd rip it in two as each contraction came and went. I was screaming for help and Cindy had started to go mental now, booting her door repeatedly, as she tried to get attention. Finally, after about forty minutes, a member of staff came.

'What's all the commotion?' he yelled. 'Get back to bed.'

'Terrie is in fucking labour!' Cindy shrieked. 'And we've been banging for ages.'

My door was unlocked and the man stuck his head in. 'What's up?' he said.

'My labour has started,' I said, unable to stop my face clenching in pain. 'I need to go to hospital.'

He sighed and I caught him roll his eyes a little.

'Look, labour takes a very long time and I can't call an ambulance as I'm alone on duty tonight. Wait there.'

He disappeared and returned with two pills and a glass of water. I was so upset. I knew he could call 999 if he needed to, but he obviously couldn't be bothered with the hassle of it all.

'These should keep you going,' he said. 'Paracetamol should take the edge off it for now.' I swallowed them quickly, but it did nothing for the pain.

He returned half an hour later to see how I was doing, but I was still contorting with agony on the bed. 'Please,' I begged, grimacing. 'Please just get an ambulance. I won't run off. I'm about to have a baby!'

He sighed again. 'Listen, you'll have to ride it out until daybreak. The next staff are on at 6 a.m. Not long to wait.' Then he locked my door again. I wondered if he knew there was every chance I would need a C-section, or if he even cared what was happening to me? But I couldn't dwell on it for long, the pains were overtaking me and any other thoughts.

By now I was almost passing out with the pain, and was so frightened that my knees had turned to jelly. I didn't know whether to lie down or kneel. I ended up almost in a prayer position by my bed.

'Please help me,' I whispered, knowing that no one could hear me and that I was in this by myself. I kept looking at my watch. The pains were coming every ten minutes or so now. After an hour and a half I was almost physically sick with the pain. The only way I could comfort myself was by rocking gently to and fro. After what felt like a lifetime, the worker looked in again.

'Please give me something!' I screamed, as another powerful contraction tore through me. 'I can't give you anything as it was less than four hours ago I gave you the Paracetamol, and I can't let you out unless you need the toilet,' he said. 'Sorry.' Then he was gone again.

I started sobbing as I waited for the next contraction to wash over me. I'd never in my life felt so alone.

By 6 a.m., I'd been in agony for several hours and was trying desperately to breathe. I was almost climbing the walls with the pain.

Finally, the day staff came on duty, and I started banging again. Cindy had woken and realized that I was still there, so she started banging furiously.

'She's been in labour all night, for God's sake. Someone help her!' she screamed.

Staff rushed into quieten Cindy while one of them looked in on me.

'I need help,' I sobbed. I was sweating so much now with the pain that my hair was stuck to my forehead. 'Please, please, please.'

Jane, another member of staff, looked at me. 'Okay, Terrie,' she said. 'Have you had a show yet? That's a mucus plug that drops out.'

I looked down at myself and saw blood. 'I'm bleeding!' I cried. 'Is that enough?'

'Oh, okay,' she said. 'I guess with the pain, too, it must be happening.'

She disappeared to call an ambulance. Our doors were unlocked by now and Cindy dashed to my side. She gripped my hand in hers and smoothed my hair.

'Poor baby,' she said, gently. 'You've been so brave. No thanks to those arseholes.' She held me gently as I winced through another contraction.

'It really hurts,' I sobbed. 'I didn't know it'd hurt this much.'

By the time the ambulance came I was having contractions every few minutes. Roseanne, a member of staff I didn't particularly get on with, hopped in with me. After being strapped to a stretcher I was rushed to Bishop Auckland Hospital in County Durham. All the way I was begging for pain relief but by the time we reached the hospital, the midwife told me that it was too late.

'Sorry, love,' she said. 'You're too far along now. You're ten centimetres dilated so that means the baby is nearly here.'

I started sobbing even harder. I couldn't stand any more. The only thing I'd been holding out for all night was pain relief.

'Why?' I screamed. 'Please!'

I had started to feel something else by now. The pain was subsiding as an urgent need to push was taking over. 'Urgh!' I cried, as my whole body tensed and I gripped the corners of the pillow. A midwife told me that the baby's head was crowning. But, after I screamed again, another nurse turned up with some needles and tubes.

'Let's just give her some pain relief, to shut her up,' she said.

My veins in my hand felt cold as I felt something push into me, but at the same time my baby was emerging, and someone else told me that they were cutting me down below to help her out.

Then, suddenly, there was a loud cry. My daughter had emerged into the world. She was whisked away from me to be checked and cleaned, and all I caught sight of was a flash of hair. Ginger hair. Just like Adam's.

Then, just as I tried to sit up, the pain medication kicked in. My legs felt heavy and numb and I was ordered not to move.

'I want to see my baby,' I said.

'Stay still,' snapped a nurse. 'You can't be walking around after pethidine!'

I lay back down and had to wait half an hour before it wore off. Meanwhile, the baby was put in a cot a few metres away from me. She was all wrapped up in a blanket, and was very quiet.

I stared at her. She was here. I was finally a mum. But I didn't feel anything. I thought I was just tired. I needed to hold her and then I'd love her, I was certain.

Finally, I found the energy to move, and Roseanne told me to go and have a shower, so I shuffled off.

When I came back, feeling a bit more refreshed, I just couldn't wait to gather the baby up in my arms.

But as I walked into the room, Roseanne was feeding her. I felt so gutted. I wanted to be the first one to feed my baby.

'Oh, I wanted to do that,' I said, disappointed.

'Well, your baby needed feeding and you were in the shower,' she said briskly. 'And you're terribly young to be having a baby, anyway, aren't you?'

I ignored her, although I could feel my cheeks burning with emotion. All I wanted to do was to focus on my baby now. Finally, I could look at her properly. I peered inside the blanket. Again, the first thing I noticed was the ginger hair. Then she looked at me with her big eyes, exactly the same shape as her father's. I almost gasped in shock. She looked the absolute image of Adam.

'Isn't she lovely?' cooed Roseanne.

'Yes,' I said. 'Can I hold her?'

I felt all shaky as I awkwardly picked up my daughter for the first time. She felt all warm and heavy, but I was terrified I'd drop her. Roseanne kept telling me to be careful of her head.

She looked so delicate and pretty. But so much like Adam that I just couldn't believe it was possible. I so badly wanted to love her but this didn't feel right. The reality was kicking in. I'd given birth to a part of Adam.

For three days I stayed in hospital. The midwives were kind on the whole and showed me where the ready-made bottles were so that I could feed my baby, who I'd named Louise Shannon. She looked like a Louise to me.

I desperately wanted to love her and was certain that once I'd got enough sleep and had recovered from the labour and we were left alone, I'd be able to. But by the time I was ready to leave the hospital for the house, I still didn't feel anything towards her. No love, no hatred, nothing but indifference. I was determined, however. I wanted to be a good mum and to love her. I wanted to keep her safe in ways I'd never been safe. I was certain that all the feelings a mum feels about her child would come flooding in in no time and that we'd be so happy.

On the day we left for our new house, I felt almost giddy with excitement. I wanted this to be our fresh start, a new way of living. I said goodbye to the nurses at the hospital and Louise and I were taken, with all our belongings, in a taxi to our new home on the other side of the compound.

Two social workers greeted me at the door. It was completely decorated in cream with matching carpets, walls and sofa. It had a kitchen, living room, two bedrooms and a bathroom. One of the rooms would be for me and Louise, the other one for the social workers, who'd be doing twelve-hour shifts and staying overnight. There were baby monitors absolutely everywhere, so wherever I went they could hear me.

'Welcome to your new home,' said Jan, who was there to greet me. She seemed lovely and I thanked her again. This new set-up was all especially for me. I wanted it to work. After all, if I could prove that I could do it myself, then I'd be allowed to live a truly free life.

'Here we are,' I muttered to Louise, as I popped her car seat on the floor. 'Our new home.'

I laid out Louise's things in our bedroom. She was feeding every few hours and I was absolutely exhausted. I'd still not slept much since the birth.

The social workers made themselves a cup of tea. 'We'll be here on standby,' they said. 'But it's up to you to get on with it. Pretend we're not here.' Then they sat down and switched on the TV.

Louise woke up and started crying so I picked her up carefully and went to the kitchen to get another feed. There were no ready-made bottles there, so I put Louise down in her carry seat, picked up the packet of baby formula left out on the side, and frantically started reading the back of it. The social workers watched me, as I scanned the packet, trying to measure out the right amount. The powder seemed to go everywhere. It all seemed so tricky and I still hadn't flicked on the kettle to get the water boiling beforehand. Meanwhile, Louise started screaming more loudly. I picked her up and tried to jiggle her as I poured in the water.

Hoping it was the right amount, I gave it a good shake, then plunged it into a sink of cold water to try and cool it, all the while wondering if what I was doing was the right thing. Making up just one bottle seemed like such an ordeal.

Eventually, with Louise's cheeks now crimson from crying, I tested the bottle temperature on my hand and then pushed the teat into her mouth. She sucked hungrily and instantly quietened. I felt exhausted, and wanted to cry myself. But I held it in. I knew the social workers wouldn't be impressed if I started sobbing too.

I soon got into a routine. Well, as much of one as I was able to. Louise didn't sleep all night. I tried everything to get her to nod off so that I could go to bed early. I put on her mobile above her cot, I walked up and down with her, I jiggled her on my knee, I even tried singing to her. I always chose the Spice Girls; I loved them. Cindy and I used to listen to them all the time in our bedrooms, quietly, away from everyone. Those times, in the unit, just a few metres away, seemed like a lifetime ago already.

'*Mamma, I love you, Mamma, I care . . .* ' I sang softly to Louise, as she stared at me, awake as usual. She looked at me with her big eyes, Adam's eyes, with such wonder. I wondered what she was thinking. I closed my eyes and held her close.

Please make me love her, I prayed. Please let the moment happen. I opened my eyes again . . . but nothing. I still felt nothing.

The midwife who visited told me to 'sleep when the baby

sleeps' but every time I lay on my bed for a nap, a social worker would shake me awake again.

'You can't be lying around when the baby sleeps,' she snapped. 'It's not reality. You should be getting on with the housework.' So I never got a chance to catch up.

The days rolled into weeks and eventually Cindy and Dopey, my two closest friends in the unit, were allowed to visit.

Cindy was thrilled for me and couldn't wait to pick up Louise and give her a cuddle. 'Aw, she's gorgeous, Terrie,' she said. 'You must be so proud.'

I grinned. I was, in many ways. But I was also so frazzled with exhaustion and confusion, I didn't know what to feel. Dopey was just as pleased for me. He kept looking at me and Louise, saying how much we looked alike. But I didn't think so. I was happy to see the two of them, though. They made me feel more normal.

They were only allowed one half-hour visit once a week; the rest of the time it was me, Louise and the social workers – although I never saw much of the social workers.

Whatever the time, day or night, they never offered to help. They never made any suggestions or tried to do anything for me. 'You wanted a baby and now you have to learn to look after it by yourself,' said one matter-of-factly.

The fact was that I was only a child myself and that, even for an adult, being a new mum is very hard work. Whatever age you are, you need supportive friends and family to see you through those first few weeks or months. Once again I had no one. Looking back, it feels like I was set up to fail. Perhaps they'd planned to have Louise fostered from the start.

*

I spent every day tending to Louise and doing nothing else – doing her washing, feeding, burping and trying to make her sleep. At night time she was up every hour, crying. By the end of the third week, I was completely and utterly exhausted. Sometimes I cried silently with her as nothing I did would soothe her. At the same time, the social workers existed in a parallel universe alongside me, watching TV, reading magazines or talking on the phone. During the eight weeks I lived there, eighteen different members of staff worked in my house.

Then, one day, Tasha came for a visit. Even though I knew that she hadn't always been a good friend to me, I was thrilled to see another familiar face.

When I showed her Louise, her reaction wasn't what I'd expected.

'Oh my God, she's got really long arms and legs, like a monkey! And she's a ginger!' she cried.

I tried to laugh it off but her words stung. Then I realized just how protective of Louise I felt. I didn't want anyone laughing at her. Even if Tasha didn't mean it.

Then, when Louise was about a month old, she started crying for three days and wouldn't stop. I was desperate and felt as though I was losing my mind.

On the third evening, after feeding Louise, I winded her and then laid her back down. But she kept crying, so I tried to burp her again, but nothing was coming up. So I sang her a song, then gently rocked her in my arms. After three hours nothing was working.

I laid her back down again.

'What do you want?' I asked her as she screwed up her face

even more and her cries reached a new level. 'Please, what can I do?'

I tried burping her again and singing but, again, nothing worked. So I put her back on the bed, and started crying myself.

'Please give me a break,' I begged her. I tried holding her close to me, but she carried on screaming. Once again, I put her down.

'Right, well, if you're sick, you're sick,' I snapped. 'You're just going to have to deal with it.' As soon as the words left my mouth I regretted them but, of course, it wasn't only me who heard them. The social workers had been listening in on the baby monitors positioned all around the house. Within seconds, one of them burst into the room, shouting with anger.

'How dare you talk to your baby like that!' she yelled. She swept Louise up in her arms and started rocking her. 'We've been listening to you and heard every single nasty word.'

'I'm sorry!' I sobbed. 'I didn't mean it! It just came out. I'm just so tired. I can't do this. I'm no good as a mum, but I'm trying my hardest.'

The social worker turned on her heels and, holding Louise close to her, she marched out, slamming the door behind her.

I threw myself on the bed and sobbed and sobbed. I so badly wanted this to work, but the first little thing I'd done wrong, they'd told me off. Not once had they offered to help. They'd been waiting for me to do something, anything, wrong and now I had. But I hadn't meant it.

They kept Louise in a room with them all night, while I cried myself to sleep. The next morning, an emergency meeting was hastily arranged for them to 'discuss the situation'. I felt so angry by now. I felt dreadful for saying what I'd said, but I knew that I hadn't meant it and that they were blowing it out of proportion. I was told I'd get 'one more chance'.

When they handed Louise back to me, all eyes were on me constantly. I felt like a child abuser but, in my mind, that was the last thing I wanted to be. Even though I had mixed feelings towards her, I could never harm a hair on her head. I knew I wasn't like my dad or Adam. I considered myself a better person than they were. Cindy came round a few days later. She was only allowed a few minutes with me.

'Oh, sweetie, you look awful! What's happened?' she asked.

I explained and she shook her head.

'It's just a blip, Terrie. You'll get through this. You're a good mum and doing your best. Life won't be like this for ever,' she said.

I so desperately wanted to believe her.

SEVENTEEN

Runaway

The weeks all merged into one. I rarely got to leave the house, although one of the social workers called Jemma was lovely and would sometimes let me go for a walk on my own, just for a ten-minute break. She was an older Irish lady who used to tell me how good I was with Louise. Also, I met a new member of staff called David. He'd just joined the unit but popped in from time to time to see how I was doing. Although I'd never completely lost my distrust of men, there was something I liked very much about him. He had a very gentle, fatherly way about him, and when he spoke to me, I could tell he genuinely cared. Gradually, we got to know each other. He was married with a couple of kids. Once he turned up with a plate of crumble and custard, my favourite dessert.

'I know how you like apple crumble, without the apple,' he laughed. 'So here's a plateful for pudding.'

It was just a small gesture, but it meant the world to me. I was continually told that social workers were looking for a foster carer placement for me, someone who would take both me and Louise. They kept telling me that they could only find someone who'd take me or my baby. Not both of us. Angela was no longer an option. I didn't know why. I think it was because they knew she'd not stopped me from seeing Adam and she was so close to all the old connections. So until they did find someone, I was to stay in the house on my own.

By week eight, I was feeling ill with exhaustion. The pressure of being watched all day in case of 'abuse' was making things even harder. But, determined to carry on, I just had to make this work. I didn't want to be a bad mum, just like my own mum had been.

One night, Louise was screaming and I needed to make up another bottle quickly. I stuck the kettle on and poured in the powder. Thankfully I was now becoming a dab hand at it. Holding Louise in one arm, I eased the kettle off its plug and poured with the other, as Louise squirmed around. Then, out of nowhere, Louise kicked her foot hard, sending the boiling hot liquid from the bottle over her foot. Her cry instantly switched from a hungry one to one of pain.

'Oh my God!' I shrieked, as I rushed her to the sink, pulling off her babygro and plunging her foot under the cold tap. In front of my eyes, the skin of her tiny foot seemed to peel off.

'Help me! Someone call an ambulance!' I screamed.

The social workers came running through. 'What the hell is going on?' one cried, grabbing Louise from me. We all bundled into one of their cars and drove off at breakneck speed to the hospital as both Louise and I cried.

To say that I felt terrible doesn't even come close. I knew it was an accident, but the guilt was immense. I could literally feel her cries of agony tearing at my heart. Nobody said outright that it was my fault, but the social workers certainly acted as though it was.

'Well, these things happen,' one said, but it didn't sound like she meant it. I knew they'd been waiting for something like this. This would be their excuse to tell me that things weren't working, that I couldn't be a mum. I just knew it. Thankfully, any injury Louise suffered was only minor. Doctors believed me when I explained that it was an accident, and they even soothed me when I cried.

'Not to worry,' said one nurse. 'No permanent damage done.'

I was so relieved, I started crying again.

After the check-up we were discharged and driven back to the house. Louise was happier now, gurgling away in her car seat, but every time I looked at the bandage on her foot, I started weeping again.

Back at the house, Jemma was there. 'You've been a very good mum up till now,' she said, trying to comfort me. 'Don't let this pull you down.'

I so badly wanted to believe her, but all my confidence had been shot to pieces. The fact was that Louise had been burned while I was holding her, and I knew all the other social workers blamed me. It was all too much. Over and over again visions of Louise's red face as she screeched in agony kept firing through my brain. Even though she was calmer and even smiling occasionally now, I couldn't get it out of my head.

That evening, as I went to make Louise's bottle, a social worker took it out of my hands.

'I'll do it,' she said, briskly.

'What?' I asked. My head hurt from crying and I didn't want a row. 'I want to feed her.'

'Well, we've decided that it would be best if you just observe for now, she said, flicking the kettle on. 'We can't risk any more accidents, can we?'

I started weeping again. I just couldn't control the tears any longer.

'Crying won't solve anything,' said the social worker. 'We all have to work together to look after Louise, but for now we think it's safer for you just to watch.'

Social workers said that they wanted to 'help' now, but the reality was, they no longer trusted me at all. I spent another sleepless night listening for Louise's cries as a social worker got up to feed her, and feeling a pain of helplessness in my chest, I fell asleep crying.

I can't do this, I thought. *I just can't.*

In the morning, I woke up and, as if on autopilot, grabbed a stash of notes I'd been saving up. Every week I got pocket money and as I never went out anywhere, I had managed to put aside £120. It was enough to do what I needed to do.

I went to see Louise, who was being fed in the living room, kissed her soft warm head, then told the staff that I was popping out for ten minutes for some fresh air. While outside, I looked left and right as I walked quickly towards the open unit gates. As soon as I crossed them, I started running as fast as I could. Away from the unit. Away from the watchful eyes. And away from a baby I knew I could never love in the way she deserved.

I kept running, until my face was red and sweaty, and my lungs felt as if they would burst. After a few minutes I realized I had no idea where I was, but when I saw an old man walking on the opposite side of the road I ran over to him and breathlessly asked him where the train station was. He told me the way before adding, 'Are you OK, dear?', but I didn't trust myself not to cry if I answered him, so I just turned and ran in the direction he'd pointed. When I reached the train station, I bought a one-way ticket back to Stevenage. As the train pulled away, I watched the sign for County Durham whizz past and wanted to cry with relief. I was leaving this strange northern town behind for good. But what did I have to look forward to? My destination might not be any better. With nothing except £70 in my pocket, I'd left to start again. But how and where I'd no idea. My choices were Tasha's or Mum's. And I couldn't face Mum and Pervy Pat, so I opted to go straight to Tasha's. I arrived a few hours later, hungry, tired and full of guilt. But as Tasha opened the door, her face dropped.

'Where's the baby?' were her first words.

'I-I couldn't do it,' I said, my voice breaking.

Tasha was holding her son Ross on her hip as she stared at me.

'What do you mean, Terrie? You didn't leave your baby, did you?' she asked. She nodded for me to come in, so I did and she made us both a cup of of tea.

'You've probably just got the baby blues,' she went on. 'Terrie, you need to go back and get her, or they'll take her away from you for ever.'

Tasha suggested that I needed antidepressants and that then I'd feel differently about everything. I knew the social workers wouldn't prescribe them as I was still underage, but, more importantly, I also knew that I wasn't suffering from the baby blues. This went much deeper than that.

She let me stay the night and said we'd talk again in the morning. Despite everything, I was so grateful for her friendship. She was always there for me, even if she lacked sympathy sometimes. In the morning, though, Tasha was in a bad mood as Ross had kept her awake all night.

'Look,' she snapped. 'I've called Adam. I've got enough to deal with and he might be able to help you get Louise back.'

I felt a shiver down my spine. It hadn't crossed my mind that she'd do that, but then I'd been in a daze on the train journey down. Of course there'd been a chance that she'd just ring Adam.

At this point I almost didn't care. I had no one. Now Adam was coming for me again. An overwhelming feeling of resignation washed over me. Adam was always going to be there, wasn't he?

I sat in silence, watching *Corrie*, when there was a knock on the door. Adam had arrived. I shivered slightly as he walked in.

'Terrie,' he said, grinning, leaning in for a kiss. 'Babe, you're back. But I've heard you left the baby.'

Tasha nodded. They'd obviously been talking.

'Yes,' I said quietly.

'Well, we can't have that, can we?' he said. 'She needs to be here, with her mum and dad, where she belongs.'

I felt my heart pounding in my ears. Although I loathed Adam, it was still my wildest dream to give Louise the life I had never had. Two parents, a nice house, a normal life.

'Do you think we could?' I found myself asking him.

He looked excited suddenly. 'Yes,' he said, kneeling down by me. His eyes were shining as though he meant every word. 'We could get a flat, like I said before. Go and live somewhere where no one knows us. We can raise the child together and when you're old enough, we'll have a proper wedding . . .'

I started to cry. I had too many thoughts whirling around my mind and I didn't know what to say. I'd heard this all before and it had never happened. I wanted to run away again, but had nowhere to go.

Looking at Adam talking, I desperately wanted to believe him. Still. Even though part of me hated him, he was an adult and I was a child. I wanted him to take control of this situation.

I nodded. 'What should we do?' I asked.

'We'll kidnap her,' he said. 'I'll borrow my mate's car and drive up, then you go in and get her, and we'll be home in no time. Then I'll rent a flat where no one will know us.'

I just kept nodding. Deep down, I didn't believe him, but of course I wanted to. But also I knew that there was another reason he wanted Louise with him. If social services kept her, they could do a DNA test on her to prove that he was the father, and I knew as well as everyone else that this was a crime.

That evening, Adam snaked his arm round me, just like he always did. 'Come back to mine, babe,' he whispered. 'I'll take care of you until we work out what to do.'

I knew what it meant. More sex. But also more boozing, which gave me the oblivion I craved, and a nice, comfy place to stay. I just didn't want to think, I wanted to be taken care of and to get wasted so that I could forget my emotions, forget that I'd dumped my baby. And in my position, what else could I do? Going back to the detention centre meant dealing with the fall-out from abandoning Louise. And at that moment I felt too weak to even contemplate that.

The next day I rang social services. I told them I was safe, that I needed some time alone.

'But you need to come back for Louise,' one of them said.

My eyes welled up immediately, as I thought of her baby smell.

'I can't do it,' I whispered.

'You're being very selfish,' said the social worker. 'Louise needs a mum.'

'I know,' I sobbed. 'I just can't be a good one at the moment. I'm sorry. I'll come back some time soon.'

During the phone call, Adam stood anxiously by. He didn't want me to be on the phone for too long in case the police were looking for me again and were able to trace the number.

'Good girl,' he said, when I put the phone down. 'You did so well. Now all you need to do is prepare yourself to get back up there and get her as soon as you're ready.'

Despite the fact that I'd upped and left, I still rang the social workers looking after Louise daily. Like any new mum I felt anxious that she was okay, I asked about her feedings and how she was sleeping, and everything, thankfully, seemed to be fine – except that at the end of every phone call they asked me to come back.

I kept putting both them and Adam off. 'I'll go some time soon,' I kept saying.

I knew I was going to do everything in my power to prevent Adam from seeing his plan through, and I never mentioned to him that during the last phone call social services had talked about having her fostered. I had been able to get some sleep and to start to think about everything with a clearer head, and I'd realized that at just thirteen, with no job or family, I couldn't give Louise a good start in life. And the more I thought about it all, the more I knew I didn't want a man like Adam to be her daddy. Not really. What chance would she have then? A pervert for a dad? She'd enjoy a better life with a proper family, maybe one like Angela's. And, hopefully when I was a bit older, I could take her back for ever. However loose it was in my own head, that was the best plan I could come up with.

During the next few times we had sex, Adam used a condom. 'We don't want you getting pregnant again,' he said, winking.

The next day, he took me for a walk through town. I spotted a tattoo parlour and suddenly was struck with an idea.

'I want to get Louise's name tattooed on to me,' I said. I felt the need to do something, anything, for my baby. I knew that I couldn't look after her as a 'proper mum' could. I couldn't go back, I knew social services wouldn't let me pick up where I left off, but I also didn't want Adam to get his hands on her either. And I'd already accidentally hurt Louise once; who was to say that I wouldn't again? So a tattoo was the next best thing I could think of to get me as close to her as possible. To make her a permanent part of my life, even if she couldn't be with me right now.

Adam agreed. 'Great idea,' he said. 'But I'll only pay for it if you get my name tattooed on there with it.'

I did a double take. 'But—' I started.

'That's the rule,' he snapped. 'Otherwise I won't let you have Louise's name either.'

'Okay.' I shrugged.

So I had both the names, 'Adam' and 'Louise', tattooed on to my right arm. I closed my eyes and winced as the tattooist started up the whirring needle. I thought of Louise and all the pain of her birth, and all the pain of running away. Somehow it seemed only right for me to suffer more pain right now.

*

Two weeks later there came another knock at the door. More police. Another recovery order. This time Adam looked genuinely shocked when he opened the door.

'Ah hello, officer,' he said, in a polite voice I had never heard him use before. 'What can I do for you?'

'Terrie O'Brian,' one said, looking at his notes. 'Is she here?'

Like history repeating itself, Adam waved them in as I was sitting watching TV. I felt nothing when they walked in, asking me to stand up. I knew the ropes now. But I also thought they must think it strange that I was here again. I watched them, waiting to see if they'd arrest Adam. For the first time I really hoped they would. I knew the only way I'd escape this man would be if he went to prison, but at the same time, I didn't want to be the one responsible for making it happen. I couldn't face the backlash if it all went wrong.

By now I'd told Angela about Adam, I'd told social workers, I'd even written a statement, despite not having signed it. Surely they would arrest him now? Couldn't social services somehow take control and press charges themselves?

At the same time as these thoughts were whizzing through my mind, they were mixed with a strange sense of dread at the prospect of finally having to let him go. By now, he had made me believe that I couldn't live without him. In truth, I didn't know what I wanted, but I wanted someone else to take over, whatever happened. During my last meeting with a social worker at Angela's, about a possible case against Adam, they'd told me that I'd have to stand up in court. I'd heard that people sometimes testified via video link so I asked to do that, but for some reason they said it wasn't possible. The thought of standing in front of him, going through the account, was too horrible for words. So when they asked me again now, in front of Adam, if I would sign it, I told them I wouldn't. They led me by the elbow out of the door.

'It's not right for a girl of your age to be hanging around in the flat of a man of that age,' said one. That was the only mention of Adam doing anything wrong.

As I walked past, Adam looked me in the eye. 'I'll get you out,' he muttered, well within the hearing of the police. I glanced at him, his eyes were burning with rage, I could tell. And I knew what he meant. He needed me to get out in case I pressed charges against him.

I was driven to the police station in Stevenage. They led me into a cell again, but this time didn't clank the door closed.

'You're only a kid,' said one. 'It's not right.'

So I sat on the hard bed, my feet swinging beneath me, looking out the door at all the comings and goings of a busy police station. I felt quite detached this time, just waiting patiently to see what was going to happen next. I kept expecting to see Adam being frogmarched through the station in handcuffs.

Then a taxi turned up and the driver told me he was taking me back to County Durham, but back to the secure unit rather than the baby unit. In my last phone call, social services had explained that Louise had been placed with foster carers, in a proper family home, in an unknown location. I liked this idea; I was happy for her, even if I regretted this horrible mess.

Once again on arrival at Aycliffe I was given a strip-search, but it didn't seem to bother me this time. I felt numb, physically and emotionally. None of the staff said a word when I revealed my tattoo, still sore and crusty, of Louise's name with Adam's emblazoned beneath. When I arrived back in the secure unit, Cindy and Dopey were the first people to rush up to me.

'Hey, Terrie!' Cindy said, grinning. I gave her a big hug. Gosh, it was good to see her. The last time we'd spent time together, Cindy had been holding Louise, while I sang a lullaby to my baby. Now we were back, two young girls in the unit. My days as a mummy seemed so long ago. But, being honest, I didn't miss it. The sleepless nights and the effort of trying not to mess up in front of the watchful eyes of the social workers had been too hard to bear. And, thankfully, both Cindy and Dopey seemed to understand. Neither of them asked me anything about Louise. They'd already been told I'd left her.

'As long as you're okay,' said Cindy. 'That's all that matters.'

I blinked back tears. I didn't want to let myself break down as I didn't think I could stop the tears once they started. All I longed for now was to return to being a child myself, to let other people look after me, at least for a while. Then once I had got myself on my feet and sorted out my life, I could take Louise back and be the mum she needed me to be.

The next day I had a phone call from social services. 'Louise's place with foster parents is going well,' a voice said. 'And now we're looking for an adoption placement.'

My heart sank. I opened my mouth to speak but no words came out. 'O-okay,' was all I managed to utter. I felt like someone had ripped my insides out; I was gutted. In earlier meetings with social services, the possibility of fostering had been mentioned, but not adoption. They knew I wanted Louise to be fostered until I sorted myself out, but now they were telling me it would take years for me to do so and that that wasn't fair on Louise.

Adoption was the only answer, according to the social workers. I put the phone down and sat in tears, wiping my nose on my sleeve. I knew, despite everything, that really I was still a little girl. I knew Louise stood a better chance in life being adopted by a loving couple than having a thirteen-year-old mother and a paedophile for a dad. It made sense, for both of us. I wouldn't have the responsibility, as horrible as that sounds. I was devastated but also felt a strange sense of relief flooding over me. I could once again go back to being a teenager. Although this had all come at such a price: I'd lost two babies – one killed by doctors, another given away, who would grow up not knowing who I was. I knew I'd never forget Louise – she'd always be in my heart and in my thoughts – but at the same time I knew I couldn't be a good mum to her. I hoped she would grow up knowing only love and happiness, but I knew that for me the pain of her loss would never, ever go away.

For the next six months the secure unit was my home again. I was given an 'independent key worker', someone to help me as the adoption process began to try and help me sort out my life. This, it seemed, was going to be very hard to do, according to Colin, the new key worker. An older man in his fifties, he'd meet me once a week to 'discuss your situation'. With greying hair, he wore glasses through which, literally, he looked down his nose at me. His job was to listen to my views and not to give any of his own. But he didn't need to. I thought he was a snob, and he made me feel as if I was just a little slag.

'Where do you see yourself in ten years' time?' he asked one day, pen poised.

I looked at him blankly. I didn't know where I saw myself in ten days' time, let alone at the age of twenty-three. I'd no idea what he was on about. I asked him on a couple of occasions if it would be possible for Louise just to be fostered so that I could take her back when I had got my life in some sort of order, but he always said no. He kept saying I needed therapy, but it was never arranged. Each time we met, I found myself becoming more distant in the meetings. There was almost little point in me saying anything. His job was supposed to be to help me, yet he wasn't helping at all. He just asked me a load of questions that he would read from a piece of paper and said nothing to my responses. Once again I felt so alone.

Then, two months into my stay, I was offered the chance to see Louise.

'You can see her once a month,' stated Colin, looking disinterested as he fiddled with some pieces of paper in my file.

I couldn't help smiling. To allow myself to imagine holding her again seemed wonderful.

On the first visit, I was taken into a room to meet her foster carer. She was a friendly-looking, skinny woman in her late forties, who seemed full of energy.

As I walked in, she beamed at me as she pushed a spoonful of food into Louise's mouth. Already Louise was four months old.

My baby looked at me with Adam's eyes, but without a shred of recognition. She was opening and closing her mouth like a little fish, wolfing down her food, her eyes looking into my own, watching me with interest. She had no idea who I was.

'Can I feed her?' I asked shyly.

'No, sorry,' said the foster carer. 'Let me finish off and then you can hold her.'

Louise looked healthy and happy, with chubby cheeks and eyes that sparkled. I admired her as I would if she had been a friend's cute baby. I didn't feel a longing for her like she was my own and it made me want to cry. She was cute, she was lovely, and I wanted her to be loved, safe, warm, cared for. But as for maternal instincts, I felt absolutely none.

Looking back now, I think it was all just far too much for my young mind to make sense of – I was still only a child myself – and I'm certain that I would have felt differently had I been even just a couple of years older. But at the time, all I knew was that I was supposed to feel something that I didn't feel, and it made me so sad.

Finally, once she'd finished her purée, the foster carer picked Louise up and put her in my arms. I handed her a soft cream teddy that I'd asked one of the social workers to buy for her, and she gurgled and smiled at me. She felt so much bigger, stronger and more aware of everything around her.

'Hello,' I said, thinking, *She has no idea at all that I'm her mummy*.

I felt horribly gutted inside. I was a stranger to my own daughter.

The foster carer chatted away about how well she was feeding, how she was putting on the right amount of weight, and how much progress she'd been making.

'I work full time,' she explained. 'So Louise goes to a nanny during the day.'

I nodded in all the right places like a robot, only half listening, all the while keeping my eyes locked on Louise's, hoping for the tiniest flick of recognition. But there was nothing.

EIGHTEEN

Saying Goodbye

A month passed and it was time for our second visit. I'd been quite nervous before the first visit, but this time my nervousness had gone, and I was really looking forward to seeing her. I'd got letters and updates from the carer in the time in between and she seemed to be doing so well. But as I walked down the corridor towards the meeting room, I overheard the sound of a baby screaming. Louise was inconsolable. Inside the room the carer was desperately trying to calm her.

'Shhhhhhh,' she cooed, trying to sway with Louise on her hip.

'What's the matter with her?' I asked. The sound of her cries seemed to pierce a part of me deep inside. It made me realize that I did have a maternal instinct deep down after all.

'Oooh, I don't know,' said the carer, looking harassed.

'Can I try and hold her?' I asked, holding out my arms.

'No,' said the carer firmly. She started walking up and down the room, jiggling Louise as she went. Then she tried poking the teat of her juice bottle in her mouth. Louise pushed it away, her wails growing even louder.

'Can't I just try?' I asked. My heart felt as though it would break unless I did something. Reaching out a hand, I gently stroked her chubby arm, which was flailing around and punching the air with anger. The foster carer moved away from me as though I would pass on a disease.

'Really, you can hold her when she's calm,' she snapped.

For the next few minutes I watched as she tried everything to calm Louise, whose face had grown red and blotchy from crying. It broke my heart to hear and see it, but to be powerless to help. I wanted to cuddle her and soothe her myself. Or at least to be allowed to try. I felt like a spare part, awkward and not knowing what to do. I tried to sit down and wait but then, all of a sudden, something seemed to snap inside of me. I leaped up and started banging on the door, which had been locked behind me when I entered.

'Let me out!' I screamed at the social worker behind it. 'I want to go!' I knew I had to get out of that room. Whatever pain Louise was feeling, I could feel deep inside my heart, and I couldn't stand by helplessly for a second longer.

I ran out and didn't turn back, poor Louise's cries ringing in my ears all the way. Back in my room, I lay on my bed and sobbed. Cindy came to see me. Without saying anything she just held me tightly.

A week later, I had another appointment with Colin. He looked at me as he placed a piece of paper on the desk between us.

'Here's the shortlist of potential adoptive parents for Louise,' he said. 'Have a look and let me know what you think.'

I read them carefully. The details were sketchy, just basic ages and their work and family life, with a couple of lines about what they liked. Because it was an adoption, all details were confidential. The first couple were middle-aged, both worked full time and had a nineteen-year-old daughter. He liked golf and she liked classical music.

The next couple were young and couldn't have kids. In quotes it read, 'They would like to bring the child up as their own.'

Immediately I didn't like either of these. The older couple sounded like they'd be leaving Louise alone all day. And I hated the idea of Louise never knowing her true identity. The third choice was a couple who'd already adopted another child, and the woman stayed at home. 'We'd always be open about the adoption and keep in touch with the birth mum,' they'd written.

Straightaway I preferred the sound of them and I told Colin.

'Well, once it's decided, you can meet them,' he said.

He pushed another piece of paper across the table. 'You just need to sign this a few times,' he said.

I scrawled my signature where he pointed, my heart banging in my chest.

This was it now. Louise was going. I signed my name where he told me to, then leaned back in the chair.

'All done,' he said, simply.

I went back to join the others, feeling a strange sense of relief. Finally, it was over.

Afterwards, it was explained that Louise's new parents would send me regular updates about her progress, together with photos. Then a member of staff called Simon asked me if I wanted to leave a video message for Louise for when she was older, to explain why I'd had her adopted.

'Yeah, okay,' I said. I liked the idea of her knowing that I thought it was the best thing for her, and that it wasn't a case of me not wanting her.

He sat me in front of a camera and, without realizing that it was already on, he asked me what I'd say to her off the top of my head.

'Hello, my name is Terrie,' I began. 'Erm . . . ' I struggled to think, but then just carried on.

'I'm from an unsettled background and my dad is dead. I ended up in care as I am seen as a vulnerable teenager. I am doing my GCSEs now, but didn't think I had much going for me. I thought you'd be best off out of it and being cared for by a nice couple who could give you all the things I never could.'

I stared at the camera. 'All I want is for you to grow up happy and feeling loved and cared for. Hopefully, one day you will realize that I made the right choice and not hate me for it.'

Then Simon clicked it off. 'That was brilliant, Terrie, so heartfelt.'

'You mean it was filming already?'

'Yes, I wanted you not to stress,' he replied.

I breathed out deeply. I knew that message could some day be seen by my daughter. And, in just a few short seconds, I'd been brutally honest and had told her why she, my little girl, could never be in my life, could never be brought up with her 'real' mum. And I so desperately hoped that she'd understand.

Around this time I started to spend more time with David, the worker I had first got to know while living in the house. He was in his forties and was one of the few workers I genuinely liked and looked up to. The care in his eyes, his tone of voice and his smile made me feel so at ease. He wasn't just doing this job to pay the bills; he did it because he liked us. Best of all about him was that he spoke to me as if I was a child – which, of course, I was.

In all areas of my life, I was treated as an adult, with little compassion. But he'd be gentle, patient and listen intently when I replied. He never tried to fob me off, or beat around the bush. 'You were a good mum, Terrie,' he said. 'But that's no life for a thirteen-year-old.'

Although touching or hugging wasn't allowed in the unit, sometimes David's words were like a hug. He made me feel warm and safe without preaching at me. He was the first father figure I'd ever had and the first man I ever really trusted.

David was a father himself and used to take us on day trips with his own teenage kids. He loved chatting to us about our lives and what we hoped for. He was one of the few people I opened my heart up to about Louise. He didn't judge me and had seen himself how hard I'd tried in the mum-and-baby house. 'I tried my best,' I sobbed one day. 'I'm just not good enough. I couldn't be a good mum. I've not got it in me.'

'You're just a child who's had a bad start in life,' he told me. 'Nothing to do with you and the person you are or the person you'll become. You are a nice person, Terrie.'

And because it was David saying this, I began to believe it. We could just be sitting eating chips on the seafront or walking to an arcade, talking, but I listened and treasured every word. I loved spending time with him and felt that I could always be myself. We'd often go to the beach at Redcar, a few miles away, on our days out, and have a good run on the roller coasters and big wheel. David took all the kids from the unit, sometimes even at weekends, just for the fun of it. For once I wasn't a child looking outside on others having fun; I was a little girl, screaming with laughter and feeling the wind in her hair. So unlike the days when I was taken for day trips to the seaside with Dad.

However, I still didn't talk to David about Adam. Like all the key workers, he would have read my files, he would have known the gist of it, but I couldn't bring myself to talk openly. I just wanted to put it all behind me and move on. David allowed me to be a kid again, and I didn't want to do anything to ruin that. During the six months I was in the unit, Adam never got in touch once. There were no phone calls or messages. I heard from Tasha now and then, but thankfully she never mentioned him either.

Towards the end of my six months, Louise's adoption was about to happen. I'd stopped seeing her after our last visit but was invited to say goodbye. I asked social workers to buy me a little cardigan for her. Then I wrote her a goodbye letter, again stating why I was doing this. During the meeting, as I handed over my letter, a social worker told me something that felt like a body blow.

'The baby's father has also been given the chance to write a letter,' said the social worker.

'What?' I spluttered.

'He has every right as the father,' she said.

I was in shock. Not only were no charges being brought against Adam by social services, they were even taking his rights as a dad seriously.

Once again, I found myself ushered into a room with adults talking quietly. This time with the adoptive parents waiting with Louise.

Her new mum turned to me, her eyes shining. She was short with shoulder-length, naturally ginger hair, just like Louise's. Her freckly face crinkled as she gave me a warm smile.

'Terrie,' she said, offering me her hand. She didn't tell me her name, she wasn't allowed to. 'I just want to say thank you. Thank you so very much.'

Her husband was standing next to her. A tall man with dark hair. He showed a photo to me.

'This is our son, who we also adopted,' he said. 'He's got some disabilities but is doing well. He'll be Louise's brother.'

I looked at the snap of a boy with a squint laughing into the camera. Louise's big brother.

'He's lovely,' I said.

The new mum kissed my cheek. 'We promise we'll keep in touch,' she said. 'With lots of letters and pictures.'

We held each other's gazes. 'We promise Louise will mean the world to us,' she whispered. I wanted to tell her how grateful I was but no words would come out of my mouth.

I picked up Louise and wrapped her in her cardigan before strapping her into her buggy. She looked into my face and all I saw was a miniature version of Adam. I knew that I loved her in some way deep down, but I also knew that it wasn't enough. She needed, and deserved, so much more. Gently I kissed the top of her head.

'Goodbye, darling,' I said. 'You've got a mummy and daddy now who can love you in a way I never could.'

I turned back round to find Louise's new mum's face streaming with tears.

'Thank you,' she said again.

I smiled, said goodbye, and walked out – leaving my baby for ever.

Shortly afterwards, when my six-month detention was over, I was moved to the 'open' area of the unit. This was essentially a children's house, full of teenagers my own age, who had no one to look after them and nowhere else to live.

It was designed exactly the same as the closed unit, but with no locks on the doors. I also joined the on-site school to finish my English GCSE, passing with a B.

'Congratulations, clever brain box,' said David when he saw me next. 'You're amazing.' I was so thrilled when I got that certificate. For the first time in my life it felt like I'd achieved something 'normal'.

The relief flooded through me when I was told that the decision had been made that I would stay in the open unit until my sixteenth birthday. The thought of returning to Mum's was too much to bear, and I knew I'd never escape Adam's clutches if I was sent back to Stevenage. My time over the next two years, living in this home with lots of other kids my age, was probably the happiest of my childhood. Quickly I made friends and became one of the most popular girls in there. Helena was the first person I met. She was a bit of a head case, always up for a laugh and pushing boundaries. She told me how she liked to nick stuff from Boots. She told me the story of how she had ended up in care. She'd thrown paint down the stairs in her mum's house at the age of twelve. After the row that followed, her mother had said that she was uncontrollable and had requested that social services take her away. I never understood and always thought there must have been more to it than that. Whatever way you looked at it, it was very sad. I knew what it felt like to not be wanted by your own mother, and I only hoped that Louise would grow up not feeling that pain, that she would ⌐   ⌐w different our situations were.

Then there was Freya. She was a self-harmer, with livid red slash marks up her arms and a liking for sniffing aerosols when the staff were not looking.

The rest of the group were lads: Mike, Alex, Paul and Tyler, all in for various reasons, from being mentally ill to crimes they'd committed.

I had money of my own for the first time as well. Mum would send me £50 every two weeks from her benefits, and I'd get £10 a week pocket money from social services and £50 a month as an incentive to go to school. I found the lessons interesting too. It wasn't just boring academic work; we had vocational courses, too, and I chose to study hairdressing at NVQ level. On top of the money we still had regular outings. I loved trail bike riding, rock-climbing and going on the dry ski slope. I lived for those trips out.

The best thing was the freedom. As long as we went to school and came home by 9.45 p.m. every night, we could do whatever we wanted. There were no strict rules. It's obvious now that I would have fared better in this sort of home than at any of my foster families, where strict rules were put in place. I was from a chaotic life and although I craved security, I found it terribly hard to stick to structure.

The downside of all this money and new-found liberation, plus mixing with some guys who were happy to get up to illegal mischief, was that I found myself in all kinds of sticky situations. Our days always started the same – in school, doing our lessons like good kids. Then we'd go off into the local town, Darlington, and buy some booze from somewhere. Alex was sixteen but looked a lot older, so he'd buy all the cider, lager or Mad Dog that he could and we'd hang about the park benches, laughing and getting drunk.

The boys would often do dares, and things occasionally got out of hand. Once Alex dared Mike to steal an unlocked car. Going along with it, Helena and I found ourselves in the back seat, bumping along, with the boys driving, screaming with laughter. Mike had called someone he knew in Middlesborough to strip the car and sell the parts for it. Afterwards, the car was moved to a car park and the lads told us to get out and run away. Later, they told us they'd torched it.

Helena was scared stiff. 'I don't want to end up in the secure unit with the locked doors,' she cried.

We all laughed at her. At one point, each of us had ended up there, so it wasn't something that frightened any of us. But even though I wasn't scared of getting in trouble, it wasn't something I liked; it was just something I did to be accepted. What I craved still, more than anything, was to be a normal child. But I also needed to fit in, and I loved being in our little group – it was almost like a family, and I couldn't face not being a part of it. So before I knew it, I found myself going along with any sort of trouble they could think up.

Around this time I also started having sex with lots of the boys. I was always careful, though. After everything with Adam, I'd been taken to a sex clinic to be checked out and decided that I wanted to avoid that humiliation again, let alone not wanting to fall pregnant again. I slept with all the guys at one point or another. We did it outside, or in alleyways or cars. It was never something I enjoyed, I just liked the feeling of being attractive to boys nearer my own age and knowing that they wanted me. I wanted to be liked and I thought that was what I needed to do to make them like me. And each time I slept with a different boy, I felt as though I was moving further away from Adam, and that was a feeling I liked.

Freya and I started shoplifting just for fun too. We had enough money to buy whatever we liked, but daring each other to nick stuff was another way of passing time. Mainly, it was make-up from Boots, or sometimes we'd go into clothes shops and the lads would start running around the shop, waving jackets and coats above their shoulders like kids playing Superman. We'd fall about laughing as the security guards tried to catch them. There wasn't any reason for it, other than that we enjoyed the attention.

Once, Freya and I were arrested after being caught swiping some mascara from a beauty counter. The police only gave us a caution, as we were still only fifteen, but the unit was informed.

Later that evening, I got a telling-off from them as well. But the social workers almost seemed relieved that we'd only been nicking stuff. At least we weren't running away. One day in the kitchen, a key worker who didn't particularly like me had a go at me for the stealing.

'It's not on,' she snapped. 'You're fifteen now and supposed to be mature. You can't pass the blame.'

David happened to come in and overhear her.

'Remember she *is* only fifteen,' he said. 'And, after all she's been through, it's not surprising, is it?'

However, later on, he told me to try and stop, bless him. 'What is it you want to do one day?' he asked.

'Just leave care!' I laughed. I had never thought beyond that.

'Life isn't that simple,' David said. 'You do need a plan, Terrie. Some idea of how you'd like to make a living.'

I had been doing my hairdressing course at the unit, so I wondered if that was something I could do. But really I had no idea. Life seemed complicated enough without having to have a career plan too.

The months flew by and I began to push Adam and the whole nightmare surrounding him to the back of my mind. I rarely heard from, or saw, Mum either, aside from being given money, so I felt like I'd truly escaped my past. I kept in touch with Tasha, though, and sometimes went to stay with her at weekends. As always, I think she enjoyed having me around to help with her baby and she used to ask me for my money from the unit, which she would then use for booze. Although I never felt like I could trust her 100 per cent and was always slightly scared that Adam might turn up on her doorstep, I liked seeing her and having some sort of connection to my old life. But I was always happy to come back to the unit afterwards.

One morning, David came in to work looking haggard and pale. He looked as if he hadn't slept for a month; his eyes were red and he had big black bags under them.

I followed him into the kitchen where he was making coffee.

'Are you okay?' I asked. I'd never seen him look so upset before.

'No,' he said. 'My wife has left me.'

David had been married for over twenty years. He had always spoken about his wife with such pride. And they sounded like such perfect parents to their teenage daughters that I'd always pictured them as the perfect happy family.

'What?' I asked, genuinely shocked.

'Yes,' he replied. 'She's gone.'

He looked broken and started sobbing. 'Sorry, Terrie,' he said. 'I shouldn't be crying in front of you. It's just so hard. I don't know what to do.'

Without thinking, I reached over and hugged him tight, standing on tiptoes as he was so tall.

'It's going to be all right,' I soothed.

He sniffed, then quickly broke away. 'Sorry, Terrie. It's not appropriate. But thank you.' Then he looked at me, straight in the eye.

'You'll make something of yourself one day,' he said.

That was on a Saturday afternoon.

Two days later, on the Monday morning, I'd been looking out for him as I was desperate to find out how he was. I kept thinking that maybe his wife would have come home to him over the weekend, apologizing profusely and saying that it was all a big mistake.

'Where's David?' I asked another worker, when the whole morning had passed and he was nowhere to be seen.

'He just needs a few days to clear his head,' he said.

A whole week went by and there was still no sign of David. Then one morning a rumour began to circulate that David was dead. I didn't know why someone would say something so cruel, but something made me ask the other key workers if there was any truth to what was being said.

'Please! Can someone tell us so we can get to the bottom of this?' I asked every worker I could find all day, but no one would tell me anything.

At dinner I asked again. 'Please can you tell me if it's true? I can't even eat anything, I'm so cut up at the thought!'

But he shook his head. 'Terrie, it's not my place,' he said, sadly.

When the night staff came on, I rushed up to them, too, for news. I just needed to know. But they shook their heads and told me staff issues were none of my business. At that point I hated the lot of them. They had no respect for us kids. They didn't see us as individuals with feelings. But then that was what had made David seem so unbelievably special: he did.

Then, a day later, I walked past Freya's room and saw her sitting on her bed crying with her head in her hands.

'It's true,' she sobbed. 'David was found dead in his car. He killed himself with his exhaust pipe.'

NINETEEN

Confessions

I fell to my knees. I felt as though someone had smashed a mallet into my ribcage. The grief hit me immediately like a physical bolt from the blue.

'No!' I screamed. 'Noooo!'

Absolutely dumbstruck with grief, I sobbed so loudly that I couldn't hear any more of what Freya was saying. The thought of never seeing or speaking to David again was unbearable. I had seen him almost every day while I had been in the unit and he had been such a shining light in my life.

Freya tried to give me a cuddle, but I barely noticed. A member of staff overheard and came to help.

'Come on, Terrie,' he said. 'Go back to your room to cry it out. We're all upset.'

A key worker walked me back. My room had been painted recently, and the smell made me want to gag. I couldn't face being alone, not that night. After lights out, I sneaked back to Freya's bedroom. 'I just can't believe it,' I sobbed. Without saying a word, she moved some pillows on to the floor, and I snuggled down next to her, where I cried myself to sleep. David's loss felt like proper heartbreak. He wasn't just a key worker, a faceless social worker, a man doing a job. I had loved him like a father and the pain of his loss was indescribable. He'd been the closest thing to a dad I'd ever known.

The next few days and weeks passed in a blur. I kept breaking down – over dinner, in school, while drinking with the others, as Freya and Helena tried to comfort me. It came in giant waves of total devastation. Words he'd said to me flitted through my mind constantly. 'You'll make something of yourself, Terrie.' 'Don't lose heart.' And I just wished I'd been able to say something more comforting to him when he'd broken down in the kitchen that time. I kept going over and over our conversation. Maybe if I'd hugged him tighter, told him it'd be okay, asked him if he had anyone outside the unit to talk to. Anything. But I hadn't. He'd said himself that it wasn't appropriate, so I had backed off. But, at the end of the day, he meant more to me than a member of staff, and I felt like I should have been there more for him.

Other kids were upset too, of course, but I took it very badly. It felt as though I'd lost a member of my family, except, of course, he was a better person than any member of my family had ever been. None of us were allowed to his funeral, just as we hadn't been allowed to go to Jason's when I was at Leverton Hall. We were told it was a 'private family affair'. Even if he felt like family to us.

Then, when all my tears had dried up, I became withdrawn and quiet. Nothing I did seemed to make me feel better. I couldn't get David out of my mind. I had little interest in TV or music or messing around with the lads like I used to. Nothing made sense to me anymore.

So when a local priest popped into the unit and offered to speak to me, I decided to see him. Ordinarily, I'd have ignored any advice dished out by 'do-gooders' but he seemed like such a kind, gentle man that I thought having a chat with him might not do me any harm. The promises of counselling after Louise's birth had never materialized and I wondered if talking to an outsider might help. I was desperate.

On the first day, I felt a little nervous as I raised my fist to knock at the side door where visitor meetings took place.

'Come in,' a smooth, male voice said.

I opened the door to find a grey-haired priest wearing a shirt and dog collar standing up and beckoning me inside.

'Terrie!' he said warmly, his brown eyes shining. 'I'm Father Neil.' He shook my hand firmly, his handshake strong and warm.

I sat down, my nerves disappearing bit by bit.

As soon as I saw the cross round his neck and his kind, en-quiring face, something inside of me wanted to spill everything. I told him about David, what his loss meant to me. How much I had loved him. Then how I'd slept with all the boys on the unit to try and find love myself.

'I can't go on like this,' I sobbed. 'I hate myself.'

The priest listened patiently without judging me, and held my gaze steadily. It felt so good to unburden myself. He didn't object to the way I spoke or to the fact that swear words occasionally slipped out of my mouth. He didn't look down on me. Then, the more he listened, the more I found myself talking. Before I knew it, the whole disgusting saga about Adam began to pour out.

'He'd force himself on me on the sofa,' I said quietly. 'Make me have sex with him and give him blow jobs.'

Father Neil's eyes flashed with distress and his mouth flickered into a grimace as he looked at the floor. I wondered if this man of the cloth had ever heard of anything so horrible happening to a little girl. He recovered his composure but not before I'd seen that he was visibly shocked.

'You, Terrie, have been through a truly shocking time,' he began. 'And it should only be correct that justice should be served against those who have hurt you so badly.'

I nodded. But I'd no idea how that could happen. I wanted the police to press charges but I'd still have to sign the statement myself. That's the way it had been left. And I was still too scared and wanted someone to help me.

Father Neil arranged for me to have weekly visits. Something I was thrilled about. Speaking to him really did feel like a 'problem shared, a problem halved', just as he said it would. Now it wasn't just my own dirty secret. This kind, lovely, religious man now knew and, more importantly, he genuinely wanted to help.

For the next few weeks, more of my story poured out, about Mum, Dad, the crazy house of lodgers, how Adam kept tracking me down and how I always found myself back in his clutches. I even told him about Louise.

'I feel so guilty,' I whispered once. 'But I'm glad she's somewhere better.'

'You can move on from this,' Father Neil replied. 'God can help you to.'

I wasn't sure, but I hoped he was right.

After a few more visits and chats with him I decided to get baptized.

'I just want to forget all the bad stuff,' I said. 'I want to turn my life around. David always said I'll make something of my life and I'm determined I will.'

The priest couldn't have been happier, of course. I'd always believed that there's a God, but I was far from being a Bible-basher. For me, this was about turning over a new leaf rather than becoming a dedicated church-goer.

'I want to get my life sorted,' I said. 'I want to go to college and have a normal life and do normal things. I don't want to get drunk and sleep around anymore.'

So it was arranged. The baptism was going to be held a few weeks later.

We went to Father Neil's Church of England church. I wore a smart blouse and skirt, and everyone in the unit came along. During the service I was asked to step forward by Father Neil and I felt all eyes on me as my cheeks flushed. But, as usual, look-ing into his eyes made me feel so relaxed. As he said the words of the baptism, I closed my eyes and leaned over the font. I felt him gently splash my forehead.

Wash it all away, please, wash it away, I thought to myself, as the holy water dripped down the bridge of my nose. I was handed a white towel to dry myself with.

'Thank you,' I said, my face breaking into a smile.

Stepping back, Father Neil grinned at me as the sun beamed through the church's stained-glass window behind him. I smiled, saying to myself, *Terrie, this is a new start. David would be so proud.*

Afterwards, everyone, including Father Neil, went out for an Indian meal. I half expected some of the lads to take the piss.

But they all respected what I was doing and where I was coming from. And afterwards I truly felt as if some of what Adam had done to me had washed away down the plug hole of that holy water font.

Once I had my sixteenth birthday, I was old enough to leave the children's home. I didn't know what the next step would be – all I cared about was getting out and making a success of my life in the real world, but I had no idea where I'd do that. I could go back to Stevenage, near to Mum, but did I really want to? And if I didn't go there, where else was possible? Part of me didn't care as I just wanted to be free of the care system. By this point, I had grown sick of key workers and social services reports and all the rest of it. I wanted to live my own life now, whatever that meant. I also knew, now I was older, that I had no reason to fear Adam. I'd heard through Tasha that he'd got a new girlfriend and had moved on, away from Stevenage.

After one final meeting, the social services 'told' me what the next step was to be. I was to move into a house in Letchworth, about ten minutes' drive from Stevenage, in a home for people with either financial or social difficulties. It was called the Nacro project. With proper sadness I said goodbye to Freya and Helena. We vowed to keep in touch and we still do to this day.

Then, once again, I found myself in a social services taxi en-route to a strange destination. Letchworth looked like a grey dump to me, just grids of terraced streets and small new-builds. I'd never been there before. As the car pulled up outside one of the new-build houses, I was given £60 and a key to the door by a social worker who met me there. 'Here's your new home, Terrie,' she said, smiling. 'I hope you settle in well. It has everything you need inside – furniture, etc. It'll be up to you to make it a home now you're sixteen.' And with that, she took off in her car. I stood alone outside the house, not quite believing what had happened. After all the meetings, reports and monitoring, it felt as though the strings had been cut and I'd been cast out. I watched as the car disappeared. I'd wanted this place to be rid of all social workers and the limitations of the unit. But not like this. To be handed a key and told to 'get on with it' seemed rather cruel. The social worker quite clearly couldn't have cared less. The street was quiet, a mum with a pram walked quickly past, not looking me in the eye. I'd absolutely no idea where I was and I began to shiver; I don't know whether it was from the cold or from fear of what lay ahead of me.

Nervously, I fumbled with the key and opened the house door. It smelt musty and full of cigarette smoke inside. In the corridor, another door opened and a man stuck his head out. He looked about nineteen, and he was big, with tattoos of dragons on his arm.

'Hello, you,' he said, his voice menacing.

His stare was cold and hard and I felt a chill in my heart. I didn't like the look of him at all.

I ignored him and brushed past to get to my door. But as I fiddled with my keys, trying desperately to open the door so that I could get away from my new neighbour, I suddenly dropped them. 'You all right, darling?' he said, half laughing. His voice was high pitched and uneven, as though he'd taken some drugs or was mentally ill. I looked up and my eyes met with his, two dark pools like a shark's.

He stepped closer and began to laugh menacingly. 'Ha! Ha!' he said slowly, leaning forward so that his face was only inches away from mine.

Grabbing the keys from the floor, I turned around and ran out. I'd only just arrived but I knew that I was going now. I needed to get away, anywhere but here.

I ran down the street until I found a pay phone and called the only person whose number I knew by heart. Tasha.

She'd recently moved away to Dagenham. She'd also got married to her boyfriend Tony and had another baby on the way. For the first time in her life she sounded settled, sorted and, best of all, away from Adam.

'Hello, lovely,' she said, a crying baby in the background. 'Just come if you need to.' A few hours later I was on her doorstep, my entire possessions in one small bag. She gave me a hug.

'Look, I'm not sure how long you can stay for, but stay anyway,' she said.

For the next few months I stayed at Tasha's, living off my £47 a week, money from social services given to all new care-leavers. She let me sleep on the sofa and I helped with her baby when I could. I liked playing mum sometimes. I thought of Louise now and then, and wondered how she got on.

Then I got a letter via social services. In it was a picture of Louise laughing into the camera. She was about two and a half by now and pretty as a picture, although I still saw Adam's eyes peering back at me. Seeing how happy she looked, I knew the correct decision had been made, even if I also knew that I'd have to live with it for the rest of my life. Louise would never go without. She would always live in a nice house, with a mum who'd cook good, healthy food and a dad who would go to work and buy nice things. She would grow up knowing what love is, and feeling safe and warm. I knew I wouldn't have been able to give her that. I could barely look after myself. I couldn't even offer her a proper roof over her head.

I still didn't know what I was going to do with my own life. I just lived day to day in Tasha's house, pleased to be free of social services and free of Adam. I was enjoying peace. Normality.

A couple of months after I had moved into Tasha's, she had a little gathering at her house one evening and it was then that I met Samir. I was so attracted to his friendly face and open manner. A little on the tubby side, he was dark-skinned and dark-haired, and as soon as we met we clicked.

'Are you at college?' he asked me as he poured me a drink.

'No,' I said shyly. I felt a little sick as I worried that he was going to ask me strings of questions about my life. I had no idea what I would say. But he didn't. He asked me about my day and what music I liked. Then I switched the focus back to him.

Samir chatted about how he was doing a course in business studies. One day he wanted to be a chef and he worked part-time in his uncle's kebab shop.

He sounded so nice, normal, hard-working and kind, and I could literally feel myself going weak at the knees as he spoke. I couldn't believe my luck that a man as decent as he was, was even bothering to talk to the likes of me.

'You're very pretty, Terrie,' he told me. This was probably the first time a man other than Adam had complimented me and it made me feel nice. Not dirty or scummy.

'Thank you,' I said, my cheeks going red.

That evening when we said goodbye, he didn't ask to sleep with me, or grope me, or even kiss me. He just pecked me on the cheek and gave me a cuddle.

'I'd like to see you again,' he said.

The next morning I had to stop myself from pinching myself. Tasha was up early with the kids and making coffee when I woke up.

'Oh, I see Samir has his eye on someone,' she teased.

'I know.' I grinned.

'He's lovely, Terrie,' she said, more seriously. 'You deserve someone nice.'

The next evening Samir picked me up and took me out to an Indian restaurant for a curry. He insisted on paying.

As we chatted over our kormas, sharing pieces of poppadom and laughing, I almost felt like crying with happiness. We looked so ordinary. Like any other couple. And, for an evening, I could pretend I was, too. Here I wasn't Adam's victim or a vulnerable girl in care. I was a teenager, with a boyfriend, who laughed at my jokes. This was something I could never have imagined possible. It didn't happen to girls like me. At the end of the evening, Samir gave me a proper kiss and it felt wonderful. I've always thought of that as my first real kiss.

Over the next few weeks we grew closer. Samir loved treating me to delicious meals out but also would come over and have a chat over coffee at Tasha's.

He was so warm and caring. I'd never realized that it was possible for a man like him to look at me twice. After a few weeks,

Samir made a move while I came to his house and sat in his bedroom.

Very gently, very slowly, we laid back on his bed and he kissed me. And instead of fear, I felt butterflies in my stomach the whole time. Instinctively, I knew I could trust him.

'You're beautiful,' he said, brushing my hair. I almost had to blink back tears as I felt so happy. Then we slept together, but for the first time in my life it wasn't sex, it was making love. And I knew I was in love with a decent man. My past was never far from my mind, but for once I could ignore it.

One evening, as I sat with Tasha. I suddenly, almost without thinking, told her the entire story about Adam. She always knew there was 'something' between us. But the reality was, she had no idea of the extent. I watched her face change from wonder to shock to revulsion.

'But I had no idea,' she whispered. 'I thought he always wanted to help you. You were just a kid.'

We sat in tears as I finished my story. 'Who did you think was Louise's father, then?' I asked. I couldn't believe that she didn't realize the extent of the abuse.

'I d-don't know,' she spluttered. 'I just thought it was a cover-up for maybe another boy you were seeing.'

I wasn't sure if I believed her. But I did know that she'd always been scared of Adam and his wild moods and dodgy dealings. I know he'd threatened her at various points during his 'relationship' with me. This made me wonder if Tasha had said something to him about how wrong it all was, and whether in fact she *did* know what was going on. I looked at her, telling me how she'd had no idea, how awful it was, what a perv he must be, and I wondered if she'd just felt powerless to do anything. Maybe the tears she was crying now were her way of telling me how sorry she was.

'I'm sorry, Terrie,' she said, as if she could read my mind.

We sat in silence for a few minutes, Tasha holding my hand, but I'm sure she wasn't quite able to look me in the eye.

'I want to nail him now,' I said. 'I want to finally press charges, do what social services should have done years ago on my behalf.'

Tasha nodded.

'I'll do whatever I can to help you,' she promised. We hugged each other and for the first time in my life I felt like I could fully trust her.

Now that I had told everything to Tasha, next I wanted to tell Samir. In many ways I could feel my 'dark secret' gnawing inside of me. I felt tainted by my past and felt that it was only fair for him to know the truth.

Of course, I was scared of his reaction. Why would he want some child rape victim? A nice man like him? He wouldn't want me – I was damaged goods, and would always carry with me baggage from my past. I steeled myself for him to end it with me.

But every time I tried to tell him, I kept losing my nerve at the last moment. I didn't want our relationship to end, so would it hurt to spend a few more days together before the inevitable? Tasha kept urging me to tell him and eventually she blurted something out in the end.

'Has Terrie told you?' she said, after a few beers.

I felt sick to my stomach. The look on my face told her I hadn't.

'Whooops, sorry!' she said.

But she was right. I had to tell Samir before I went back to the police again. He'd wonder what was going on.

So that evening, Tasha left us and we sat down alone while I told him everything.

'I've got something important I want to talk to you about . . .' I began.

A horrible look of confusion and upset crossed his face.

'No! I don't want to dump you or anything!' I cried. 'It's just . . . something you need to know.'

He looked at me intently, his arms folded. Unable to look him in the eye, I felt ten years old again, as the whole sordid story poured out. I didn't go into any detail, I skimmed over the worst of it, but I told him that I'd given birth to a baby. By the time I'd finished, his beautiful brown eyes were shining with tears. He reached out and clasped my hands in his.

'Terrie, I'm so sorry,' he said, his voice choked.

I waited. I closed my eyes. I knew what was coming next. He was going to end it and walk out of the door.

But, instead, he carried on speaking.

'I love you,' he said. 'And hearing what you've been through has made me admire you even more. I think you're an incredible person for getting through all this and ending up the person you are today.'

Now it was my turn to well up. I couldn't believe what I was hearing. Here was a man who was so lovely, so kind and decent. And yet he accepted me after what had happened. I was bowled over by his reaction. I sat there while I let it all sink in, and gradually I could feel something I'd never felt before – I could feel a sense of respect for myself building inside of me. Maybe he *was* right? Maybe I was stronger than I'd ever given myself credit for? The older I had got, the more I realized how messed up my background and family were. I'd been abused for most of my childhood, but I was still here, still fighting for the truth to come out and even able to attract a lovely man like Samir.

'You deserve to find some justice now and I will be behind you every step of the way,' he said.

His words echoed those of Father Neil before my baptism. 'Justice should be served,' he'd told me and now, finally, hopefully, I was on my way to seeking it.

The very next day, I called the local police station in Stevenage. They came around an hour later with a female police officer who sat down and went through all the details. My case had been lying on file for a while and they had the original statement I'd written with Angela three years previously.

'You can expect a good pay-out from this,' said one officer. Even though any extra money would be a help, that was the last thing on my mind. This was about putting Adam behind bars where he belonged. Money didn't matter.

As I signed the paperwork, a voice rang out on the police radio in the living room. 'We're knocking on his door now,' it crackled.

Immediately, other officers had been contacted to arrest him. Now I was here ready to tell them everything and to stand up against him, they were not wasting any time. As I heard the news, more relief washed over me, and I realized that I wasn't scared any more.

The next day, the police explained to me that Adam had been

bailed. But they were getting a DNA sample from Louise to back up my claims. They took a quick swab of DNA from my cheek for testing, too, and would also get Adam tested.

Then, before I knew it, we had a court date. A policewoman rang to tell me.

'Wow,' I said, breathlessly. 'So soon.'

'Yes,' she replied. 'These things are fast tracked sometimes if the police bring the case forwards.'

I felt quite faint with a mix of excitement and fear. But it wasn't to be as straightforward as I had hoped. Adam was pleading not guilty.

'What?' I gasped. 'How can he do this with DNA evidence from Louise?'

The WPC sighed. 'You'd be amazed what people think they can get away with,' she said. 'But yes, the evidence is there. The DNA evidence is damning.'

Quickly, my fear returned. Especially when she told me again that there was no chance of me giving my statement via video link because I was no longer a minor in the eyes of the law. They told me that I would have to sit behind a screen while I gave evidence instead. But as I thought about it, something inside me changed and I felt a strength rise up in me from no-where.

'No,' I said, firmly. 'I want to face him and look him in the eye if I have to be in that courtroom,' I told my officer. 'I want to tell everyone what he did to me.'

The very thought made me want to vomit, but at the same time I knew I had to face my abuser. I wasn't going to sit behind a screen. I wasn't going to hide.

*

And so the trial started. I found myself barely able to eat or sleep for worry. I wasn't allowed in during it, only on the day I was supposed to give evidence – the last day of the hearing.

I wore the smartest black skirt and shirt I could find. I wanted to walk in there with my head held high and feeling strong and determined. I wasn't a victim any more. I was seeking a justice that I should have been given years earlier. I was standing up for the little girl I had been.

On the day, Tasha came with me. She watched me get ready in silence that morning and we took the bus together, barely looking at one another.

Finally, as we walked up to the grey, cold-looking court building, she turned to me.

'You all right Terrie?' she asked.

I nodded faintly but I couldn't speak. I was scared I'd start crying if I did. I didn't want anyone to touch me or to ask how I was. I just needed to get through this.

We had our bags searched, gave our names, and a policeman and WPC came and greeted us before taking us inside.

'You have to wait here,' said the WPC.

I sat outside the doors of the courtroom, trying desperately to take deep breaths but unable to get enough air inside my lungs. I stared at the clock as a million images ran through my mind, images of what he had done to me. I'd read through my statement the night before to refresh my mind. I didn't know what I was going to say, exactly, as I took the stand. But all I needed to do was tell the truth. That the man sitting opposite me had abused me again and again from the age of ten, how he had taken away my innocence, stolen my childhood.

It seemed as though the hands on the clock were barely moving, as though time itself was standing still. I glanced down at my smart outfit and smoothed my skirt, noticing then that my hands and legs were trembling.

Come on, Terrie. Pull yourself together. I knew this was the one and only chance I would get to tell the world what he had done to me and see him brought to justice. *He's not the one in control anymore; you are.* I had been a child when the sexual, and emotional, abuse had begun. But now I was older, and stronger, and the time had come for me to take a stand.

I pulled myself up straight, just as the polished wooden door swung open and an official-looking lady appeared, giving me a brief nod. I could hear people inside the courtroom, solicitors and court officials, speaking to one another in hushed voices.

'You can go in now, Terrie,' she said. 'Are you ready?'

I nodded. *This is it*, I thought. *This is what I've been waiting for all these years. A chance to put my sickening past behind me once and for all.* As I stepped through the doors and took a deep breath, I felt all eyes on me and became aware of the deafening silence. Then, from across the room, I saw him.

I was shocked by his appearance. He looked dirty. Wearing jogging bottoms, a jumper and trainers, his casual outfit looked out of place in such a serious place like a courtroom. His ginger hair was stuck up in ruffled spikes, and he looked as though he hadn't slept in days. I'd heard he was now seeing an eighteen-year-old girl from a nearby estate. I guessed it was the nervous-looking woman in the family area. She looked so naïve, young, vulnerable.

The sight of him made my stomach turn. I looked at him,

determined to make eye contact and let him know that he was no longer in control of me, but as he lifted his head in my direction and we locked eyes, that same unnerving smirk he had always had began to spread across his face. I felt myself shiver as I turned away, filled with a mixture of anger at myself, anger at him and a gut-wrenching fear that he was going to win. Just as he always had done. My mind was still filled with all the disgusting things he did to me and I had to concentrate to blank them out. Now I was older, now I'd left care, now I'd told people like the priest and Samir – proper, decent, nice men – and seen their reactions, I could understand finally just how depraved Adam was. Having sex with a child. A little kid who had no proper parents. Just because he could. It was revolting. I always knew it was wrong, even instinctively as a little girl, but he was a fully grown man . . . how could he? And for years he thought he'd got away with it. I just wanted this to be over. I looked down and by his feet spotted a holdall. Adam obviously didn't think he was going home. Even he presumed he was going to prison. Good.

I'd already heard how Adam had denied that there had been any sexual contact and he even said that if DNA proved Louise to be his child it must have been the result of me 'jumping on him' when he was asleep. His version of events would be laughable if they weren't such bare-faced lies. A police officer sat beside me as I bit my nails and tapped my foot under the table, the nerves building up again as the minutes passed. After half an hour of more legal wrangling, I was still waiting for the case to start when all of a sudden the judge announced that the court was adjourned.

I felt confused and a bit annoyed as I was ushered back out of the room again.

'What's going on?' I asked the WPC. 'Why do we have to wait?'

'Let's just see . . .' she said, staring at a few officials nipping in and out of a side door.

I bit my lip. This was unbearable. Didn't they know how hard I was finding this? How difficult it had been for me to psych myself to go in there and face him in the first place? But I had forced myself to do it as I knew I had to tell everyone the truth about Adam. I had to make sure he would never do this to anyone else. But now I was being asked to wait all over again. It was like torture.

'God, they take their time, eh?' muttered Tasha. I couldn't even reply.

Eventually, after what felt like hours, the solicitor handling my case and a police officer came out to see me.

'Adam has finally pleaded guilty,' he said. 'You don't need to be here now.'

I wanted to punch the air.

'The coward!' I cried to Tasha. 'He made me come to court but he couldn't bear to sit and listen to what I had to say because he knows it's the truth!'

But, deep down, I was relieved. He'd made me wait until the eleventh hour, but at least now he had admitted what he'd done.

'What did he plead guilty to?' I asked.

'Unlawful sexual intercourse and indecent assault,' explained the solicitor. 'The judge did mention that if the social services had kept the foetus as evidence from your first pregnancy, he'd be facing more serious charges as you were under thirteen then, but, as you were just thirteen when you got pregnant with Louise, then we couldn't make the more serious charges stick.'

I nodded, trying to take it all in. I didn't know what it all meant, but something told me that those charges didn't sound quite bad enough for what he had done to me. I wanted him to be put away on bigger charges, like rape and kidnap. But as long as he went to prison for a very long time, I almost didn't care what they got him on.

We returned to the court for sentencing. A hush descended on the courtroom until all you could hear were the judge's robes rustling as he walked in, and the lawyers shuffling their papers.

'All rise,' said a voice, and we all stood up. Then the judge began speaking, reeling off the charges and background information on my case. Then it came to sentencing. I held my breath as I strained to listen. 'I sentence the accused to thirty months in prison. He will also have to sign the register as a sex offender.'

I must have misheard.

'Didn't he mean years?' I whispered to Tasha.

She looked pale and shook her head. 'I'm sorry, Terrie,' she whispered back. 'He said "months".'

Her voice quivered, and we looked at each other, both of us with tears in our eyes.

I felt frantic; I didn't know what to do. A pure white rage started forming in my chest as I fought to keep breathing. I wanted to scream and wail, cry out loud so that the world would know how I felt.

The reality was that if social services had kept the foetus of my aborted child, the one I conceived at the age of eleven, Adam would have faced a life sentence under the more serious offence of having sex with a girl under the age of thirteen. Because we only had DNA proof from Louise and I'd conceived her just after having turned thirteen, he'd get away with indecent assault charges. It was devastating.

After everything I'd been through, Adam got a paltry sentence of just thirty months, meaning that he'd be set free within a year and a half. That was all the law thought my childhood was worth.

TWENTY

The Price of My Childhood

I watched as Adam was sent down. That nasty little smirk was still on his face as he glanced over to his new girlfriend, who was sniffing into a crumpled tissue. What she had to cry about I didn't know. The smirk told me everything I needed to know; even he thought he'd got away with it.

'No,' Tasha was saying. 'It can't be right.'

Very quickly, after Adam had disappeared, the judge ordered the case over and dismissed the court. Blindly now, I pushed past all the dark suits leaving. I had to get out, get some air. I heard a weird sobbing sound and realized that it was coming from me. I caught my breath as a rage I'd never experienced before started to boil over, making my head spin.

'What was that about?' I cried to my solicitor. 'He's got just thirty months in prison for raping me over and over as a child? For kidnapping me? For making me pregnant?'

The solicitor looked genuinely upset, I'll give her that.

'It was down to the charges in the end,' she said. 'We couldn't prove anything happened before the age of thirteen. The foetus of the first pregnancy wasn't kept.'

'I was still a CHILD!' I screamed at her, tears rolling down my cheeks.

One of the social workers on the case was walking efficiently past. Clutching a file to her chest, staring at the floor as she went. Probably trying to avoid me.

'And you!' I cried, shrugging Tasha off me. 'If social services had kept evidence from my abortion, we'd have had the DNA needed to prove he'd abused me at eleven and he'd have got what he deserved!'

The social worker's eyes flitted up briefly to meet mine. 'I'm sorry,' she said, quietly. 'It's out of my hands now.'

'Yeah, that's the trouble,' I spat. 'My case was never in anyone's hands. No one ever took responsibility. Call this justice?'

Tasha curled her arm around my shoulder, leading me away.

'All this! All this time!' I said. 'I've got nothing to show for it.'

Tasha was almost in tears too. 'Look, you did your best,' she soothed. 'Come on, let's get out of here.'

The emptiness I felt was dreadful. I knew Adam was going to prison, but even he had managed to smile about it – he knew he should have got much worse. We got the bus home in silence, the enormity of what had just happened hitting me again and again. I tried to tell myself that at least Adam now had a criminal record, he would be on the sex offenders register for life, and people would know what he'd done when he walked down the street afterwards. But, truth be told, the sentence just wasn't enough for me. I'd not found anything like the justice I craved.

That evening, when I sat with Samir by my side and a cup of tea in my hands, I realized that I couldn't give up now. If Adam had got away with it, I wasn't going to let social services do the same. 'I'm going after them,' I said to Samir, as I felt the feeling of desperation slowly leave me. 'I'm going to get all my files and I'm going to show the world how social services let a vulnerable little girl down. I'm going to take social services to court.'

After so many years in care, I knew all the rules, all the jargon. I was always one of the kids who liked to read over their files, the endless reports and the forms filled in about them. I liked to know what they were saying about me and was savvy enough to be able to read between the lines.

Years ago, when I managed to stay with Mum for a few weeks longer after they'd wanted to put me in care, I had been able to do so by knowing how the system worked. As they only had an interim care order, not a full care order, I knew that, legally, I could stay at home for a bit longer. I understood back then, even as a child, how it worked and now that I was sixteen I felt even more powerful. Very few people had taken social services to court but I knew my rights and social services should pay for letting me down, so other kids didn't experience what I had been through.

In my eyes, thanks to them, I'd received almost no justice in Adam's case because they'd not kept my aborted baby. Not to mention their letting me down so badly while I was in care. The word 'care' was such a flaming joke. Now, with a bit more determination, I wanted an apology from them as well.

They were supposed to protect me, but they let me down, as did my carers, the police, everyone.

The next day, Tasha rang the *Sun* newspaper on my behalf to tell them about my case. I at least wanted some publicity about it, so that people would know how wrong it was. But the journalist told Tasha it wasn't a story they could run with. My heart sank when she told me that. Maybe people wouldn't care about it? Maybe my story was already fish-and-chip paper? Maybe I was just another young person lost in the system? Suddenly, those feelings of worthlessness re-emerged. I was the forgotten child people would always overlook.

As the news of Adam's light sentence sank in, I became tired and irritable. Although Samir had been nothing but a tower of strength for me, our relationship began to suffer. We'd been seeing each other for over a year now by now, but it wasn't going anywhere. He'd boosted my self-confidence no end, and I adored him, but he was a Muslim and we could never be together for ever. In his culture he could expect an arranged marriage and that was the path he'd have to follow. Very sadly we both decided to split.

For a few weeks, I felt very low. I still had no job, now I had no boyfriend, and I didn't know what I was to do with my life. Instead, I concentrated on helping Tasha with her kids; by now she'd had her other baby so her hands were full.

Tony, Tasha's husband, worked in the security business and one day he brought a mate, Paul, home for a few cold beers after work. Funny, cute and tall, I liked the look of him. But after Samir and the court case, a new man was the last thing on my mind. That evening we all sat around drinking and Tasha started trying to encourage me and Paul to get together.

Paul made me laugh. He had such a positive way of looking at life and seemed so laid back. I noticed a twinkle in his eye. He was the complete opposite to me: calm, cool and at ease with life and his emotions. We chatted all evening and as we learned more about each other, we gradually felt more relaxed in each other's company and found that we were making each other laugh, telling funny stories and teasing each other about our differences.

'How can you listen to that rubbish?' he laughed when I told him I love reggae music, and I told him exactly what I thought of his music taste when he said he loved rock. He liked a drink and I'd given up alcohol by this point. But, despite our differences, the more we chatted, the more lovely I thought he was. Despite myself, we had a little kiss at the end of the night.

When we talked about meeting up the following week, he confided in me that he'd recently lost a place to live. 'I'll be sofa surfing for the next week,' he laughed, 'so the more evenings out I can have the better!'

'Come and live here with us, then,' I said, without thinking.

We'd had such a fun evening and he seemed so genuinely lovely that any concerns I would normally have had disappeared and I just blurted it out without thinking. When he said he'd take me up on the offer, I kept my fingers crossed that Tasha would say that it was okay. After all, he was one of Tony's closest friends, so she knew he would be trustworthy.

'Yeah,' she laughed. 'Why not?'

And so three days later, Paul was sitting in our living room with bags at his feet. 'Hope you're a tidy house guest,' I laughed.

Looking back, it was quite a bizarre situation. As soon as Paul had moved in we started to see each other as a couple, even though I wasn't sure how I really felt about him; I hardly knew him after all. I still had problems trusting men, and I still wasn't quite over Samir. But, like everything else in my life, I just went with the flow. He found out about the court case almost straightaway but I didn't go into details. Like always I felt ashamed about what had happened and feared scaring him off with my tales of abuse and pregnancies. So I brushed it under the carpet, gave him sketchy details, and he sensed not to ask any more questions.

Each evening after work, we grew closer and closer. Paul always confided in me what was happening in his life. He was from a lovely, normal family, had a stable job and was hard working. Best of all, he seemed really keen on me, and although I didn't know exactly how I felt, I liked the idea of having a decent bloke in my life again.

When things first became serious between us, though, it felt like all the laughter stopped and we seemed to argue all the time. Sometimes Paul would go out and get drunk with the lads and not come home for days on end. At other times, he'd put his arm round me and tell me he loved me. I didn't know what to believe, and I never knew what he was up to.

'You need to find somewhere else to live!' I screamed at him once.

He looked so upset. 'But it's you I want, Terrie,' he said.

We always ended up making up, at least for a while, and so gradually the weeks rolled into months. When things were good between us we laughed lots and hugged all the time; Paul gave the best cuddles and had a way about him that made me feel safe and protected. But it felt like things were rarely good anymore. I still wasn't sure whether I loved him, but what I did know was that I hated the prospect of him not being there. Then, three months after he had moved into the house, I found out that I was pregnant.

*

Deep down, I think that, unconsciously, I'd planned it. I'd been thinking about Louise so much lately; being around Tasha and her kids made me realize once again that motherhood would be a role I'd find so much joy in, and that had Louise arrived now, there would have been no chance that I would have given her away. Watching Tasha play with her kids and seeing the way their eyes lit up when she woke them in the morning, just made my heart mourn the loss of Louise and everything that could have been. Now that I was living outside the care system and Adam was becoming a part of my past, I felt ready, even though I didn't discuss any of this with Paul. And we weren't being careful . . .

I dreaded telling Paul and I felt like a child who'd been playing with fire when I found myself holding a positive pregnancy test once again. But I was happy. It was all I'd ever wanted: a family and a child. And this time my baby's father was a decent man. Not Adam.

I told Paul that evening. He looked a bit shell-shocked but then he smiled.

'What do you want to do?' I asked Paul matter-of-factly. Even if he was going to leave me, I knew I'd cope. By now, I felt so independent. I knew that whatever life threw at me I'd manage. 'I'm keeping it,' I said firmly. I held my breath, praying that he'd say he wanted the baby, but knowing that regardless of what he said, nothing in the world was going to stop me having this baby and giving it all the love and care I wasn't able to give Louise.

'Whatever you want to do,' he said. 'I'll stand by you.'

I felt the relief flood over me, but I couldn't speak; I could only nod. Then we cuddled for ages, while Paul stroked my hair.

'I'll always be there for you both, no matter what. You know that, don't you?'

Again I nodded, although there was still a part of me that didn't quite believe him. But if he was staying for now, I was happy. For the first time in my life, I could look forward to something resembling a normal life and how amazing was that? *This really is it*, I told myself. *This is what I've been waiting for my whole life.*

I rang the housing office and was grateful to hear that the council would offer me a flat. I didn't get pregnant to get one, but now I was pregnant, I knew that I couldn't stay with Tasha any longer. So Paul and I were planning to move in together properly. Even then I wasn't sure I loved him. But, in my eyes, now that I was pregnant, we at least had to try and make it work. And, of course, he was a decent man. He worked hard and cared for me, and even though he was a young lad who still liked to go out and get drunk with his friends, I knew he would make a wonderful dad.

This time, my pregnancy felt wonderful and the excitement was overwhelming. Every day as I grew bigger, I talked to my bump, making plans for the future and promising my child the world.

'I will always be here for you,' I kept saying to it.

To know that I was now seventeen and no one could take my baby away made me want to burst with joy, but while my belly grew so did a worry in my mind. Would I love this baby any more than Louise? Would I bond with it? What would happen if I didn't? I kept pushing the thought away, but it gnawed away at me sometimes. Often I would lie awake at three or four in the morning, tossing and turning as these thoughts rolled through my mind.

But as the baby's imminent arrival became more real for me,

nothing seemed to be any different for Paul. I let him get on with what he wanted. Sometimes he still went out all night, sometimes he came home drunk. We rowed about housework, and what programmes to watch on TV. But when we weren't rowing, we were laughing; he always knew how to make me smile. And even when Paul and I were rowing, it was a relief not to be thinking about Adam or court cases. I was still wrangling with social services to get hold of files so that I could start proceedings, but everyday life was taking my mind off it all.

On 7 February, while lying in bed, familiar clenching pains gripped my tummy and I knew the contractions had started. It was two months before the due date, I was thirty weeks pregnant, and I was terrified.

'What if I lose the baby?' I cried to Paul as he tried to calm me down.

'You won't,' he kept saying.

I tried desperately to remain positive as I held back the tears. We jumped into a taxi and he held my hand as I twisted in agony on the back seat.

'Stop the car!' I yelled. 'I need to be sick!'

'No, we need to keep going,' ordered Paul. 'The baby is on the way.'

'It'll be a fifty-pound fine for a clean-up if you don't stop,' moaned the driver.

'I'm not paying that!' I said. 'Stop the car.'

He pulled over as I stepped outside and sucked in the fresh air, instantly feeling better. Then we got going again. By the time we reached the hospital, the pains had become agonizing, and as I was taken to a room and examined, I noticed the worried looks on the midwife's face. She said she needed to get a doctor, who arrived shortly after and began pushing and prodding my bump as I writhed around on the bed in agony.

'You need an emergency C-section,' he said. 'The baby is in a breech position.'

He didn't need to say it. I had known that something wasn't quite right and I could feel that the baby was in an awkward position; Louise had been breech, but it didn't feel the same this time round. But hearing the doctor say it sent a wave of panic through me. 'Just keep my baby safe,' I whispered as the tears ran down my cheeks.

I'd never held anyone's hand so hard, as Paul ran alongside the trolley. Lying on my back watching the lights overhead, I was beside myself with pain and fear.

'Don't let the baby die,' I sobbed. What if my dreams of being a good mum came to nothing again? I couldn't bear the thought.

Just an hour later, I was lying on my back as my new daughter was pulled screaming into the world. She arrived at 9.50 a.m., on a Monday morning – strangely, exactly the same time of day, and day of the week, as her sister Louise had done. Tears slid down my face as I waited for her to be cleaned and I was wheeled into a room with Paul, dressed in a green cap and gown, holding our little bundle in his arms.

'Here she is,' he whispered.

As he placed the blanket with our baby into the crook of my tired arms, I felt a rush of love and devotion I'd never experienced before. Looking down, I could see tiny fingers and a pair of big dark eyes like my own peering back at me, and I knew, absolutely knew, that I would do anything for her.

'I will never ever let anyone hurt you,' I whispered, trembling. Those words felt so powerful. Words I'd longed to hear from my own parents but had always been denied.

This is what it's supposed to feel like, I thought. *This is it.*

Our beautiful daughter, who we named Chloe, had to stay in the special care unit for a few weeks before being transferred to the neonatal unit, and she was in hospital for almost three months altogether. I was allowed to stay in hospital with her for the first few nights, but then I was sent home and Paul and I would arrive early each morning to sit by her side, or he would drop me off and come back after work. To begin with she was on a respirator and fed through a tube, but once she was able to breathe on her own and have a bottle, the midwives helped me to feed her and bathe her, and I was happy to pretend to be a first-time mum, soaking up all I needed to know to give my baby the best.

Then, finally, one day the doctors arrived and said we would be able to take our little bundle home with us, so we packed up all her things and headed away from the hospital that had become a second home to us. We went back to Tasha's before we moved into our new flat nearby in Dagenham a few weeks later. It was a massive two-bedroom place in a high-rise. As I was a care-leaver now on benefits, the social services gave me an Argos catalogue and told me to choose what I wanted to furnish it with. For once I felt very lucky. Soon we were living in a lovely flat with our beautiful baby girl and lots of new furniture around. It felt wonderful. This was how life was supposed to be.

For the first time in my entire life I felt as though I belonged where I was. I was almost giddy with happiness and contentment.

I had my baby, my man, and at long last a flat of my own. It was all I could do to stop from pinching myself every morning.

But life was still far from perfect. I was finding it hard relying so heavily on Paul as he was bringing in the only wage with his job as a removal man. And being a full-time dad wasn't something he found easy. Paul went out drinking a lot still, and didn't help out much with Chloe. She was the apple of both our eyes but when it came to the everyday stuff like nappy-changing, feeding, washing and housework, Paul wasn't interested. He often left me alone to cope while he went out boozing with his mates.

Every night I was up, feeding Chloe, then exhausted in the day. Paul would leave for work without so much as making a cup of tea. The day was a whirlwind of nappies, washing and feeds, and as much as I loved making sure Chloe was happy, I needed a break sometimes. Paul would come home, bolt down his dinner and, by the time I was giving Chloe a bath, he'd already be downing his first pint.

We rowed furiously when he got back, often with me losing my temper and him storming off to bed. But the next day we always forgave one another. We always seemed to be able to put it behind us. After all I'd been through, I didn't care about the rows or whether he helped or not. It was enough to know that he was there and that he was staying.

When Chloe was six months old, we were having a ferocious row about something petty like washing up, when Paul started laughing.

'Oh, stuff it!' he said, trying to lighten the mood. 'Let's just get married.'

Despite my anger, I found myself laughing too.

'You nutter!' I cried. 'Go on, then!'

And so, on my eighteenth birthday, I married Paul at Barking and Dagenham register office, with a party to celebrate afterwards. We decided to have our reception at home. Word soon spread about the party we were having as the music boomed from our flat, and before long, the entire house was filled with banging tunes and half the neighbourhood. It was less an intimate affair with friends and family and more like a riot! Mum came along, but it was all too much for her. She stood in the kitchen, hiding, stayed to watch us cut the cake, and then left. I knew she was struggling at the time. She'd had a recent spell in hospital and had met a dodgy boyfriend in there. He was also mentally ill and briefly moved in with Mum. Mum rang me around this time in tears to say that Kim, our German Shepherd dog, had died.

It turned out later that Mum's boyfriend had been injecting Kim with orange juice. I was absolutely cut up as I'd loved that dog when I was at home. But I couldn't blame Mum. As usual, she had no idea what was going on and thankfully she soon broke up with her deranged boyfriend.

I was touched that Mum had come along for a while as I knew how big a deal it was for her. But once she'd left, I was pleased that I could put everything to do with my family to the back of my mind for what was left of my big day.

This whole new life felt a world away from the care system, the court cases and everything else. I knew through Tasha and her old mates in Stevenage that Adam would be getting out soon after serving just over a year or so, but I decided not to dwell on that and to enjoy life instead. I wanted to concentrate on Chloe and Paul. Life was far from perfect, but then again, it was also a world away from being abused by Adam. I was a mum, Chloe needed me, and that was all that mattered now. After all, he didn't know where I was any more. For the first time in my life I could breathe easy, feel safe – even if I knew that I'd not got proper justice for what he'd done.

Despite the fact that we were now married, mine and Paul's relationship didn't improve. I knew Paul loved me and, most of the time, just having him to rely on was enough. But occasionally Paul's drunken nights out would really get to me and I wished he would just grow up.

Then, when Chloe was just over a year old, I did something that was textbook stupid. I made myself fall pregnant again to try and 'save' the relationship. Looking back now, I think that it was a crazy thing to do, but I thought that having the two kids would somehow make us even more of a 'proper' family. Maybe it'd give Paul more of an incentive to grow up. Paul was shocked, but said he'd stand by me regardless of our rocky relationship. The pregnancy sped by and soon I was giving birth to a little boy, whom we named Matthew. Again, I felt the surge of maternal love, just like before. And I was bowled over. Now I had a girl and a boy, the perfect combination.

'Our family is complete,' I said to Paul.

The look on his face said it all: absolute pride and joy.

But our happiness wasn't to last. When Matthew was five days old, we'd both been awake all night with him screaming. The poor thing had terrible colic. As usual, Paul stayed in bed, while I was up and down, trying everything to soothe Matthew. I felt so exhausted, I would have done anything for a lie-in or for Paul to take a turn.

'Why don't you frigging well help more?' I snapped.

He looked at me, bleary-eyed, and rolled over. 'Got work in the morning,' he muttered. We'd been rowing like crazy towards the end of the pregnancy when my tiredness had kicked in and Paul didn't step up to help with Chloe, and the previous few days since Matthew had arrived had felt unbearable at times. But I knew early days with a baby were hard and that it would be worth it in the end.

But when I got up for Matthew's morning feed, Paul had a face like thunder. 'I'm sorry,' he whispered. I spotted the bag full of clothes in his hand and my heart skipped a beat. 'I can't do this, Terrie. I'm going . . . '

'You what?' I snapped. 'What do you mean?'

'All this aggro, no sleep, I can't do it!' he said.

At that moment I really saw red.

'I just can't do it, Terrie,' he cried. 'Sorry.'

'Good. Just go, then!' I raged. 'You're nothing more than a guest in this house anyway. It's like a hotel where you come to eat and sleep when you're not at work. It's not a family you want. It's a convenience store!' I was sick of Paul coming and going, doing whatever he liked, while I cared for the kids and picked up the mess. But as I heard the door click shut, it felt as though my heart had shattered into a thousand pieces. I didn't want this. I didn't want to be a single parent. I was nineteen and alone again, but this time I had a toddler and a baby to depend on me. I wanted so desperately for them to have a loving mum and dad, the perfect family, something I'd never had. But now that had been taken away from them. After losing two babies, I wanted to do everything in my power to protect Chloe and Matthew, but already I felt that I'd failed my beautiful children.

TWENTY-ONE

Back to Haunt Me

As always, I decided to just get on with things as best I could. I needed to keep my little family going, whatever Paul was doing with his own life. We remained friends and he saw the kids whenever he could when he wasn't working.

I quickly settled into a new routine for myself and the kids, without Paul being there in the mornings or evenings. I got the kids up, took Chloe to nursery, did a few bits and bobs in the shops, then went for a walk before heading home to do the housework. It wasn't a thrilling life, but I did what needed to be done. But it was hard. I missed having Paul around and missed his cuddles, even though I didn't miss the rows. I only saw Tasha or a few mum friends I'd chat to at nursery. I didn't have anyone else. I felt so lonely. Getting by on the benefits wasn't easy either. Paul did his best to help out by giving me extra money, but he was also contributing to rent and bills at his mate's house where he was staying now. Life was tougher than ever.

For once, though, I had nothing else to focus on except my family and that gave me a sense of freedom. I could forget about Adam, the court case, Mum's madness, the past. All I could do was live firmly in the 'here and now', caring for my babies and giving them all the love I never had, and that made me happy. In a way, by loving Chloe and Matthew, I was healing myself.

This new simple, peaceful life wasn't to last, though. One day when Matthew was just a few months old, I was struggling home with some bags of shopping, when I spotted a flash of ginger hair on a man leaving my block of flats.

I didn't register who it was until I reached my front door. A breeze was blowing through, as the door hung half off its hinges. Splinters of wood were scattered by my feet. Someone had come and kicked the whole door in. I knew that Adam had recently been released from prison and I knew that he'd be angry with me for what I'd done. There could only be one explanation for this . . .

My stomach churned, as I fumbled for my mobile phone.

'Paul,' I screamed. 'I think Adam's paid me a visit.'

Paul rushed over and we called the police. 'Adam must've done it,' I said, over and over. He had served just eighteen months. I didn't know where he was or how he'd found out where I was living, but there was no doubt in my mind that it was him.

The police listened sympathetically and took notes, but said that they couldn't press charges unless they found proof. They helped us board up the door and left. That night, Paul stayed with us. He held me tightly as I trembled in bed. I hated Adam for scaring me like that. I might not have had the proof that it was him, but who else could it be? I felt sick to my stomach as I imagined what would have happened if I'd been at home with the kids. But then again, maybe he'd been stalking my flat to see when I was out? I didn't know which was worse.

*

The next day, Paul moved back in. For the first time since we'd got together, I told him I loved him – and I really meant it. He said it back to me and the look in his lovely eyes made me believe he meant it too. It sounds crazy, but that's the way it was between us; we never had to say lots to know what the other one was thinking. And now I felt sure of his feelings, I felt safe enough to tell him about Adam and what he had done. Obviously, he knew some of the story behind the court case, but that night I poured out my heart to him.

He listened intently, sometimes tears sprung into his eyes, sometimes he said nothing and shook his head with horror. Then when I'd finished he grabbed my hands.

'You are amazing, Terrie,' he said simply. 'I can't believe you have got through all of this and emerged into the fantastic mum and strong person you are. I had no idea.'

Samir had been the first person to say this to me, and the first person who had made me begin to believe in my own strength. But with Paul it felt even better. I just welled up with tears and, for the first time, I believed it wholeheartedly. Yes, he was right; I was strong and did the best for our kids, no matter what. I could handle anything on my own, I knew that then. But I also knew that I didn't want to; I wanted Paul by my side. We had got married, had two children, split up, and were now back together. This time I knew it was for keeps.

'But now what are we going to do about Adam?' I asked.

Understandably, Paul wanted to kill him. But I told him to forget that and to focus on moving on with our lives.

'I've dragged him as far as I can through the courts. It was the social services who let me down in the end. But I've done what I can,' I explained.

Paul was incensed at how short his prison sentence was, but realized that it was out of our hands now.

'We have to look to the future now. Finally, I'm free – well, as free as I'll ever be from it,' I said.

Adam, however, had other ideas. Although I found myself always looking over my shoulder, I never saw him. So I tried to carry on as normal, but two days later, when Paul was out at work again and I'd taken the kids to the park, I returned to find the door kicked in again.

This time the police arrived even faster and seemed to take it more seriously. But afterwards I didn't hear anything. Although I had Paul there at night, he was out at work during the day and I was really scared at the thought of Adam turning up one day when the kids and I were at home, so I called the council.

'I know Adam has tracked me down,' I explained. 'Would it be possible for us to move?'

They told me they'd look into it, but I didn't hear back. The whole situation was horrifying. Each time it sent out a clear message to me: I know where you live, and I'm bloody furious. He didn't do anything else except batter the door down; nothing was taken or broken inside. But, then again, he didn't need to. The fact that he was watching to see when I was out and was angry enough to kick my door down in broad daylight was terrifying.

We didn't know what to do. Our neighbours said they never saw anything and the police still insisted that they couldn't arrest him without evidence.

'We have to leave,' I cried to Paul. 'We can't stay here. He's kicked the door in twice. What will he do next?'

Paul was furious. He wanted to protect his family but felt the authorities were letting us all down.

'We shouldn't be forced out,' he said.

Then, a week later, just like Groundhog Day, I returned from dropping Chloe off at nursery to find the door smashed in yet again.

Again, I rang the council and begged them for help.

'Please,' I said. 'The door has been kicked in three times in two weeks. We don't know what to expect next.'

They agreed to help us find somewhere to rent privately. So, the next day, I packed up as fast as possible and we drove back to Stevenage, leaving Dagenham behind. It was a quick decision to go there. Tasha had told me that she had heard through her old mates that Adam had left the area, and it was the only place I knew well. The downside, though, was that Paul would have to leave his job in Dagenham and try to find another one. But even he didn't care by now, he just wanted us to be safe. So much for our fresh start.

We arrived back in Stevenage with a few suitcases, the kids' buggy and little else. We were so desperate to get away from there and take the kids somewhere they would be safe that we left pretty much everything else, including the furniture behind.

'Right,' said Paul, determined to put a brave face on it. 'This really is our fresh start.'

In a way, I was pleased to be back. Although I had few happy memories, it was an area I knew well and it felt good to be back there with my new family now. Mum was still there, living in the same house I'd grown up in. The only lodger she had now was Pervy Pat.

I rarely heard from Mum, or Fraggle, as I still called her. Now I was older and a mum myself, I understood even less how she could have treated me so indifferently as a kid. I blamed her mental illness; it was the only explanation, and easier for me to cope with than the thought that she just didn't care.

After settling into our new flat, a small, run-down two-bedroom place nearby my old estate, we went to visit Mum to tell her that we were back. I hoped the council would find us a bigger place fast, as our new place was nowhere near big enough for a family of four. By now Paul had had to sign on the dole. He had been looking for work, but nothing was around at the time.

As we knocked on the door to Mum's house, all the painful memories came flooding back. We heard her shuffle towards the door, and then she opened it and just stood there, dressed in a nightie and ripped cardigan, staring at me blankly; she didn't even look at Chloe or Matthew.

'Where's Pat?' I asked, straightaway.

'Upstairs,' said Mum. Neither one of us had even said hello.

'Right, well, that pervert stays well away from my kids at all times, do you understand?' I said.

I stepped inside, and for a moment I felt faint and had to grip hold of Paul to steady myself. The smell of the house hit me immediately. Paul looked at me as if to ask me silently if I was okay, and he squeezed my shoulder reassuringly as I nodded and we walked through to the living room. I kept a very tight grip of Chloe's hand, while Paul pushed Matthew inside in his buggy.

I'd already told Paul about Mum and Pat. He was appalled, quite rightly, but also I think a little bit curious as to what they were like. He accepted me, warts and all, and he accepted my mad family too, even though it was a million miles from the nice family environment he'd been bought up in.

I looked around the house. The same sofa, the same dresser, the same wallpaper. All the same from my childhood. Just the sight and smells of the place turned my stomach. It was even dirtier than usual. Piles of washing-up lay in the sink and the whole place smelt musty. Pat mainly did the shopping, but I was sure he didn't do much for Mum. She seemed worn out, her hair was even more of a frizzy mess than usual and her clothes smelt of urine. She didn't look like she had anyone looking after her at all.

I stuck the kettle on and made Mum a cup of tea and we chatted for a bit.

'Are you okay?' I asked her.

'Yes,' she said, her eyes blank.

I didn't know what to say. I didn't know how to help her. I hated the fact that Pervy Pat was still hanging around, but it was her house and I couldn't tell her what to do.

After a fairly awkward half-hour of small talk from us and one-word answers from Mum, I said goodbye with a heavy heart. Despite it all, all the abuse and horror, Mum was still a vulnerable person, in need of someone to look after her. I decided to ring social services to make sure she had carers coming in.

After our move back, I threw myself into being a full-time mum as much as possible. I loved making sure the kids were fed, clean and cared for. I loved tucking them up in bed at night and reading them stories. I was hoping to settle Chloe into a new nursery as well soon.

Sometimes, when Chloe had a nightmare, I'd just hold her close to me, stroking her hair.

'Mummy will never ever let anyone hurt you,' I soothed.

She would often bury her head into my neck and say, 'I love you, Mummy', and my heart melted every time.

Those words felt like magic to me. I was giving my children the childhood I had never had; they would grow up knowing what it felt like to love and be loved. Gradually, the old wounds began to heal.

But at the same time, watching my children's innocence, I felt a white-hot anger brewing inside of me. When I thought of how social services had let me down I couldn't contain my rage any longer. I thought about how, ever since I was very young, the authorities who were paid to protect me just passed the buck. And I was plagued by the idea that they were probably doing the very same thing to other children who desperately needed their help at that very moment. I hated the idea that they had allowed my childhood to be stolen from me, and became determined that I would do everything in my power to stop it from happening again.

One morning, after putting Matthew down for his nap, I grabbed the phone and rang the social services.

'I'd like to make a complaint,' I said. 'Against the children's department about my upbringing in care.'

A bored-sounding lady took down my details and said she'd get back to me. I replaced the receiver feeling a little better. Now I'd got the ball rolling I was determined to try and get some sort of justice. I'd only talked about it before, made plans in my mind, but what with having the babies, splitting with Paul, and Adam returning, it wasn't something I could follow through with. Now I was telling them and I knew how slowly the social services operated, but this time I was willing to wait.

As always happened in my life, just as things had begun to tick along nicely, something else came along to knock me sideways. I got the results of a smear test and it was abnormal. Tests revealed the cells were one step away from being cancerous.

'The risk of cervical cancer is raised if you have lots of sexual partners or if you began having sex at an early age,' explained the doctor.

Once again, I felt myself boiling with rage. I'd been forced into having regular sex from the age of ten. Now, at nineteen, I was facing cancer. Once again I was having to live with the consequences of Adam's actions.

'Okay, what do I need to do?' I asked, thinking of my kids. I just had to get better, there was no other option.

I was given a barrage of tests and had to have the cells removed by laser, which was painful and horrible. While it was being done, I just prayed that it would work and that it would get rid of the risk completely. I had to be there for my kids. The treatment was awful. Every week for three weeks I had to have the laser burned into my cervix and was given two types of medication, which made me feel so sick. Several times the hospital asked me to stay in overnight but I always refused. I never wanted to leave the kids even for a single night.

Paul was my rock throughout the whole ordeal. He couldn't believe I had to go through this now either, on top of everything else. But I refused to feel sorry for myself for long. I just wanted it over with so that I could get on with my life.

Of course, with the diagnosis and treatments, I forgot about pursuing my case with the social services. Once again my fight against social services would have to be put on the back burner.

As I recovered from my treatment, Mum's situation seemed to go from bad to worse. She'd started to panic when she went into shops, so could no longer even go and pick up a few bits from the newsagent's. She'd become even more vacant, stopped doing even the smallest household tasks, and become very moody. Although she was still being looked after by a mental health team, she wasn't doing very well on a day-to-day basis. Paul would get her bits of shopping and check in on her while I was in hospital and having my treatments. But she started to turn up at our house more often.

She liked to see the kids, although I never let her be on her own with them. I didn't think she would hurt them, exactly, but I didn't trust her. Mum's only way of showing them any real affection was to give them expensive presents. She'd ask Chloe what she wanted and buy it. Once, she turned up with a really expensive doll's house based on Chloe's favourite kids' TV programme, *Balamory*.

She also wasn't allowed to be 'Nanny' to them. I didn't think she deserved such an important title, and she wasn't able to look after them like a normal nan would. So I told Chloe that she could call her 'Fraggle' and that she was like a 'friend' to her. I didn't mind Mum having a relationship with them, but it had to be on my terms.

One day, Mum turned up, and instead of the usual blank look on her face, she was in floods of tears.

'I can't do it anymore,' she sobbed, covering her face in her hands. I'd never seen her like this before, not since Dad had died.

'Mum?' I asked. I sat next to her, I could feel her trembling.

'What's happened?' Paul had overheard and joined us on the sofa. 'You can tell us,' he said, gently.

I loved the way Paul was around my mum. He knew our history, but he always treated her with respect, like a small child who needed looking after.

We listened as she told us how Pervy Pat was up to his old tricks again. Except that this time he wasn't targeting little kids, he was using Mum as his victim. Taking pictures of her and even forcing himself on her.

Once again, a familiar feeling of nausea washed over me. Despite it being her own house, even Mum wasn't protected from the perverted goings-on there. She was being abused in her own home. And even though never once had she protected me, it was my instinct to try and help her now.

'Right, that's it,' I snapped. 'It's about time Pervy Pat got his comeuppance. I want him out of your house.'

Mum looked at me, all confused.

'But how?' she asked.

'I'm going to look after you now,' I said loudly, as if talking to a deaf person who could only lip read.

We let Mum stay over, always careful, though, not to leave her alone with Chloe and Matthew. Then I called the police.

Immediately, they took my complaint seriously and sent an officer to go and search the property. I told them to look out for perverted pictures dating from the 1980s. Finally, something was being done, even though, as usual, it was me instigating it. But the next day, they called me to say they'd drawn a blank.

'We can't find anything at all,' they said. They had kept Pat in custody overnight, in order to give them time to gather more evidence. They wanted to search his room more thoroughly and to question him about my allegations. I'd already told Paul the whole sorry story, so he said he'd go round there himself to help find Pat's disgusting stash. Mum handed him her keys. A look of relief that something was being done passed across her eyes.

I went with Paul, but couldn't face being in Pervy Pat's room, so I left him to it.

'You need rubber gloves and a gas mask,' I tried to joke.

Within ten minutes of rooting through his bedroom, Paul came downstairs, pale-faced and holding a cardboard box of sordid photos. He'd found it under the bed.

'I can't quite believe what I am seeing,' he said. 'It's revolting.'

One by one, Paul picked up Polaroid snap after snap, of various members of my family over the years, all in a state of undress. It was like a pornographic 'who's who' of my relations.

There were some of Liz, bending over with her skirt over her head. Of Nan, looking startled as she climbed out of the bath. Of Nan half holding her towel down, exposing a wrinkly boob, looking startled at the flash. All of them had handwritten 'receipts' on the back, in Pervy Pat's writing. He'd paid them around £50 a shot. Then there were a few of me, aged six, shyly trying to scramble into my knickers after a morning bath. I turned my head.

'We've got to call the police,' I said to Paul, unable to bear it any longer. I dialled the number of the station in Stevenage and they came over instantly.

The policemen left with the haul, thanking Paul for his help.

Paul was silent with shock as we got the bus home. We both felt quite enraged that the police hadn't bothered looking properly the first time, but then again, Pat's stinky bedroom was such a minefield, unless you knew where he hid things, and it needed someone with a strong stomach. Even so, they obviously hadn't tried very hard.

'Seeing those pictures of you as a small child really brought it home,' Paul said quietly. Later, he told me about the other hideous items he'd found in there including see-through clothing and children's knickers. The revolting man had even kept a pair of my old underwear I'd had as a ten-year-old.

'It's just disgusting,' said Paul, shaking his head sadly. 'Horrible, dirty old pervert festering in that room for sixteen years. Well, his secret is out now, isn't it?'

'You don't know the half of it,' I said, thinking of Pat dribbling, his eyeball up against the bathroom door trying to catch a glimpse of my naked flesh. Urgh. Even today the memories of him make my skin crawl.

I hadn't been in his bedroom for years and I didn't want to even think about what else might lay lurking in it. The thought made me shudder.

But, now that Pat was out of the house, albeit temporarily while he was held in custody, Paul and I decided that we should take the plunge. The council wouldn't let Mum move in with us, so we decided to move in with her instead. This was a big decision for me as the last thing I wanted to do was to move back to the house where such terrible memories existed. Just stepping over the threshold brought them straight to my mind. But Mum couldn't look after herself anymore and the council had made it clear that they wouldn't give us anywhere bigger any time soon, so it seemed to be the answer to all our problems. It was also the perfect way to make sure that Pat stayed away. Some distant relatives, who I didn't know very well, got in touch when they heard what we were doing.

'He's an old man,' one said in a phone call. 'You can't just kick him out.'

By now Pat was living on people's sofas, whoever would give him room.

'We didn't,' I replied. 'The police arrested him for being a pervert.'

I was disgusted that they were sticking up for him. They wouldn't listen to my accusations so I gave up. 'If he needs someone to look after him, you do it then,' I stated matter-of-factly. 'He's not our problem anymore.'

After we had moved our suitcases in, I put on a pair of rubber gloves and gave some to Paul.

'Right,' I said. 'The only way I could exist in these four walls again is if everything is gutted . . . '

Paul looked at me in surprise. 'What do you mean everything?' he said.

'Everything means everything,' I replied.

We started with Pervy Pat's room. As I opened the door, images of my childhood and rifling through his things came flooding back. How anyone could wander into this room and not believe the man who lived in it wasn't some major weirdo I didn't know. The walls were covered in 3D posters of Disney characters, including Minnie Mouse and Betty Boop – hardly the sort of thing you imagine seeing in an old man's bedroom.

There were hundreds of Corgi cars still in their boxes pinned to the walls. Bric-a-brac, including dozens of dusty ornaments of naked women, lined every surface. He was also obsessed with Princess Diana and had plates, mugs, calendars, posters and silver spoons with her face beaming from every one. Paul pulled out a collection of yellowing magazines from under his bed. It was full of pictures of naked men and women with big hair and moustaches, porn from the 1960s and 1970s.

Paul managed to laugh as he flicked through them.

'Wow,' he said. 'Vintage porn!'

He shoved them all in the bin bag.

'At least the pictures are of adults,' I muttered.

There was children's clothing strewn everywhere and the Coca-Cola sleeping bag I always had as a child was lying open on his bed. He'd taken it and used it to sleep in himself. When I picked it up, the filthy brown sheet underneath was crawling with tiny black bugs.

'Urgh!' I cried, recoiling backwards.

Paul looked over my shoulder.

'Blimey!' he shuddered. 'He slept on that?'

Together we grabbed the sheet, screwed it up, and binned it.

'All this gets burned,' I said grimly.

In his room were sixteen years worth of things he'd collected and never once cleaned.

'Ewww, what's this?' I said, putting my hand on a tissue under the bed. Wrapped inside was some weird sex toy that was like nothing I'd ever seen before. I started laughing as I waved it at Paul.

'It's Pervy Pat's little friend,' I said, half laughing, waving it at Paul. If I hadn't laughed I would have cried and I'd already done enough of that. Once again I felt sick as I opened a bin bag and dropped it in. But however disgusted I felt by it all, I also had a strange sense of power as I was the one in control now; I wasn't being chased around the house by his Polaroid camera. This time I was here to get rid of Pervy Pat and his disgusting filth for good.

I looked up and noticed that Paul was looking quite upset and had tears in his eyes.

'You okay?' I asked. His lips were set in a grim line. His face was white as porcelain.

He nodded. 'I'm just so flaming angry on your behalf, Terrie. You had to live next door to this heap of filth with this horrible old man throughout your whole childhood. It's not right . . . ' His voice tailed off, choked with emotion.

I put down the bin bag I was holding and squeezed his arm. 'Yes, you're right,' I said. 'But now you can help me by clearing the bastard out. Let's burn the lot in the garden.'

We literally pulled Pervy Pat's room apart and then piled up the collection of rubbish, clothes and ornaments in the garden. After a few hours, the job was done.

'Phew,' said Paul, wiping away the sweat from his forehead with the back of his hand. 'That was a serious amount of absolute filth.'

'In every sense of the word,' I replied.

But I didn't want to stop there. I knew that the only way I could live with my children in this house was to pull it apart bit by bit and remove any trace of my childhood. As it stood, it was stuck in a time warp.

So, for the next few weeks, we carried on. I stripped all the units off the walls, all of Dad's brass ornaments, including the big plates, swords crossed above the door, all the cupboards, the stinking sofa, all the fly papers still stuck to the ceiling, the bedding, the beds, the cushions, everything. I only kept a few family photos and Mum's clothes.

When all the big items were piled in the garden, waiting to be burned, I started on the wallpaper, ripping it off in satisfying strips.

'Even the wallpaper?' asked Paul.

'Most definitely the wallpaper,' I replied, thinking of Dad's horrible brown paper in his bedroom.

It took eight weeks, and it was exhausting, but we managed to completely gut the whole house. Then Paul threw some petrol on top of the piles of stuff we'd gathered in the garden and set it alight. Watching the flames curl into the sky was one of the best sights of my life. I'd done it. I'd returned, reclaimed the house, and got rid of the setting where so much of the sexual, physical and mental abuse took place. Where the loss of my childhood began and never ended.

If only Dad could see me now, I thought, as his brass plates turned black with soot.

Someone from the council came round to see it afterwards. I'd rung them beforehand and told them what I was doing. They knew that I'd have to somehow pay for the decoration and repairs myself afterwards, so they didn't seem to mind.

'Wow,' he said, marvelling at the bare walls. 'I've never seen any house quite like this. It's quite a feat!'

'Yes, it is,' I said quietly, knowing he had no real understanding of why I'd done this.

'It's saved the council a fortune in repairs,' he enthused. 'The place was a bit of a pit beforehand anyway.'

'You can say that again,' I replied.

TWENTY-TWO

Starting Over

Once again, we had nothing and had to start from scratch and, with little money, it was difficult. We were both living off benefits now and didn't have a stick of furniture. However, I couldn't have had it any other way. The stinky carpets, Dad's trinkets, and all evidence of Pat had finally disappeared. Thank God. Now everything had been stripped from the house, I thought the sense of relief would last. That the memories would be erased. But I was wrong. The following night after our fire, I found myself feeling panicky as I walked into the bathroom to brush my teeth before bed.

I stared at myself in the mirror above the sink. We hadn't removed all the bathroom suite as it would have been too expensive to replace, so there were bits and pieces still left from my childhood, including this mirror. As I gazed into my reflection, behind me it felt as though Dad was there. Looking over my shoulder, I threw my toothbrush in the sink and ran back downstairs, trembling.

'It's like he's haunting me,' I sobbed to Paul. 'Looking over my shoulder! All the memories are still here. In the walls, in the smell of the place!'

He held me tight. Part of me couldn't believe I'd ended up back where I'd started. The terrible irony of choosing to move back with my own children to a house I'd been determined to escape wasn't lost on me. But we'd made the decision and I was determined to make a good home for my kids too. They deserved nothing less. Paul did his best, bless him, but it was hard. We managed to buy some paint and Paul started redecorating. One day, I had the idea of building a wall to separate the living room and the kitchen. But as soon as he'd built it, I told him to tear it down again.

'Sorry,' I said. 'It just feels so claustrophobic now!'

Thankfully, Paul was patient with me and simply tried to help. Picking up a mallet, he started knocking the wall down, once again creating more dust.

'I just want you to feel better,' he sighed.

I was convinced that I could still smell the hideous stink from Pat's room. I scrubbed the walls and the floor with every type of cleaning product and bleach, but the stench seemed to be in the fabric of the brickwork.

About eight months later, Pervy Pat's court date came up and he was appearing at Stevenage Magistrates Court, charged with possession of indecent pictures. Determined to go along and watch justice taking place, we went for his sentencing after he had pleaded guilty.

I was pleased that he'd owned up to it, but then again, with such damning evidence, he had little choice. The box of pictures with his writing on it was under his bed. There was no way he was getting away with it now. Paul and I found ourselves standing right next to him in the waiting room. I stared at him. He looked stooped, even older than his years, and very sorry for himself. As always, he had a wet patch of dribble down his jumper. 'Dribbler,' I could hear my voice taunting him from years earlier. He didn't dare glance up in my direction. He just sat there, looking like a lonely, sad old man.

We walked into the courtroom to hear him plead guilty. I couldn't wait to hear his sentence, but wish that I'd not bothered staying to listen. Despite it all, the judge handed him a suspended sentence. Due to his age and ill health he wasn't considered fit for prison.

I fought back tears as we left. 'What kind of justice is that?' I said to Paul. Once again he agreed. But the law of the land has tariffs for these kinds of crimes and, sadly, they are not very long sentences. People with driving or tax evasion offences would get longer inside. However, finally, it was over. Pervy Pat was no longer in the house, Mum was safe and Pat now had the criminal record he deserved. I managed to get Chloe into a lovely school nearby and Paul started working again as a removal man. Things were looking up for once.

Dealing with Mum didn't get any easier, though. The only way she could live with us was if I became her full-time carer, so I did. I had hated caring for her when I was a child, but now I was older I felt a bit more resilient. The only way I could bear it was by treating her with the same respect I would any invalid, and by not viewing her or treating her as my mum. That way I could stop expecting any kind of maternal care from her, care I'd never received anyway. Events from my past were always on my mind, and now, with Pat's court case, I was having to confront them again. And that meant confronting her own role in it all, even if it was just a passive one.

After Pat pleaded guilty, I tried to talk to her about our past. I wanted her to acknowledge some of it. I needed her to say 'I was wrong, I'm sorry.' I thought that would help me move on.

'You know he deserved to get locked up,' I explained. 'He took so many filthy pictures of me, and you let him.'

'It wasn't like that,' she kept saying. She looked confused, frowning, as if trying to remember details.

'You were the mum in the house,' I said, trying not to lose my temper. 'And he took perverted pictures of me.'

Mum looked as if she was about to burst into tears, then her features changed again, as though a veil had been drawn across her face.

'I just don't remember,' she said helplessly.

I grew so angry. To hear her refuse to face up to all the pain and hurt I experienced throughout my childhood was too much.

'You don't remember?' I cried. 'Well, how lucky you are, then! You can rest assured that I'll never forget any of it.'

But she looked at me blankly again. I wanted to scream but knew there was little point. Although she was genuinely mentally ill, it felt as if she was hiding behind her condition. She had doctors and pills to protect her. What did I have? Nothing. I had to face the truth, alone as usual, while Mum refused to help. I could see that I would never get the apology from her that I so desperately needed.

Day-to-day life soon took over again and with two kids, it was, of course, non-stop. Instead of brooding over Mum and her refusal to admit anything, I pushed it to the back of my mind. Once I stopped wanting her to say sorry, or to own up to what had happened, things grew easier. I just needed to make sure she was safe, fed and clean. I was still her daughter and I saw it as my duty.

I suppose I did love her, in a way. Not as a 'mum' figure, but just as a person who had always been in my life in some way or another.

A year after our move, we'd managed to redecorate the house, but I still found it hard to settle. The slightest resemblance to how it had looked when I was a child sent me into a blind panic. I even refused to allow Paul or Mum to dry any washing on the radiators because, back then, Mum was always drying stuff and it brought back childhood memories again. Once, Paul casually hung up a coat on the back of the door and I just lost it.

'Take it down!' I cried, knocking it off. 'We always had hundreds of coats hanging up everywhere and I hate it.'

I knew I sounded over the top. But if I had to live in a house full of memories, I wanted nothing inside to resemble the family home where so much misery had taken place. Our coats hang neatly in a cupboard now.

Try as I did to settle, though, I was becoming almost neurotic about 'not being reminded of back then'. So we applied to the council for new accommodation. But they refused. They told me we'd made ourselves 'intentionally homeless' by leaving the place in Dagenham when Adam had kicked our door in three times. It was all so unfair. I felt so trapped, like a caged animal in a mental torture chamber. Dad's 'ghost' seemed to follow me around; however hard we scrubbed, we could never quite get rid of the smell and the house always seemed cold to me. But, according to the council, I'd just have to put up with it.

Six years passed, and during that time I had been a carer for Mum and my kids were growing up into wonderful little people. Paul and I were still together too, despite our ups and downs, and, luckily for me, my health was still good.

But gradually I had been feeling my longing for justice returning. I had time to think and this time I was in a place where I could take action and follow it up. Chloe was now eight years old, approaching the age I'd been when I'd ended up in care. In some ways, when I looked at my own daughter, it made my past feel even worse. She was so young, so innocent and naïve. Things I was never allowed to be. I was forced into having sex at the age of ten. I was pregnant by the age of eleven. I was a mum by thirteen. I'd watch her laughing on her bike with her friends outside and listen to their childish games with dolls, and it made my heart want to break. She was nothing like I'd been at that age, when I was already used to Dad abusing me. And thank God she wasn't. But watching her innocence also fuelled my anger. How dare the authorities, who were supposed to care for me, let me down so incredibly badly? How could social services have allowed me to stay with Adam so often? Why was I given the responsibility for whether action could be taken against him or not when anyone could have seen how scared of him I was? It was all too much.

One evening, when the kids were safely tucked up in bed asleep, I sat down with Paul and brought up the subject again.

'I just want people to sit up and listen,' I said. 'I want social services to admit that they neglected me.'

'It'll mean going to court again,' said Paul. 'I'm guessing it won't be easy . . .'

'I know that,' I said. 'But I have to try and prevent any other kids going through what I went through. I want them to learn from their mistakes.'

'I'm a hundred per cent behind you,' Paul added.

He reached out and squeezed my hand as we turned back to

the TV. But I couldn't concentrate on any of it. My mind was racing now about how I was going to start my fight. How I was going to seek this justice. I couldn't wait to get started.

The first step I needed to take was to get hold of all my social services records. They'd sent a few last time, but this time I wanted all of them, no questions asked. I called the department again and said that I wanted to make a complaint, but also that I'd like to get hold of the records too. Over the years, hundreds of documents had been drawn up concerning me. I wanted to look through them properly so that I could prove where they had gone wrong.

After applying in writing, I waited and waited, but nothing showed up. It took eight months of phone calls and more letters before the files arrived. When they did, they weren't in proper date order. It was a chaotic mess and very difficult to understand.

Reading through some of my notes brought back the memories. All the way through, one name had been consistently 'blanked' out: the name of Adam. The only reason I could think of for why they had done this was to protect themselves. After all, if they admitted that they were aware that Adam was 'on the scene' since I was ten, and was the father of my baby, too, and had even jotted it down in my files, they'd have to admit responsibility for a big failure of care. They'd have to admit that they'd allowed him back in my life time and time again.

So, after sifting through the files and getting nowhere, I gave up and decided that I knew exactly where they'd gone wrong anyway. I sat down to write my letter. Point by point I jotted down paragraphs of how social services had failed to protect me when I was at my most vulnerable.

I told them how my dad was a known sex offender and had

been imprisoned after fathering my half-sister's child, and yet somehow I was still allowed to be brought up in his care. I wrote about how my mum went into a mental hospital when I was seven and I was left to fend for myself, cooking and cleaning. How I then went to live with Liz and no proper checks were made to see whether or not I had adequate accommodation and a healthy lifestyle. I also pointed out how I'd had no counselling following my abortion, and if I had received help, I might not have become pregnant again. Then I asked why the police didn't press charges against Adam and why I was pressured into signing a statement, despite being threatened by him. Once I had typed it all out, I felt bubbles of anger rising in my chest again.

I reread the letter a few times, tears springing to my eyes. It was a catalogue of errors, really. A terrible string of mistakes, let-downs and failures by the police and social services and I had been just a little girl stuck in the middle of it. Abused by men all along the way. My childhood ruined. As I dropped it in the letter box, I silently hoped this would be the start of some proper justice. But after Pervy Pat's and Adam's sentences, I wondered if it was ever possible?

A few weeks later, social services called back and said they were taking the matter seriously and would be speaking to their solicitor about my case and, a couple of months later, I was invited to a meeting with some managers.

As I walked into the room, I found myself feeling like the young child I had once been. Three people in smart suits sat behind a desk as I sat in front of them. I could feel them looking me up and down as they shuffled papers and put reading glasses on.

'Now, Terrie,' said one, 'your case has been examined very closely.'

I leaned forward in my chair.

'Our solicitor has looked over all the facts and figures and, yes, the social services department must be held to account for some of the failures in looking after you in care . . . '

Part of me wanted to leap from the chair. I couldn't believe they were admitting it so quickly, but then again, it was all there in black and white where they'd failed me. How could they deny it?

'And you will be compensated accordingly,' they said.

This had never been about the money for me. But, with our house still desperately needing decorating, I also didn't want to turn anything down.

'How much compensation were you looking for?' one man said, peering over his glasses.

I shifted uncomfortably in my seat. This wasn't the way I had imagined things going. I wanted them to admit their failings and tell me it would never ever happen again. I wanted them to tell me who the managers were who had made these terrible decisions about me, and I wanted them to be sacked or disciplined. But all they wanted to talk about was money.

'Erm, I don't know,' I stammered. 'If I did get any money, it would be for my children, for the house. It's in a disgusting state and I've asked to move as it brings back so many bad memories.'

They all nodded in unison, scribbling notes, making me feel like a money-grabber.

I wanted to shout, 'This is not about the money!' But no sound came out. I didn't want to turn down anything either. They kept conferring among themselves and asking me questions about money, and then as quickly as it had started, the meeting was over. I left feeling so unsatisfied. A million new things I wanted to say flitted through my mind as I got the bus home. Was I really just going to be offered money and nothing else?

Back home, Paul chatted it through with me. We both knew money would make a big difference to the kids and our lives. In fact, it would be a godsend. But no amount of money would change what I'd been through. And how much money did they think I deserved? What I really wanted was a day in court, a chance to stand up and tell the world how they'd failed me and for them to say sorry, not a wad of cash, money designed to shut me up.

A few weeks later, I got another letter from the solicitor. It explained that if my case went to court, the social services might have to pay out thousands of pounds for the defence, and if I lost, I might not get a penny. So they were willing to pay me some money up front. It would be £15,000. To my little family this was an enormous sum of money. It all seemed so final, and still wasn't the result I wanted. But could we really turn it down and risk losing a sum that could change all our lives for the better? I was still desperate to redecorate again after we'd lost the chance to find a new place. There was no prospect of us moving any time soon and I still felt desperate to change our house anyway we could afford to. I couldn't work, as I had to care for Mum full-time. I received a carer's allowance, and Paul wasn't bringing much money home. It was a horrible decision to make. I talked it through with Paul and with a heavy heart we both agreed to take the money.

A few days later, a meeting was set up for me to go to a room at the offices of Hertfordshire County Council, to be handed the compensation. I knocked on a door leading off a long corridor and was ushered in by an official-looking man in a suit with a wonky tie. He barely looked at me as he pushed a piece of paper across the desk.

'We want you to sign this to state that you will never sue us again,' he said, matter-of-factly.

I picked up the pen and paused. I didn't know why this was an issue. I didn't plan to sue them again but, at the same time, I still had so many questions. Why were the people involved in my case not held to account? Was anyone going to investigate the failings? Could this happen again? I took a sharp, silent breath and scribbled my name on the paper. Then I dropped the pen as if it was a hot coal. Without saying a word, he handed me the cheque. As I took the slip of paper, a familiar sickness lurched over me. I felt dirty, contaminated. As if all the disgusting things that had happened to me were happening all over again. I was being bought, sold off. All the horrors and all the let-downs were for this measly piece of paper. Outside, I broke down in tears, handing Paul the cheque. I didn't want to touch it.

'Is that all my life is worth?' I sobbed. 'Is it? A few thousand quid handed to me in a cold office room?'

Paul wrapped his arms around me and held me tight as I allowed myself to cry, with anger, frustration and relief.

'You've done everything you can, Terrie,' he whispered into my hair. 'I'm so proud of you.'

We stood for what felt like ages as I felt my tension melt a little.

'It just doesn't feel enough,' I said, wiping my nose. 'But you're right, I am proud too.'

A day later, a letter of apology dropped on to my mat. I have read it many times, hoping against hope that they have learnt from my case and will never ever allow what happened to me to happen to another child. Reading it meant more to me than any cheque. They'd finally admitted that they had done wrong. They hadn't got away with it. But I also knew in my heart of hearts that it didn't guarantee that they would change. I still don't understand why they didn't help me in the first place. I was tied to Adam, they claimed in defence. They said they couldn't prove that he was a risk to me, and that I was unable to tell them enough so they could protect me from him.

Although these facts are all true, the reasoning makes no sense to me. I was still a child, regardless of how mature I might have thought I was. I was just a frightened little child. A child who had been in the system for years with a known history of being in and out of care and possible abuse issues. (There are numerous notes in my files by one social worker or another stating that they believed I was abused by my father, yet no one ever followed that up or related it to the situation with Adam.) I couldn't extricate myself from Adam because I'd been groomed from a very young, impressionable age to be reliant on abusers. Such abuse situations are not straightforward, but surely knowing my history, bearing in mind my age and his, it should have been clear to everyone that Adam was a risk to me, regardless of what I said or didn't say. Wasn't it obvious that the relationship must have been unhealthy – it was illegal after all? They were right to say that I couldn't help myself, but that is why I thought the social services and the courts were there: to help vulnerable children. So, although it felt good to get the apology, I still didn't feel as though I could trust them not to make similar mistakes again.

EPILOGUE

As time has gone by, I've learnt to push what happened to me further and further to the back of my mind and to live in the here and now as much as I can, rather than allowing myself to be forever haunted by my past. But I'll never be completely free of the scars of my childhood.

I still live in the same house in Stevenage, where all the abuse took place, with Paul, Chloe, Matthew and sometimes Mum, who has a place of her own now, but who likes to comes and stay with us a few days a week. We've redecorated the house several times, and although as the years have passed the memories held in its walls have begun to fade, I still can't go upstairs on my own late at night when it's dark. The house always feels cold, even with the heating on. I've told the council on numerous occasions about my associations with this house. We've been on the waiting list for years to swap or move, but are always told that nothing is available for us.

I'm still my mum's full-time carer. We already knew that Mum had bipolar disorder, and she was also diagnosed with manic depression a few years ago. She spends most of her days picking her nose on the sofa, and chain-smoking roll-up cigarettes. I do all of her shopping, including buying her clothes, every week. She doesn't like going out anymore, so I always get her what she needs. I cook for her whenever I can – she insists on having liver and mash for dinner twice a week – and I try to go along with whatever makes her happy. I still don't see her as a mother figure – she never has and never will be a proper mum to me – and my kids still call her 'Fraggle', not 'Nan'. But she is still my mother and despite everything I am still her daughter and am determined to do what's right for her.

I occasionally see Liz around, but we don't even acknowledge one another, and when I go into town I often spot Pervy Pat out and about. He is in his late eighties now and appears to stick to the same routine he's always had, cashing his pension in the post office before going to the market once a week. He just looks like a frail old man, hunched over with a walking stick, the Polaroid camera around his neck long gone. He looks better cared for these days, and I have heard that social services pay for a full-time carer for him, so his jumpers are not covered in patches of dried dribble like they used to be. He never looks at me when I walk past, although I'm sure that he sees me and Paul. I hold my head up high whenever I see him.

My nan Margaret is living in an old people's care home alongside Ron, her brother. She's very frail and, with all her mental-health problems, can't cope on her own. Ron is now in his late sixties and in poor health. Simon found himself a girlfriend and cut himself off from the family. I don't know where he is now.

Meanwhile, the most important role in my life is bringing up my kids. Chloe is ten now and Matthew is eight. Although they live in the same four walls as I did during my childhood, their world couldn't be more different to the one I lived in. After finishing their homework, they play outside with their friends every evening in a spot I can see from my kitchen window, and they always come home to cuddles and a hot, home-cooked meal. They are loved, safe and secure, enjoying the childhood I never had, and that in itself has a healing power for me and my past.

Christmas is a huge affair in our house. I save as much money as possible during the year and spoil them rotten. On the big day, we can't move in our living room for presents under the tree. And when they sit down to open them, I film them, savouring every last moment of their joy. Watching their faces light up and hearing the sounds of their excited screams and laughs gives me no end of pleasure. But much more important than all the presents in the world is that they know they are, and always will be, the most cherished things in mine and Paul's lives.

I still get a letter from Louise's adoptive parents at least once a year, and they always include a picture of her with a beaming smile on her face. I think about her often and feel a pang of sadness when I do, but that smile always reminds me that I did the right thing. She's a teenager now, the same age I was when I had her, and I'm so grateful that her life is so very different from mine. They tell me that she's doing well at school and dreams of becoming a vet. I hope with all my heart that her dreams come true.

Over the years, my relationship with Paul has gone from strength to strength. Now we are truly in love and have just celebrated over ten years together. Nothing will ever tear us apart. He has grown into an amazing dad and husband. He lives for us now and is a hard-working, proud man who stays because he chooses to. I am so glad to have him by my side. He's from a good background and family, and even though he can't even begin to imagine what my life used to be like, he has never flinched in his support for me. In my moments of weakness, he tells me how strong I am, and at last I can believe him.

Years ago, I had the 'Adam' tattoo removed from my arm but I left Louise's name. I don't want to ever forget her, even if I had to give her up.

I found out that after leaving prison Adam got married but then separated from his wife and was awarded custody of one of his children. I've also learnt that because his conviction was only for thirty months, he will by now have been taken off the sex offenders register, meaning he's free to do as he pleases. In my view, he shouldn't be allowed near any kids, even his own. He is a monster who in my eyes never served a proper sentence for his crime. I don't believe he's learned any lessons.

I'm also disappointed that the people who were directly involved in my case have never been called to account. They have never been investigated or made to pay for their neglect or the wrong decisions they made. It stands to reason that things will not change if lessons are not learned from my case. But I have to have faith that somehow, some day they will.

However, despite that, I can't help but feel proud. The little girl who was passed from pillar to post, abused by every man she encountered, fought back and was awarded with at least some kind of justice, however small. I might not have always got the results I wished for, but the man who abused me for years, who stole my childhood, ultimately received some sort of punishment and, for a while at least, was rightly branded as the sex offender he is. I'm also one of the first children brought up in care to sue the social services for neglect and win. If it stops one child living through what I went through, it's worth it. And I feel even more proud knowing that my children, my babies, will never feel the isolating pain of being uncared for that I remember so well.

I wanted to tell my story as I was a victim for many years, but I am a victim no longer. For at least two generations my family was destroyed by sickening paedophiles; abuse breeds abuse, it's a proven fact. But, for some reason, I grew up with my own sense of right and wrong and the spirit to fight for justice. I wasn't broken by what they did to me, and I've managed to break the cycle. As long as I am alive, no one will ever, ever harm my own kids in the ways in which I was harmed. All those years ago, Dad was right when he saw a spirit in me, when he nicknamed me Terrie the Terror. All the court cases, all the police statements, all the phone calls, all the letter-chasing, has been worthwhile in order to be able to finally stand up and say that the people who should have cared let me down. And if, by reading this book, one single victim of abuse finds the courage to stand up and find justice of their own, then every step of my journey for justice will have been worth it.

ACKNOWLEDGEMENTS

I would like to thank my ghostwriter, Shannon Kyle, my agent, Diane Banks, and my editors at Pan Macmillan, Ingrid Connell and Lorraine Green, as without them none of this would have been possible. My neighbour – she knows who she is – has been a wonderful friend and pillar of support, so thank you for always being there. I can't put into words how grateful I am to Paul, my husband, for picking me up when I'm down and showing me how strong I really am, but most of all for loving me no matter what. And finally there are my children . . . They have made my world complete and I hope they know just how loved they are. It is the love I have for them that inspired me to put pen to paper once and for all, in the hope that my story might prevent other children from suffering in the way I did.

extracts reading groups

competitions books new

discounts extracts

competitions

books

new

events

books

extracts

new titles reading groups

interviews

events extracts

discounts

new books events

events new

discounts extracts discounts

www.panmacmillan.com

extracts events reading groups

competitions books extracts new